American Indians in U.S. History

American Indians in U.S. History

Second Edition

Roger L. Nichols

University of Oklahoma Press : Norman

ALSO BY ROGER NICHOLS

*The Missouri Expeditions, 1818–1820: The Journal of
Surgeon John Gale* (Norman, Okla., 1969)
Natives and Strangers, with Leonard Dinnerstein and
David M. Reimers (New York, 1979–2003)
Black Hawk and the Warrior's Path (Arlington Heights, Ill., 1992)
Stephen Long and American Frontier Exploration (Norman, Okla., 1995)
*Indians in the United States and Canada: A
Comparative History* (Lincoln, Neb., 1998)
American Indians in U.S. History (1st ed.; Norman, Okla., 2003)
Warrior Nations: The United States and Indian Peoples (Norman, Okla., 2013)

Library of Congress Cataloging-in-Publication Data

Nichols, Roger L.
American Indians in U.S. history / Roger L. Nichols.—Second edition.
    pages   cm
Includes bibliographical references and index.
ISBN 978-0-8061-4367-5 (pbk. : alk. paper)
1. Indians of North America—History.
I. Title.
E77.N553 2014
973.04'97—dc23

                    2014000605

American Indians in U.S. History, Second Edition, is Volume 248
in The Civilization of the American Indian Series.

The paper in this book meets the guidelines for permanence and
durability of the Committee on Production Guidelines for Book
Longevity of the Council on Library Resources, Inc. ∞

3 4 5 6 7 8 9 10

To Bradley and Laura Hawk

Contents

Illustrations

Photographs

Maps

Preface to the Second Edition

S ince I completed the manuscript for the first edition of this book in 2002, scholars have written hundreds of books and articles as they continue to expand their work in American Indian history. This edition has several goals. It incorporates new material using recent ideas and scholarly approaches, corrects errors and critical omissions noted by readers, and responds to reviewers' questions and suggestions. While doing those things the book's central focus remains. It is designed to provide a brief, general description and analysis of Indians' dealings with other Indians, invading Europeans, and the United States to the present. It makes no effort to include all groups, events, ideas, or people that comprise the overall story. Rather, the narrative is designed so that instructors can build on it, adding their favorite varieties of history—social, cultural, gender-focused, economic, military, or comparative—to suit their individual courses.

The book has four parts. Part I, comprising the first chapter, deals with Indian America prior to the European invasions. "The European Colonial Era," Part II, examines tribal experiences during the sixteenth through eighteenth centuries. Part III, "Facing the United States," focuses on invasions of Indian country after the founding of the United States. The final part covers the late nineteenth century to the present. The dates used in chapter titles are approximate: events can rarely be categorized so neatly.

The colonial era story follows issues related to borders, frontiers, and invasions as it considers intertribal relations and Native dealings with the incoming whites. Later chapters use the same categories but shift focus to analysis of Indian initiatives such as trade, diplomacy, migration, religious adaptation, defensive warfare, incorporation of Anglo-American economic practices, and cultural blending.

While this book chronicles three centuries of cultural and military invasions of Indian North America, it is not designed as a narrative of Indian-white conflict. Native people had a long history of invasion, conquest, and enslavement of each other predating whites' arrival. Even after Europeans reached America, this continued as groups such as the Iroquois, Comanches, and Lakota Sioux spread terror and misery among their neighbors for generations. The United States fought at least forty wars against Native groups between the 1780s and 1890, but this book considers military actions as just one of many elements of Indian-white relations.

This new edition gives more attention to Indian social and cultural issues as well as their incorporation of ideas about personal property and Anglo-American economic activity. I have added material on Spanish-Indian relations in colonial Florida and the Southwest, overlooked somewhat in the first edition. All but the first chapter include new one-paragraph biographies of men and women who were not chiefs, shamans, or warriors but who made important contributions to their peoples. I have also added material about how individual Indians' lives intersected with larger-scale events covered by the narrative. Social historians often criticize others for presenting tribal groups as victims. No honest analysis of the Indians' story can ignore that label—Native people have been on the losing side during three hundred years of repeated invasions—yet it is it is imperative to move beyond victimization and to explore the resilience, determination, and success of Native groups in retaining their identity, culture, and land to the present. While some reviewers faulted the first edition for focusing too heavily on federal policies during the twentieth century, those actions and court decisions laid the foundation for many of the paths Indians have taken in the last seventy-five or eighty years. The 1934 Indian Reorganization Act (IRA) established many reservation governments, and today those have considerable local sovereignty, a circumstance nearly impossible to have been attained without federal actions. The same may be said about the more recent Federal Acknowledgement Program that continues to officially recognize new tribes. Present-day Indian successes are entwined with national trends and federal actions. To reduce the focus on those relationships would give an entirely unbalanced view of the current situation.

It is my hope that this revised edition offers general readers, students, and instructors a clear, accurate, and lively guide to Indian experiences in U.S. history.

Preface to the First Edition

The history of American Indians can be as appealing and exciting to general readers or to college students as reruns of 1950s western films are to twelve-year-old boys. As a result, since the 1960s authors and scholars have written to meet this appetite for adventure and excitement. Hundreds, perhaps thousands, of books and articles chronicling the lives of famous chiefs, the history of warfare, reservation stories, and tribal annals now line bookstore and library shelves. Some of this new work is excellent, but often the texts are lengthy. There are few comprehensive, interesting books for the general public. This briefer narrative is meant to highlight the main issues in American Indian history and to point readers toward more detailed analyses of events or people they find particularly interesting.

I make no pretense here of giving a comprehensive discussion of all the central questions—that would require many volumes. Rather, I present a broad outline of Indian experiences throughout American history. Generally the history moves through three stages. Prior to the European invasions, Indians enjoyed local independence, unless they had fallen under the domination of some other tribal group. From the start, they experienced, for lack of a better term, a frontier situation. That is, they had some contact, cooperation, competition, or conflict with their neighbors. Once the discoverers and those who followed them from Europe to the Western Hemisphere arrived, the situation changed. Gradually, as whites became more powerful, they began taking tribal lands and resources. By the last decades of the nineteenth century, Indians moved into the second stage in this broad history, becoming reservation dwellers. For many, this lasted until the twentieth century. The third stage begins with individuals and groups leaving their reservation bases to mingle with the general population, finding their way in contemporary society. Within this framework, my first chapter examines the precontact Indian world, and the rest of the book presents the post-1500 era, with five of the remaining seven chapters focusing on the period since American independence.

At first glance, the central issues seem clear. The Native people in the United States held the land and its resources, and the invading Europeans wanted those things. Although accurate, this version of the story is much too simple and gives the Indians no role other than that of victim. What actually happened from 1500 to the present proved far more complicated. During those five centuries, tribal groups and their European neighbors vied to control the situation. Indians wished to live their lives in traditional ways, and whites were determined to force them to change. Certainly both sides tried to impose their forms of government, diplomacy, and economic activity. Warfare gets lots of attention, but often the central disputes between whites and Indians focused on how people were to live. Issues such as social organization, family relations, language, food, clothing, housing, religion, education, and medicine were major points of conflict.

Tracing the history of American Indians in the United States presents several difficulties. With at least six hundred identifiable groups to consider, one faces hard choices. A general narrative cannot analyze the experiences of each tribe, trading partner, military ally or enemy, reservation, or particular leader, and this book makes no effort to do so. Another challenge is determining which events, spanning five centuries, to include. For many Americans, knowledge of Indian-related issues, events, people, or cultures may not go beyond what popular culture and the news media have offered, meaning that much of the story remains unknown. Then there is the question of which sources provide the most accurate and usable basis for understanding the events being discussed. Although prior to the twentieth century most Indians did not write, a variety of sources indicating their perspectives does exist. These sources include oral traditions, drawings, calendar sticks, and similar materials. Other information comes from a careful reading of non-Indian accounts of trade encounters, treaty negotiations, ceremonies, and even conflicts.

All this challenges the writer to uncover and analyze tribal points of view and then to place Native Americans at the center of the action, as they were at the time. The incorporation of tribal customs and practices into the narrative emphasizes ideas, movements, and individuals that often have not appeared in traditional American histories and also clarifies what motivated Indian communities to take particular actions. However, the historical record is opaque much of the time. Often little remains extant from those who could write, so scholars must depend on comments from angry pioneers, frustrated bureaucrats, missionaries, teachers, and ambitious army officers—and of course one must use extreme caution when examining such sources.

Americans have written a lot about Indians since the seventeenth century, with some of the first descriptions coming from the so-called captivity narratives. Often prepared after major wars, these narratives depicted tribal peoples as children of the devil, as heathen barbarians. Views about Native Americans became more varied in subsequent generations, but many Europeans and white Americans considered Indians to be savage and dangerous enemies down through the 1880s when the Apache Wars in the Southwest reinforced that idea. Novelists, radio authors, and film writers perpetuated stereotypes into the last half of the twentieth century, when the image shifted to an equally erroneous one of the peace-loving, ecologically aware victim of American national aggression. All of these views fall short of a usable analysis. Like people in any group, Indians fit into many categories—good, bad, or somewhere between.

Since the onset of "political correctness," officials, scholars, and Native American groups have debated which terms are the most accurate and appropriate for discussing American Indian history within the United States. When asked, many Indians prefer their tribal name, for example, Ho Chunk rather than Winnebago, but few use anything other than *Indian* for the entire group label. Anthropologists pale whenever they hear the word *tribe* because they insist that the Indians never belonged to tribes until long after encountering the European invaders in North America. Nevertheless, the federal government uses *tribe* as part of the legal definition of a group of Native people. *Native American* has some popular use, but technically all people born within the country are natives. *American Indian* has the most widespread acceptance, and many pan- or multi-tribal groups use it as part of their official names. The Indian rodeo and Indian powwow circuits use it, and many universities have American Indian Studies programs staffed by people calling themselves Indians. All of these terms will be used in this book, simply to spare the reader what would otherwise be an endless repetition of any one of them.

Acknowledgments

W hen I was first asked to consider writing a book that presented the story of American Indian experiences from the beginning of time to the present, I laughed in surprise. The book was to cover the entire range of American history, yet it was to be brief. To these criteria my response was something like, "You have got to be kidding, right?" The answer sobered me. The University of Oklahoma Press really wanted such a book and asked me to consider the project. In a few weeks my initial lack of enthusiasm gave way to serious consideration of the request. Could the book be written, and was I the person to do it? Having recently recovered from the seemingly unending project that resulted in my 1998 comparative study of Indian experiences in the United States and Canada, I had vowed to steer clear of another far-reaching study. At the same time, it was that book which finally persuaded me to undertake this one, as a possibly less monumental project.

As with all my books, many people and institutions provided support and encouragement. Jeff Burnham, then an editor with the Press, got me started. Jo Ann Reece took over the project in midstream. As project editors, Marian Stewart and Abby Hayes have guided it through production with care. Others on the University of Oklahoma Press staff have played important roles too, and all have my thanks and appreciation. Several of the scholars who read the manuscript for the Press made good suggestions and helped me to avoid both factual and interpretive errors. Among my colleagues, Leonard Dinnerstein read the entire manuscript, offering both support and trenchant comments as well. As usual, my wife, Marilyn Nichols, read the chapters more times than she would care to remember, and made telling comments that improved the manuscript.

Staff at the Library of Congress Reader Service Division and at Photographic Services there helped me locate material and illustrations that appear in the book. My home institution, the University of Arizona, assisted in a variety of ways. As always, the Interlibrary Loan staff located items beyond our collections. The aid provided by our technical support person, Jeff Block, proved to be of particular importance because the first edition was my first book done entirely without a typewriter. Despite some grumbling on my part as pages disappeared into the ether, the manuscript came together well, if occasionally despite my best efforts. To the individuals and groups who assisted me throughout this process, I offer a sincere "thank you."

Chronology of Important Events

1676	Bacon's Rebellion in Virginia
1680	Pueblo Revolt drives Spanish from New Mexico
1680s	Plains tribes acquire horses
1691	Spanish reconquer New Mexico
1701	Iroquois make peace with France and England
1703–1704	English and Indian allies raid Florida missions for slaves
1711–12	Tuscarora War in Carolina
1715	Yamasee War in Carolina
1720–30s	French-Fox Wars around the Great Lakes
1722	Abenaki War in Maine
1729–31	French destroy most of the Natchez tribe in Mississippi
1738	Smallpox ravages Southeastern tribes
1741	Russians open trade with tribes on Gulf of Alaska
1751	Pima Revolt drives Spanish from Arizona
1755	French and Indians defeat British at Fort Duquesne
1756–63	French and Indian (Seven Years') War
1759–61	Cherokee War in Carolina and Tennessee
1763	Treaty of Paris, French out of North America
1763–64	Pontiac's War
1763	Royal Proclamation establishes "Indian Country" idea
1769	Spanish begin settlement in California
1774	Lord Dunmore's War
1775–83	American Revolution
1778	First U.S. treaty signed with Delawares
1779–81	Major smallpox epidemic in North America
1783	Treaty of Paris recognizes American independence
1789	Constitution gives federal government control of Indian affairs
1790	Alexander McGillivray signs Treaty of New York for Creeks
1790–94	War between Indians and United States in Ohio Valley
1794	Indians defeated at Battle of Fallen Timbers
1795	Treaty of Greenville
1799	Handsome Lake begins Long House religion among Senecas
1805	Tenskwatawa begins a new religious movement in Ohio Valley
1807–11	Tenskwatawa and Tecumseh work for a northwest confederacy
1811	Tribes defeated at Battle of Tippecanoe in Indiana
1812–15	Many tribes join British in War of 1812
1813–14	Creek or Red Stick War in Alabama
1817–18	First Seminole War in Florida

1819 Congress establishes Indian Civilization Fund

1821 Sequoyah develops Cherokee syllabary

1824 Office of Indian Affairs established in War Department

1827 Cherokees adopt a tribal constitution

1830 Congress passes the Indian Removal Act

1831 *Cherokee v. Georgia* finds Indians "domestic, dependent nations"

1832 *Worcester v. Georgia* finds state laws do not apply to tribes

1832 Black Hawk War

1835–42 Second Seminole War

1836 Creek Removal

1837 Smallpox epidemic in Missouri Valley

1838 Cherokee Trail of Tears

1848–49 California Gold Rush

1849 Office of Indian Affairs moved to new Department of the Interior

1851 Treaty of Fort Laramie

1861–65 American Civil War

1862 Minnesota Sioux War

1864 Sand Creek Massacre
      Navajo "Long Walk"

1866–67 Red Cloud's War closes Bozeman Trail

1867 Peace Commission treaties at Fort Laramie and Medicine Lodge

1869 Board of Indian Commissioners established

1871 Congress ends the treaty system

1872–73 Modoc War in Oregon

1874–75 Red River War in Texas

1876–77 Great Sioux War and Custer defeat

1877 Nez Perce War

1878 Indian police forces begun

1879 Carlisle Indian School established

1881 Sitting Bull surrenders
      Sun Dance outlawed

1882 Indian Rights Association founded

1883 Lake Mohonk Conferences begun
      Courts of Indian Offenses established

1884 Beginning of modern Peyotism

1885 Major Crimes Act passed

1886 End of Apache Wars in the Southwest

1887 Dawes Allotment Act passed

1890 Ghost Dance and Wounded Knee Massacre
      Sitting Bull killed

1903	*Lone Wolf v. Hitchcock* rules that Congress can end treaties
1908	*Winters v. United States* defines tribal water rights
1911	Society of American Indians founded
1917–18	United States enters World War I
1918	Native American Church established
1923	Committee of One Hundred
1924	American Indian Citizenship Act passed
1928	Meriam Report published
1934	Indian Reorganization Act passed
1930s	Navajo Livestock Reduction Program
1941–45	Twenty-five thousand Indians serve in World War II
1944	National Congress of American Indians founded
1946	Indian Claims Commission established
1953	House Concurrent Resolution 108 and Termination
1956	Relocation Program begun
1961	American Indian Chicago Conference and self-determination
	National Indian Youth Council founded
1964	Fish-ins
1966	Navajo Rough Rock Demonstration School founded
1968	American Indian Movement (AIM) founded
	Indian Civil Rights Act passed
1969	Activists seize Alcatraz
	Navajo Community College opens
1970	Taos Pueblo regains Blue Lake
1971	Alaska Native Claims Settlement Act
1972	Trail of Broken Treaties and occupation of BIA building
1973	Sixty-seven-day confrontation at Wounded Knee, South Dakota
1974	*United States v. Washington* (Boldt decision)
1975	Indian Self-Determination and Educational Assistance Act
	Council of Energy Resource Tribes founded
	Leonard Peltier conviction
1978	American Indian Religious Freedom Act
	Tribally Controlled Community College Act
	Federal Acknowledgment Program established
	Santa Clara Pueblo v. Martinez decision
1980	Penobscot/Passamaquoddy claims settled (Maine)
1985	Wilma Mankiller becomes principal Cherokee chief
1988	Indian Gaming Regulatory Act

1990   Native American Graves Protection and Repatriation Act
        Employment Division v. Smith decision
1992   Mashantucket Pequots open Foxwoods Casino
1994   Tribal Self-Governance Act
2002   Thirty-two tribal colleges in operation
2005   National Museum of the American Indian opens
        NCAA bans use of Indian mascots
2009   *Cobell v. Salazar* decision

PART I

Indian America

CHAPTER 1

Peopling the Land

Debating Human Origins in America

At a hydroplane race along the Columbia River in June 1996, two students watching the competition saw more than they had expected. They found a skull that later proved to be part of a skeleton poking up through the mud. That sent them hurrying to call the local sheriff. At first the authorities assumed the bones were those of a recent murder victim. Soon, however, James C. Chatters, who did skeletal forensics work for the coroner, realized that the remains were much older, and in fact the bones ultimately proved to be those of a human from approximately ninety-three hundred years ago. News of this discovery might have attracted only modest media attention except for one startling fact: Chatters claimed that Kennewick Man, as he became known, had few physical features that might link him directly to the ancestors of modern American Indians. Other scientists concluded that the skeleton showed similarities to Ainu from Japan or Polynesian Pacific Islanders. This discovery brought immediate public attention to long-standing academic and scientific debates over how and when humans had reached the Americas. It also caused bitter disputes between Northwest Indian tribes seeking to claim the remains for burial and scientists eager to learn more about human origins in North America. Since a 2004 federal court ruling against the native claimants, the skeleton has lain in a vault at the University of Washington's Burke Museum.

Until well into the 1990s most scientists agreed that humans crossed the modern Bering Sea by walking from Siberia to Alaska on land that now lies far below the ocean surface. According to this theory, during the last Ice Age, the nearly unending cold locked much of the world's water in vast glaciers that stretched across large parts of the Northern Hemisphere. With so much water removed from the oceans, their levels dropped hundreds of feet, exposing an eight-hundred-mile-wide land bridge called Beringia connecting Asia and North America. To call this route a bridge is deceptive because at that width it was broader than the expanse between the Mississippi River and the Rocky Mountains. Clearly, people could cross Beringia without ever seeing the ocean at all.

Supporters of this overland-migration theory note that sometime between thirty-five thousand and fifteen thousand years ago the earth's climate began a gradual change. Warming initiated glacial melting, and as the ice sheets shrank, gaps opened in what may have been impenetrable barriers of ice. The newly formed passes allowed groups of hunters from northeastern Siberia to follow the herds of big game animals into the Americas. For several thousand years, small bands of people from Asia trekked eastward and southward, taking advantage of the passages around and through the ice fields. By about thirteen thousand years ago these Paleo-Indians had spread across North and South America. Time erased most signs of their presence, but ancient sites where they killed large game have provided scientists with stone spear points found resting among the bones of their prey. Around ten thousand years ago the gradual climatic warming and perhaps the increasing numbers and skills of the hunters combined to drive such large animals as mammoths, giant camels, and ground sloths to extinction. Prehistoric humans stood supreme!

This version of the prehistoric settlement of the Western Hemisphere now faces challenges from several quarters. Traditional Indian accounts offer sharply differing versions of tribal origins and history, explaining how their ancestors came to be in America. Most groups have creation stories that say little or nothing about traveling great distances to reach their modern locations. A sampling of those accounts reveals differing descriptions of ancient events and actions. Often these say that "the People" or "the only True Men," as they called themselves, came from under the earth. For example, the creation story of the Zuni people who live on the Arizona–New Mexico border describes how they "first emerged out of Mother Earth's fourth womb at a sacred place deep within the Grand Canyon." From there they migrated slowly along the Colorado River, building and abandoning villages as went. Finally they came to what they call the "Middle Place" near the headwaters of the Zuni River, where they still live.

Although many tribal origin stories recount similar tales of coming up from the underworld, others tell of descending to earth from above. The Iroquois of New York describe human origins as beginning with a pregnant woman who fell to earth through a hole in the floor of the sky. A Maidu version has the creator descending from the sky to a water-covered earth, where the creator used mud brought by a turtle from the sea floor to make the earth's land and its people. The Cherokee version also describes the earth as covered with water. After a water beetle brought mud to the surface, the land grew so that the animals, plants, and people could descend from the sky to live on the earth. Except for a Paiute story in which Raven helped to crack ice that blocked their ancestors' travels, these legends include nothing suggesting that the tribal people had any memory of glaciers or having lived anywhere other than in the Western Hemisphere.

Whatever cultural or religious value these tribal accounts have for their listeners, like accounts of Moses descending from Mount Sinai with the Ten Commandments, they offer little real data for scientists seeking clues to prehistoric migrations or settlement. As a result, scholars in such fields as archaeology, paleontology, geology, and linguistics continue their efforts to learn about humans in the early Americas through other means. The 1990 congressional passage of the Native American Graves Protection and Repatriation Act accelerated their efforts. That law called on museums, universities, and historical societies to examine their holdings of tribal artifacts and funerary remains to determine if present-day Indian groups had any religious or other claims on these materials. This demand focused renewed attention on items long locked away in collections but rarely studied. As curators and scientists examined their holdings, often for the first time in decades, they made discoveries that challenged not only tribal ideas about their ancestors' location of origin but also existing theories of early human activities in the Americas.

At the beginning of the twenty-first century, repeated and sometimes acrimonious debates have focused on several questions. The first of these is "When did early humans first arrive in the Americas?" The long-accepted theory held that between fifteen thousand and ten thousand years ago small bands of hunters moved east from Siberia. Their descendants left behind spear points found at Clovis, New Mexico, early in the twentieth century; thus they came to be known as the Clovis people. Early skeletal remains found at their kill sites in the Southwest date to 11,000 B.C., but the hunters spread rapidly across North America, reaching the Atlantic coast of Nova Scotia in Canada as early as 8500 B.C. and eastern Virginia at about the same time. Until the 1990s, most scholars accepted the theory that the Clovis people represented the earliest group of so-called Paleo-Indians to arrive in North America.

Since then, a variety of new techniques, including work with human DNA taken from skeletal remains and discoveries of petroglyphs and implements that predate Clovis materials, have pushed back estimates of early migrations and settlement. The etchings found in August 2013 at the site of ancient Pyramid Lake in northern Nevada may be as much as 14,800 years old. The time and skill needed to produce them suggests that the Native artists had a much higher level of sophistication than investigators had initially thought. At a second site, Monte Verde, in Chile, researchers located a village of about thirty hunters who lived in mastodon-hide shelters some 14,500 years ago, which predates by one thousand years any Clovis materials found thus far. Thomas Dillehay, chief archaeologist at the site, faced such opposition to his findings that eventually he invited a blue-ribbon panel to visit Monte Verde and evaluate his data. To their surprise, the "experts" came away fully persuaded by Dillehay's data.

Meanwhile, other scholars working at sites in the eastern United States began to present evidence that pushed early human occupation of those areas farther back in time than the Clovis era. At Saltville in Virginia, archaeologists have uncovered tools of stone and bone amid mastodon bones thought to be at least fourteen thousand years old. Farther east, at Cactus Hill, Virginia, scientists decided to dig below the earth level containing Clovis era spear points. To their amazement, they found, in layers, different and older weapon points and the stones used to make them, now estimated to be at least 15,500 years old. Still older dates have been suggested for the Meadowcroft Rockshelter in western Pennsylvania. For several decades researchers there have sifted through remains that include implements, charcoal they believe to be the residue of cooking fires, and even woven materials dating to at least seventeen thousand years ago. A dig in Kenosha County, Wisconsin, has found piles of bones from butchered mammoths that are at least 13,500 years old. Other sites, ranging from eastern Brazil north to Florida and west to Alaska, have yielded prehistoric items that scientists agree push back by centuries the previous estimated time frame for early human occupation of the Western Hemisphere.

The evidence of pre-Clovis settlement has increased the debate over a second question: "Where did the early people originate?" If the glaciers remained in place, blocking migration across Beringia until nine or ten thousand years ago, how did the early people get here? On this question researchers have found little evidence. Small boats, whether of wood or skin, have long since disappeared, and coastal lowlands that might provide evidence of human activities now lie under the oceans. Yet it seems clear that some of the migrants must have traveled by water. Recent findings suggest that they probably journeyed from island to island or along the edges of the ice fields, hunting for maritime animals and following the flights of land birds to find their way across the oceans. In response to skeptical colleagues, those who support this interpretation note that humans had traveled from mainland Asia to Australia at least forty thousand years ago. If they could do that, there seems little reason to reject the possibility that early hunters worked their way along the edges of the ice fields across both the North Pacific and even perhaps the Atlantic Ocean while finding their way to the Americas.

The theory that people might have traveled west from Europe has only recently found some scientific acceptance, or even a willingness among a few scholars to consider it. This claim is based on at least two kinds of archaeological data. Evidence of pre-Clovis occupation in both Virginia and South Carolina raises interesting questions. The spear points found at several sites differ markedly from the later Clovis ones. They resemble artifacts from the Solutrean culture of southern France and Spain far more than anything now recognized as having come from Asia. The discovery of red-ocher burial sites containing non-Mongoloid skeletal remains also raises questions. Such burial practices also existed in western Europe but not in Asia. If these materials have been dated correctly as having been laid down hundreds or even thousands of years before Clovis era people occupied those sites, then they must have come from migrations that predated the land-bridge migrations or from Europe, because the glaciers blocked land migration from Asia at that time.

Scientists have unearthed specific sets of bones that suggest that some of the early people who came to the Americas might not have come from northern Asia at all. For example, the Spirit Caveman, found near Fallon, Nevada, dates to ninety-four hundred years ago. Had he been a part of the overland migrations of Asian hunters to Alaska, he should resemble modern Indians, but he does not. Rather, he appears to have descended from the ancestors of the aboriginal Ainu of modern Japan or groups from Southeast Asia. The Buhl Woman, found near Buhl, Idaho, is thought to be 10,600 years old. She too bears almost no physical resemblance to members of any modern tribal group. These tentative identifications resulted largely from the 1990 federal order requiring museums to examine the burial items in their holdings and, when possible, to return these materials to the tribes considered to have descended from the ancient groups. That action brought archaeologists and other scientists into direct confrontations with Indians and with the federal government.

As a result of the federal directive to examine their holdings carefully, scientists developed a highly detailed set of ninety measurements for each of the nearly two thousand skulls held in various museums. Often, however, their findings have angered nearly everyone involved. While individual tribes demand that the bones be returned to them for proper burial, the archaeologists insist that physical evidence proves the skeletons came from individuals who could not have been the ancestors of modern Indians. Not only do the skulls bear little or no resemblance to present-day Indian physical types, researchers continue to assert, they also clearly have far more in common with Ainu, Polynesians, or even early Europeans than they do with contemporary groups in the United States. As arguments escalated, they led to threats of suits in the federal courts and produced rulings by the Department of the Interior that particular skeletons be given to individual tribes.

The suggestion that the earliest settlers in America might not be the direct ancestors of modern Indians infuriates some tribal activists and religious leaders. Pointing to their creation stories, many Native Americans believe that their ancestors have always lived in North America. Certainly they never consider the possibility that others may have arrived here first. Elders have taught that Indians have not always looked exactly as they do now, and some scientists agree. They accept the possibility that during the last ten thousand years the appearance of humans in North America most likely changed, perhaps drastically. That claim provided the basis for demands that museum skeletal holdings be turned over to the tribes for interment. The Shoshone-Bannock tribe of Idaho pressed their claim to the Buhl Woman successfully and reburied her. Both the Northern Paiutes from Nevada, who asked to be allowed to rebury the Spirit Caveman, and the Umatillas of Washington, who demanded that the Kennewick Man be turned over to them, moved aggressively to assert what they considered their tribal rights. However, in both cases the skeletal profiles scientists developed do not support the tribal claims, and so the debate continues.

The ongoing story of the Kennewick Man bones since their uncovering shows how contentious the issues surrounding the treatment of skeletal remains have become. Shortly after the discovery, researchers judged the skull to be that of a non-Indian, perhaps a Pacific Islander or even a European. Within two months of that announcement, the Army Corps of Engineers took possession of the skeleton. When scientists asked for permission to examine the engineers' study of the bones, the Corps of Engineers denied them access. This led quickly to the publication of notices that the Confederated Tribes of the Umatilla were to get the skeleton for reburial. In October 1996 scientists filed a complaint that challenged the actions of the Corps of Engineers. What they wanted was a chance to do Carbon-14 and DNA testing on a tiny portion of the bones. Meanwhile, archaeologists, physical anthropologists, tribal leaders, and bureaucrats all argued about what was to be done with the remains. The major news outlets and television networks ran interviews and articles, all of which brought the question of early human presence in the Americas to public attention as never before. In August 2002, Judge John Jelderks of the U.S. District Court in Oregon ruled against those tribes demanding immediate reburial of the skeleton. He found that under federal law the remains could not be defined as "Native American." Two years later, in April 2004, the federal Ninth Circuit Court of Appeals upheld Jelderk's decision, so the bitter dispute between local Indians wanting to bury Kennewick Man and the scientists hoping to continue research on his bones continues.

The newest and in many ways most interesting part of the search for early humans in the Western Hemisphere has arisen from the recent tracing of the human genome. DNA researchers now claim that all humans descended from early peoples who came from sub-Saharan Africa as recently as one hundred thousand years ago. From there they migrated across Asia and Europe to the rest of the world. More specific studies of DNA have uncovered a rare genetic factor called haplogroup X DNA that is passed down through women. Some geneticists claim that this factor shows that the earliest migrants to the Americas had "no obvious ties to any Asian groups." They could have been earlier pioneers to the New World from Asia, or they could have come from Europe, where the haplogroup X still exists among a small portion of the population. Whatever scientists make of the new evidence, it seems clear that the older theory of a migration over the land bridge and the tribal ideas about their ancestors' origination in the Americas are too simplistic. The prehistoric process of peopling the Western Hemisphere was far more complex, and for Indians it is contested bitterly.

The scientific findings have received their sharpest criticism from Lakota Sioux writer Vine Deloria, Jr., who objects to both the methods and the theories scientists have developed when studying early human presence in North America. Mercilessly heaping ridicule on the Bering Sea–crossing theory, Deloria asks how the herds of Pleistocene animals the hunters supposedly followed east from Asia could have crossed Beringia when ice covered the region. He also says that scientific data based on Carbon-14 dating techniques are flawed or even entirely wrong. Deloria agrees with some scholars when he claims that early humans may have been in the Americas much earlier than the Clovis era, but he asserts that a human population lived here for several hundred thousand years and may even have evolved here independently from those peoples in the rest of the world. With the recent DNA findings, almost no scholars accept his multisite theory of human development, but debate continues over how and when humans came to this continent.

Though the disputes remain unresolved, the new evidence has convinced nearly all researchers that the story of prehistoric migrations to America is much more complicated than previously thought. It now appears that repeated movements of small groups took place over thousands of years, stretching back much farther in time than earlier findings had suggested. Many of those migrations brought people not just from Siberia, but also from Southeast Asia, the Pacific Islands, and possibly even western Europe. As scientists continue to find new artifacts and reexamine Clovis era sites looking for evidence lying beneath them, they develop a more complete understanding of how, when, and from where early humans came.

The Archaic Era

Whatever direction these debates take, at this point the issue of human occupation and development in North America after 9000 B.C. is less contested. Scientists have concluded that the climate in the Northern Hemisphere moderated around that time, and the ice fields gradually melted. Most agree that these climatic changes drove such large mammals as mammoths, sloths, and camels to extinction, although a few scholars claim that the early hunters destroyed them. As people sought new animal sources for food, they spread across the continent rapidly, and by 8500 B.C. they had migrated as far as the Atlantic coast of Nova Scotia in Canada. Wherever they lived, Paleo-Indians faced a variety of environments. Archaeological remains suggest that during what scientists call the Archaic Era (8500 B.C. to 1000 B.C.), these people developed a relatively common culture. Most lived in small family groups or bands. Together they hunted, fished, gathered, and used food sources found within an area perhaps one hundred miles across. They made their tools out of stone, bone, or wood and fashioned household implements out of wood, bone, shells, and reeds.

Scientific data for the Archaic Era remain modest, as few artifacts have survived. This means that archaeologists must work chiefly with weapons, pottery, and tools, and these items provide only a limited amount of information about how early people lived. Because researchers unearthed mostly weapons from that era, they began to name groups of people according to the sites where their spear points were found. Thus, one can read that people such as the Sandia, Clovis, Folsum, or Cascade made unique implements and lived in towns or regions bearing those names. The first three of those sites lie in present-day New Mexico, where the dry climate preserved the evidence. The Cascade people got their name from an area along the Pacific coast. All of these groups left behind implements and weapons, and some of these can be dated by various methods. Scientists consider the Sandia items to be among the oldest in the West, assigning them dates of between 15,000 B.C. and 10,000 B.C.

Of these early groups, the Clovis people left the most extensive remains. Scholars have found their delicate, well-crafted stone spear points at sites ranging from the Southwest deserts to the Atlantic coast. Their makers lost or abandoned the weapons among the bones of the large animals they hunted. Based on clues from existing remains, archaeologists depict these people wearing animal skins and hide or fiber sandals, using their long, slender, fluted spear points successfully for thousands of years, and subsisting primarily on meat from their hunting. Despite being limited to little more than spear points, the Clovis evidence shows clearly that these people adapted to life in various regions of the country.

Gradually the small Clovis bands disappeared or mixed with people who made Folsum points, first discovered during the 1920s near Folsum, New Mexico. Nomadic hunters like their predecessors, these people tracked early bison, deer, and elk. They may have been more numerous than earlier Paleo-Indian groups, based on evidence they left of cooperative hunts. Tactics such as driving animals over cliffs or into marshy river bottoms made their food gathering more effective than the efforts of earlier small hunting bands. Like the Clovis people, the Folsum groups spread over much of North America and left evidence of their activities all the way to the Atlantic coast. Except for a different type of spear point, the items researchers have found from these groups suggest that the roving hunters shared a similar culture and a similar level of technology.

Sometime between 7000 B.C. and 4500 B.C. the Folsum group disappeared or evolved into people who developed the Plainview culture, a group that scientists see as a sort of link connecting the early hunting cultures with their more modern Indian descendants. These Plainview or Plano people began hunting the increasingly large herds of bison on the plains. They learned to preserve meat by drying it in the hot summer sun or by mixing it with fat, seeds, and berries that they packed into containers made from animal intestines. This gave them a sort of trail mix—called pemmican today—that resembled sausage but without much meat. Another climatic shift occurred between 5000 B.C. and about 3500 B.C. The new weather patterns seem to have reduced the herds of large animals the hunters followed, and so the Plano people migrated after the animals or had to change their subsistence patterns. For whatever reasons, their culture disappeared, and almost no evidence of human occupation of the plains for the next thousand years has been discovered.

Artifacts from approximately 3000 B.C. suggest that people living in America at that time had developed new skills for using the environment effectively. They had begun making and using pottery, which allowed them to store and prepare food. Some groups had begun to cultivate grains and squash as well. Although physical evidence for that era is limited, what has been found suggests continuing improvement in hunting weapons and an increased knowledge of edible plants, as well as more efficient fishing and harvesting of seafood along the coasts. All of these changes resulted in a gradual expansion of populations. In every part of the country, people settled into routines that depended on their local resources. For generations, even centuries, they lived in what became accepted as their home areas, becoming "Natives" in their particular locales.

Because humans reached North America at different times, separated by hundreds or even thousands of years, the cultures that emerged differed widely. The societies that developed depended on the individual groups' knowledge and technology, but also on available local resources. People who settled along the Pacific coast from Oregon north to Alaska established the Cascade culture, making their living from the products of the rich coastal waters. Some became seafarers, hunting whales and sea lions, often far from shore. Others dwelling near the coast or along the rivers that flowed into the ocean depended heavily on the annual salmon runs for their basic food supply. Inland bands living near the mountains spent less time fishing and subsisted by hunting deer and elk and gathering seeds and bulbs. All of these groups depended on roots, berries, nuts, seeds, and plant fibers to make their lives comfortable.

Vastly different lifestyles emerged among those who dwelt between the Sierra Nevada Mountains and the Rockies farther to the east. Sparse resources there limited the population. The arid climate meant that hunters had to depend on small animals such as rabbits and ground squirrels. As a result, these people lived in small bands and supported themselves by hunting and by gathering seeds, fruit, and nuts whenever possible. Working with reeds and other plant fibers, they made baskets, twine, nets for trapping birds and small animals, and sandals. Excavators have unearthed baskets and twine dating to roughly 9000 B.C. made by these desert peoples. The Spirit Caveman found near Fallon, Nevada, was a good example of this early culture, one that lasted for at least five thousand years in parts of the desert West.

Other hunting groups lived at the fringes of the plains, gradually coming to depend on the herds of bison that came to dominate the central grasslands. These people hunted cooperatively, often driving frightened animals over cliffs, into pens or corrals, or toward the marshes and quicksand bogs along major rivers. Although these animals provided meat, hides, bones, horn, and sinew for successful hunters, the bison herds often held less attraction for them than one might expect. The plains dwellers hunted on foot and had only dogs to help them transport the hides and meat from hunting sites. Also, the animals moved frequently, often staying hundreds of miles from the hunters' villages. As a result, the bison provided an erratic food supply at best for those who lived at the edges of the Great Plains or at the base of the Rockies. This encouraged people in those places to begin cultivating food crops in order to supplement their diet. Centuries later, their descendants would acquire horses from the Europeans, revolutionizing their lives.

The Golden Age

By about 1200 B.C., the inhabitants of America entered what scholars have labeled the Golden Age of their early history. The term fits well because by that time many of the early societies had learned how to use local resources effectively. Not only did they plant and harvest crops successfully, they used repeated and large-scale fires to shape their local environments. In the Pacific Northwest they burned grasses and bushes, clearing land to encourage the growth of bracken and camas. In the Midwest and East other groups burned the undergrowth to thin the forests and thus encourage the growth of berry bushes and other shrubs. The more open woodlands attracted large numbers of browsing animals such as white-tailed deer. On the prairies people used fires as part of their hunting, driving animals into traps, over embankments, or into marshes. These tactics developed over several centuries and at different speeds, bringing long-term changes to much of the country. By this era the Native peoples in many regions had learned to process and store foods for several years at a time, so they no longer had to worry continually about their daily supply. Certainly by 1000 B.C. agriculture had spread from west to east, and across much of North America large-scale, well-organized societies emerged. Some of these societies still functioned at least a thousand years later, but several disappeared "mysteriously," or at least for reasons not yet determined.

During the Golden Age, ancestors of later desert dwellers of the Southwest struggled to settle in that region because of the limited resources they found. Between 1000 B.C. and A.D. 1000 at least three distinct cultures developed there. The Hohokam settled on lands along the rivers that stretched southward from the Gila River in southern Arizona into the Mexican state of Sonora. There they built towns with square buildings on or near the river floodplains and irrigated hundreds of acres of land, raising corn, beans, pumpkins, and squash. Like other early peoples, they welcomed traders who brought such things as sea-turtle shells and turquoise from California. Highly successful farmers, they continued to live in what is now southern Arizona until after A.D. 1300, when their society appears to have disintegrated. The causes for this collapse remain unclear, but scientists offer several possible explanations. During the thirteenth century, gradual climatic changes and a series of droughts brought chaos to these sedentary communities. Heavy winter rains flooded the fields, and silt blocked the irrigation canals that had taken so much labor to construct and maintain. Because the people had watered the same fields for generations, the soil became clogged with mineral salts, which led to smaller crops. The crop shortages and an increasing population apparently overwhelmed the people's ability to feed themselves. As a result, by A.D. 1400 they had left their large towns, as small bands scattered across the countryside for survival. Their descendants, the present O'odham groups, refer to them as the Hohokam, people "who are used up."

At about the same time, a second desert culture, the Mogollon, developed in what is now central Arizona. These people lived in the mountains east and north of what is now Phoenix. Another farming people, the Mogollon produced some of the most beautiful prehistoric pottery made in the Southwest. Active participants in the extensive trade networks that then existed, they had many connections with other early peoples in northern Mexico and in California. These influences appear in their pottery designs, which include many kinds of ocean fish not found within hundreds of miles of their settlements. Archaeologists have identified artifacts from at least twenty Mogollon villages along the Mimbres River, marking these people as the producers of the most varied and beautiful ceramic work in the region. Like the Hohokam, this culture faded from the scene during the A.D. 1300s, and scholars assume that the climatic changes of that era and perhaps early Apache raids explain the disappearance. No one is certain which modern Indians may have descended from the Mogollon.

Perhaps the most intriguing of the prehistoric people in the Southwest, the Anasazi, or "ancient ones" or "ancient enemies," as the Navajos call them, appear to have been the ancestors of modern Puebloan groups. By A.D. 700 they had settled at the southern end of the Colorado Plateau and in what are now desert lands in Arizona, New Mexico, and Colorado. Expert basket-makers, they hunted, gathered, and farmed across the rugged countryside. Between A.D. 900 and 1000 they constructed modest adobe and stone buildings, and during the next several centuries they erected large towns with multistoried stone buildings. A series of well-paved roads stretched out from their apparent cultural center at Chaco Canyon in New Mexico, connecting them to many other communities. The seven pueblos there had at least thirteen hundred rooms and housed some six thousand people. Pueblo Bonito, the largest of these, stood four stories high and included four hundred rooms.

Communities that size depended on agriculture. The residents at Chaco Canyon farmed small plots of ground that they watered by hand as well as others they managed to irrigate using a series of canals. During the late thirteenth century, regional droughts devastated the crops, and in a few generations this society vanished. At Chaco Canyon the thousands of people split into smaller groups and scattered across the region. Until the 1990s, scholars attributed the abrupt collapse of Anasazi culture almost entirely to the recurrent droughts that struck the Southwest. More recently, however, some have suggested that warfare may have been part of the drama as well. Substantial evidence of human slaughter and cannibalism has been found. For example, specimens of human tissue in preserved samples of ancient human feces found at one Anasazi site provide incontrovertible evidence that some cannibalism took place there. Large numbers of human bones bearing marks that could only have resulted from their having been butchered and stirred in cooking pots have been discovered there as well. Whether the cooking and eating of people resulted from invasion and conquest, was part of symbolic religious ceremonies, or occurred for other reasons is uncertain. What remains clear, however, is that, whether because of these actions or despite them, by A.D. 1300 this culture had collapsed and the people had left Chaco Canyon.

In the Mississippi Valley region far to the east, the later Archaic Era population developed what is known as the Woodland culture. Unlike the West, which offered only limited amounts of good cropland and lacked dependable water supplies, this area had a variety of resources. As a result, many small settlements developed, often connected by wide-ranging traders who carried items for exchange over hundreds of miles. The earliest known settlement of any size stood at Poverty Point, Louisiana, so named because these people left so few pottery shards behind for scholars to examine. Apparently these people preferred to carve their bowls out of soapstone rather than to fire them. Perhaps they never found clay that made good ceramics. In either case, little of their pottery has survived. Begun shortly before 1400 B.C., this community built large-scale earthworks that are among the earliest known north of Mexico. There, near the Mississippi River, they built a series of six octagonal earthen ridges that enclosed more than ten square miles of land. On the terraces inside the ridges they built conical and bird-shaped earthen mounds ranging from twenty to seventy-five feet high, where they buried some of their leaders.

The inhabitants situated many of their houses on the earthen ridges, and the community seems to have used most of the enclosed space for ceremonies, public business, and play. Some scholars contend that the leaders and merchants from Poverty Point were Olmec people who had come north from Mexico. In what is present-day Louisiana, they dominated the local population and patterned their community on what they had known at home. They built mounds like those common in parts of Central America at the time. Wherever these people originated, they had skilled stone workers, who made axes, hollow drills, and other tools as well as pendants shaped like humans, birds, and insects. The community had considerable astronomical knowledge, identifying the equinoxes and solstices that marked the changing seasons. There is evidence that they understood magnetism, and it appears that they used magnetic stones in some of their ceremonies. Whether they developed their skills and knowledge independently or learned from trade and other contacts with people across the Gulf of Mexico is unclear.

Like most of the prehistoric cultures in America, the Poverty Point people disappeared or merged with groups that later became prominent. By 800 B.C. another Woodland culture, the Adena, emerged in the Ohio Valley to the north. Their villages dotted riverbanks in present-day Ohio, Kentucky, and West Virginia, and they too built earthen mounds sometimes more than sixty feet high. Often these covered burial huts or chambers. Like the Poverty Point people, they laid out earthen ridges or embankments but on a smaller scale than their predecessors. The Adena buried some of their dead in mounds, which they built by the hundreds in the Ohio Valley over a period of more than a thousand years.

They enjoyed a varied diet that included seeds, nuts, fish, shellfish, birds, and other animals. Their technology resembled that of other late Archaic Era people, including stone axes, chipped weapon points, and stone pipes, as well as bone, wood, and copper personal ornaments.

By about 100 B.C. a new group, the Hopewell, emerged in Illinois. They seem to have benefited from a gradual warming trend that made farming more successful than it had been several centuries earlier. Using hoes made from the shoulder blades of deer or other large animals, they planted and raised corn in several of their communities. Hundreds of Hopewell villages stretched along the major rivers in the East, as these people came to dominate the area from what is now western New York to the edge of the plains and from the Gulf of Mexico north to the Great Lakes. The use of mounds begun by earlier cultures continued, as the villagers built embankments often stretching several miles in length. These people buried wealthy and powerful individuals in earthworks too, but now often included wives, retainers, servants, and personal goods as part of the rituals. While some mounds stood sixty to seventy feet high, others, not as high, took the shape of birds, animals, and snakes and could stretch for hundreds of yards and contain thousands of tons of dirt.

Throughout all of these early Woodland cultures leaders wielded enough authority to persuade or force extraordinary amounts of toil from their citizens. All of these vast engineering projects resulted from hand labor. These Indians had no domesticated animals to assist with the work. Such control over the common people could not achieve everything, though, and by A.D. 350, when the climate began cooling again, the Hopewell villagers saw their orderly world begin to unravel. In Illinois and the Ohio Valley region the shrinking growing seasons endangered food supplies, and individual villages began taking independent action. It seems likely that intervillage warfare occurred as the people faced increasing competition for diminished resources. The efforts needed to erect and maintain defensive walls around many of the towns took much of the time previously used for mound-building. Farther to the south, where the climate remained mild, Hopewell villages continued to function in the old ways. Sites in Tennessee, Louisiana, and Florida all suggest that some mound-building continued there long after it had ceased in the North.

The cool, wet climate that initiated the Hopewell decline encouraged other Midwestern Indian farmers to develop crops that required a shorter growing season. Gradually the weather shifted again so that by A.D. 800 the Mississippi Valley was experiencing warmer and drier weather. By this time, maize cultivation had spread across much of the East, and corn became an essential staple for feeding people in existing villages and towns. A new society evolved into the Mississippian culture, which remained in place until the eve of contact with intruding Europeans centuries later. Again, scholars lack evidence to pinpoint the origins of this group, but they theorize that this culture grew out of the existing societies in the lower Mississippi Valley.

Cahokia

The city of Cahokia, standing near the Mississippi River across the water from the site of present-day St. Louis, became the center of this society. Established as early as A.D. 950, it appears to have resulted from an intrusion onto the local scene, because for much of its history it had a strong log palisade for defense against attacks by local groups. The people there enjoyed trade and cultural contacts with others in eastern Texas, Mississippi, and Illinois. They chose the site for the community wisely: an area with excellent soil, a dependable water supply, and plentiful stands of timber. These qualities attracted people, so that by the time the city was strong enough to dominate the entire center of the country, large subsidiary towns had grown up along major streams nearby. Cahokia itself covered nearly five square miles and had an estimated population of nearly thirty thousand. At that size, it represented the largest urban center to develop north of Mexico in the prehistoric era.

To its neighbors, Cahokia's stout defenses, large population, and obvious power had to have been impressive. However, the huge earthen mounds its inhabitants built characterize the community more than anything else. Some of them still dominate the local landscape. Monk's Mound, so called because a small monastery once stood atop it, reached a height of more than one hundred feet. Even today it covers an area larger than a football field and includes some twenty-two million cubic feet of soil. It is by far the largest of all extant earthworks found within the United States. Built entirely of dirt, it grew in stages over several hundred years. More than one hundred other mounds of various shapes and sizes remain at the site today. Cahokia's hierarchical leaders used extensive slave labor to build their community, and slaves and personal property were often buried in the leaders' graves.

By A.D. 1000, the city had grown to its full size and served as the economic, political, and religious center for a vast network of towns and villages that reached across half of the continent. As they spread their influence outward from Cahokia, the Mississippians established communities as far apart as Red Wing, Minnesota, and Etowah in Georgia. Their expansion, however, brought resistance from some groups living at the edges of the Cahokia sphere of influence. Evidence from one site includes the skeletal remains of young men, presumably killed in fighting, that had been chopped to pieces and then dumped into the refuse piles. It is not possible to know whether the victims came from the ranks of the victors or the vanquished, or perhaps from prisoners executed later. Nevertheless, their presence indicates that some local groups resisted stoutly. Scholars think that by A.D. 1400, Cahokia had collapsed. By then its large population had denuded the nearby hills, taking all the timber for housing and fuel. This increased flooding and erosion, thus damaging food production. It seems likely that centuries' worth of refuse, garbage, and sewage polluted local water sources and brought disease and occasional deaths as well.

At the End of the Archaic Era

When the Golden Age cultures went into decline or disappeared, life for most aboriginal groups continued, often taking several centuries to change. Between A.D. 1000 and A.D. 1500, many of the ancestors of modern American Indians moved into the regions they occupied when the first Europeans arrived. In the Southwest, descendants of the earlier desert cultures dispersed and became the Puebloans of northern Arizona and New Mexico or the desert dwellers of southern Arizona. At the same time, small groups of Apacheans drifted southward east of the Rocky Mountains and moved gradually into the region. Ancestors of the Utes and Navajos followed, apparently reaching the area only a short time before the earliest Spanish invaders arrived.

On the plains the culture that had developed by A.D. 1500 gave rise to such later tribes as the Blackfeet, Cheyenne, Arapaho, Comanche, Crow, and Siouan groups. These people followed the bison, and that activity led them into a mostly nomadic existence. Long before they acquired horses from the Spanish or their tribal neighbors, they had become effective hunters. Some groups like the Lakota Sioux came to the plains from their previous home north and west of Lake Superior many generations after the hunting cultures had attained predominance there. Because of their numbers, they retained the nomadic way of life longer than some others and so came to represent the hunting cultures of the region in popular culture.

East of the plains along the Missouri, Platte, and Kansas Rivers, other groups settled during this era. To the south, the Wichitas and later the Kansas combined buffalo hunting with farming along the rich bottomlands. They built lodges of grass and reeds in summer and sturdier earthen dwellings for winter. Each year after planting their fields in late spring, they hunted on the plains. By late summer they returned to their villages for the rest of the year. North of them, Caddoan groups, who became the Pawnees of Nebraska and the Arikaras of South Dakota, followed a similar annual cycle. The Arikara villages became some of the major trading centers in the upper Missouri Valley. Plains hunters traveled there to exchange surplus meat, hides, and horns for food crops the villagers raised. These trading patterns continued well into the nineteenth century.

East of the Mississippi River, three cultural groups—Muskogeans in the South, Algonquians along most of the Atlantic coast, and Iroquoians in New York, Tennessee, and Georgia—came to dominate the area. All three lived in agricultural villages, although the Iroquois had substantially larger towns than the other groups. They combined farming, hunting, and gathering, but the coastal Algonquian groups also obtained much of their food from the rivers and nearby ocean. The presence of strong palisades used for defense of some Iroquoian villages suggests that raiding and war played important roles in their lives. All three cultures shared economic practices and technology, but their languages and religious practices kept them apart as competitors if not enemies.

Like people in other parts of the country, the eastern villagers shifted their locations gradually, depending on hunting success, the presence or absence of enemies, and modest climatic changes. Ethnologists estimate that by A.D. 1500, nearly six hundred distinct groups had emerged across the country. Numbering perhaps four or five million people, these groups took part in wide-ranging trade networks that made available ocean shells from each coast, mica from the Appalachians, copper from the Great Lakes area, precious stones from the Far West, and even tropical feathers. Yet, despite the extensive trading, suspicion resulting from raiding and warfare continued to separate groups. Actually, few Indians lived as part of formally organized tribes at the time. Rather, most dwelt in nearly independent villages, armed camps ready to defend themselves, attack their enemies, or raid for slaves and property. Occasionally they joined with nearby communities that shared their language and culture for trade or war. By A.D. 1500 dozens of cultures existed that linked the prehistoric people with the groups who occupied what would become the United States several centuries later.

Suggested Readings

Chatters, James C. "The Recovery and First Analysis of an Early Holocene Human Skeleton from Kennewick, Washington." American Antiquity 65, no. 2 (April 2000): 291–316.

Cordell, Linda S. *Ancient Pueblo Peoples*. Washington, D.C.: Smithsonian Books, 1994.

Deloria, Vine, Jr. *Red Earth, White Lies*. Golden, Colo.: Fulcrum, 1997.

Dillehay, Thomas. *The Settlement of the Americas: A New Prehistory*. New York: Basic Books, 2000.

Fagan, Brian M. *Ancient North America*. New York: Thames & Hudson, 1995.

Jennings, Jesse D. *Prehistory of North America*. Mountain View, Calif.: Mayfield, 1989.

Kehoe, Alice Beck. *North American Indians: A Comprehensive Account*. 3rd ed. Upper Saddle River, N.J.: Pearson/Prentice Hall, 2006.

Parfit, Michael. "The Dawn of Humans: Hunt for the First Americans." *National Geographic* 198, no. 6 (December 2000): 40–67.

Preston, Douglas. "Cannibals of the Canyon." *New Yorker*, November 1998, 76–89.

Young, Biloine Whiting, and Melvile L. Fowler. *Cahokia: The Great Native American Metropolis*. Urbana: University of Illinois Press, 2000.

PART II

The European Colonial Era

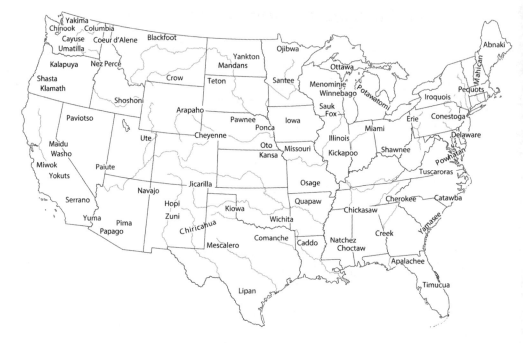

Indian America, 1500

CHAPTER 2

Meeting the Invaders, 1500–1700

They came from all directions. Some had fur on their faces and looked like dogs, others gazed out through eyes the color of the sky, while a few had hair the color of sand or dried grass. Often word of their arrival raced ahead of them, so that even villages far from any ocean learned something about the strangers. The Europeans' descriptions of early encounters depended on when and where they met Native people. For example, a member of the 1539 de Soto expedition to Florida reported that the Spanish invasion had terrified the Indians as it moved from Florida through land that is now Georgia, Alabama, and Mississippi. Given the explorers' violent tactics and destruction of tribal villages, this should have come as no surprise. Nearly a century later, in 1620, the Pilgrims saw Indians as dangerous enemies. Ten years later another New Englander claimed that the coastal people thought the first ships bearing settlers were floating islands. Clearly that was nonsense because by then the villagers there had dealt with explorers, fishermen, and traders sailing offshore for at least a half-century. Few Indian accounts of early contacts with the invaders have survived, and many of those give only vague descriptions. A traditional Sauk story described their first encounter with whites rather differently. After dreaming for several decades of meeting a white man, the leader, Na-na-ma-kee, met the French. They gave him a medal, shirt, blanket, and other presents and promised to remain friends. Certainly the Indians in this encounter were neither astonished nor terrorized. In New England Wampanoag leader Massasoit hurriedly forged a defensive alliance with the Pilgrims against his traditional Indian enemies. The variety of experiences produced widely different accounts.

Wherever they met, Europeans and Natives brought vast differences in thought and custom to the encounter. While European societies operated within guidelines laid down by centralized governments, authoritarian religious groups, and often well-defined class structures, societies in aboriginal America had little in common with them or sometimes with each other. In widely scattered places tribal and even multitribal organizations existed, such as the Five Nations Confederacy of the Iroquoians in New York, the confederation led by the Powhatans in Virginia, and the chiefdoms in the Southeast. Often, even they operated one village at a time, each having a council of respected elders that made recommendations for the group but held only modest enforcement power. A reverence for nature stood at the center of Indian thought and practice, as the villagers assumed that the earth, sun, and moon as well as the plants and animals around them all had spiritual powers. Obviously, this belief put them at odds with the Europeans, who saw nature as a set of resources to be developed and used, and certainly not as entities having spiritual powers. In fact, to Christians then, that idea was heretical. Because at least six hundred distinct groups inhabited the land in 1500, making valid generalizations is difficult. Still, from almost any aspect, tribal life differed from that of the newcomers.

Whether Indians realized it or not, the European invasions of North America would alter their lives forever. In fact, one scholar who analyzed the meetings between the tribal people and the invading English said that they created a New World, not just for the invaders but also for the Native peoples. Generations of villagers had mastered their environments. They knew the countryside and its resources, plant and animal. When vegetation threatened prized hunting areas, they simply burned the offending shrubs. If the soil in their fields became depleted, they moved a few miles away, allowing the ground to lie fallow as it recovered. They dealt with their neighbors effectively through trade and diplomacy. The Europeans' arrival changed many of those early Indian patterns of subsistence, trade, and warfare abruptly. While villagers near the coasts or other entry points for the newcomers encountered them first and may have suffered the most consequences, the invaders' impact spread across the continent. They came from several directions, and nearby tribes had little chance to avoid contact for long.

Even groups living hundreds of miles from intruding Europeans could not escape the disruptions, as new patterns of trade, diplomacy, and warfare developed and came to affect everyone. More importantly, unknown diseases, animals, and plants forced Indians to remake their lives. Epidemics of smallpox, influenza, and measles ripped through Native communities, often killing many of the most productive adults who held the villages together. Repeated waves of contagion moved across the countryside, destroying entire populations in places and thoroughly disrupting most village societies repeatedly. Demographers have estimated that in the heavily populated areas in central Mexico and on some of the islands in the Caribbean, up to 75 percent of the Native population died from epidemic disease during the first several generations after the Spanish arrived. Although tribes in the southeastern United States had extensive populations, many of the people lived in modest-sized villages, so the epidemics that swept through that region seem to have brought somewhat fewer fatalities there.

The farther people lived from regions the Europeans visited, the less impact imported diseases had. Yet even tribes living hundreds of miles from colonial settlements suffered, as visiting Indians and white traders carried sickness with them. At the same time, domesticated animals such as cattle, horses, sheep, and hogs changed the landscape forever. Cattle trampled village cornfields while eating much of the crop. Hogs rooted through marshes, destroying long-used clam beds along the coastal waters. Grazing and browsing animals competed with the native deer and later with the bison on the plains, reducing the supply of animals available for Indian hunters. Eventually the introduction of firearms and alcohol brought other difficulties. This combination of new diseases, technology, and animals affected groups far beyond the troublesome newcomers.

Encountering the Spanish

The Indians' first experiences with the Spanish proved more violent and disruptive than their meetings with most other Europeans. By 1513, when Ponce de León's expedition reached Florida, some villagers along the Atlantic coast already had met Europeans. As much as five hundred years earlier, Native people on the coast of Newfoundland encountered these strangers. Skraelings, as the Norsemen called the Indians there, fought so well that they drove the Greenlanders away. Other villagers met small numbers of fishermen, traders, and men hoping to seize people they could carry off into slavery, long before the Spanish reached Florida. Those minor incursions alerted some coastal groups to the dangers newcomers posed, and in the Southeast violent clashes marked the meetings between Spaniards and Indians from the start. Ponce de León's Florida experiences illustrate this clearly. When he first landed on the Florida coast in 1513, the Calusa tribe there attacked almost immediately. Eight years later, in 1521, Calusa arrows gave the explorer a mortal wound and drove his men back to Cuba.

Other southeastern tribes failed to defeat the Spanish a generation later, when Hernando de Soto invaded the region. In 1539 de Soto landed at Tampa Bay leading an army of six hundred men plus an interpreter who had lived with tribes in the region for several years, and hundreds of horses, mules, pigs, and dogs. This force crisscrossed the region during the next four years, bringing misery to every group it met. Many of the village societies there had descended from the earlier Mississippian cultural groups. They lived in multitribal chiefdoms that had prosperous farms, large populations, and well-built communities constructed around temple mounds. Despite their wealth, they lacked the gold or silver de Soto craved, and his demands brought repeated violence. The expedition seized a town abandoned by the Apalachees and then had to fend off several attacks there. A year later, the Cofidtachequi people near Camden, South Carolina, welcomed the invaders, giving them clothing and freshwater pearls. Not satisfied with these gifts, the Spanish looted the villagers' graves and temples and seized the young female "queen" before marching away.

The invaders left a trail of destruction as they murdered, looted, raped, and enslaved Indians throughout their entire four-year invasion. However, not everything went as they had hoped. The tribal "queen" slipped away from her captors, and as news of the Spaniards' violence and greed spread, villagers along their route all resisted or fled. This enraged the Europeans, who feared that it decreased their chances of finding gold or other precious items. Repeated Indian raids against de Soto's party reduced its numbers steadily. Several times the tribes attacked successfully, inflicting heavy casualties. In 1540 ancestors of the Chickasaws, led by Tuscaloosa, assaulted the Spaniards, killing and wounding many. The next spring they mauled the weary invaders again. In a surprise raid, they killed many horses and hogs and also burned clothing, food, and equipment. Despite these setbacks for the Spaniards, the leaders' greed kept the tiny army going in its futile search for wealth. When leaders of the Natchez tribe ridiculed de Soto's claim that he had descended from the sun and rejected his demands, the weary Spanish continued down the Mississippi River. By May 1542, their leader had died and the remainder of the contingent struggled back to Mexico. Their four-year invasion of the thickly settled Southeast brought violent deaths and spread European diseases that weakened many of the Native societies. This invasion permanently disrupted aboriginal life as the ancestors of the upland tribes who later became the Choctaws and Chickasaws moved into areas replacing the groups destroyed by Spanish violence.

A generation later the Spanish returned to Florida. Led by Pedro Menéndez de Avilés, they landed in the mid-1560s and quickly destroyed a French outpost near present-day St. Augustine. Then they built a few small forts along the Atlantic coast, and by the 1570s Franciscan friars arrived to open missions. Between 1595 and the 1650s they started at least thirty-four missions from the Atlantic coast west to what is now Tallahassee. In each they persuaded the villagers to build a small church and began trying to teach Catholic Christianity to their hosts. From the start the friars worked to change Indians into copies of Europeans in dress, language, and religion. Some of the Native people just adapted bits of Christianity to their own beliefs or new foods to their diets. The less nutritious mission fare led to iron-deficiency anemia, lower birthrates, and lower resistance to European diseases among the converts. Yet other villagers added new European crops and livestock, and this encouraged people to settle in larger towns. The Franciscan friars hoped this would bring them more converts, but they rarely had more than forty people at any one place. One friar reported that the Indians refused to move to the missions because when they became Christians "the Spaniards treat them as slaves, they no longer have liberty, nor are they masters of their possessions." Whatever else they did, the friars helped the Florida mission towns grow into prime targets for later white and Native raiding parties.

Although far from any coast, tribes in the Southwest did not escape Spanish incursions. Continuing stories of richly clad Natives who lived in wealthy cities far north of Mexico caught the interest of authorities in northern New Spain. In 1540 Francisco Vásquez de Coronado led the largest expedition up to that time into the future United States. With some four hundred Spaniards, another three hundred servants and slaves, one thousand Indian allies, and at least as many horses, cattle, mules, and sheep, he traveled north into present-day New Mexico. Having followed the advice of Fray Marcos, who had visited the region earlier, the invaders faced bitter disappointment when they reached the first of the Zuni pueblos, which they thought was the legendary city of Cíbola. This was no city of gold. Rather, it was a three-story mud adobe structure that looked less inviting than some of the farming villages Coronado's men had passed in New Spain. The Zuni offered some food, but when they asked the Spanish to leave, violence erupted. During the fighting, the soldiers' armor protected most of them from injury, and after their defeat, the villagers had to accept the invaders' presence for some time. It seems likely that the Zuni resistance stemmed from rumors they heard from people who had met the invaders earlier about what to expect from the strangers.

Although Coronado seems to have been less greedy and destructive than de Soto, who marched through the Southeast at the same time, his force entered a region with a smaller population and a much weaker economic base. With less fertile land to cultivate, little water for irrigation, and violent Apachean neighbors, the New Mexico tribes experienced severe demographic shocks from the Spanish invasion. Meanwhile the explorers continued their hunt for riches, with one party finding its way north and west to the Grand Canyon. The rest of the expedition reached the vicinity of Albuquerque, where they robbed the nearby Indians repeatedly. When men from various pueblos raided the Spaniards several times during the winter of 1540–41, the invaders struck back. In a vicious attack, the soldiers destroyed the pueblo of Arenal and immolated its defenders. By spring they had destroyed about a dozen of the nearby villages. Soon afterward, in 1541, Coronado led his force east onto the plains, seeking the fabled city of Quivira, but somewhere in Kansas he quit. Instead of a golden city, he found Caddoan people living in villages of grass shelters. Having failed to do anything more than spread destruction and disease among villagers, he returned to Mexico.

While the Indians probably celebrated when the unwelcome intruders left, their freedom lasted only another fifty years. In 1598 Juan de Oñate led some five hundred soldiers, settlers, and friars up the Rio Grande Valley into New Mexico. These people had no intention of hurrying through on a search for gold; they had come to stay. Pueblo leaders welcomed the Spanish cautiously, soon moving out of one Tewa town to make room for them. When the newcomers also demanded laborers, food, fuel, and clothing, the villagers reluctantly complied. After a short time, some of the soldiers complained about their inactivity and lack of opportunities to find wealth in the new land, and so Oñate sent them exploring. At Acoma Pueblo the soldiers' actions quickly outraged the Indians, who attacked, killing the commanding officer and twelve of his men. At first it seemed that they had succeeded in driving the Spanish away, but the soldiers soon returned. Seventy well-armored fighting men stormed into the village, and in bitter combat they killed nearly eight hundred people. Then the victors hacked off one foot from each of the surviving adult males and enslaved the women and children for the next twenty years.

At least temporarily this barbarity seems to have terrified the Puebloan groups in New Mexico and others nearby. The uneasy peace that followed allowed the Spanish settlers along the Rio Grande to spread slowly, as they established small farming communities near the river and its tributaries. Friars lived at many of the pueblos, and nearby troops tried to retain control over the region. The invaders' atrocities did little to help persuade the Indians to accept Christianity. In fact, one of the Puebloans asked a friar "if [you] who are Christians caused so much harm and violence, why should [we] become Christians?" The cleric had no persuasive answer, and repeated efforts to disrupt and destroy Indian religious practices and to seize and burn sacred items enraged the villagers. Despite their anger toward the Spanish, language and cultural differences often kept them from uniting against their oppressors. Still, individual pueblos rebelled, and the Spanish had to subdue outbreaks at Zuni in 1632, Taos in 1639, and Jémez in 1644 and 1647, as well as among the Tewa in 1650. These Indian efforts to regain their independence taught the Spanish little, because neither civil nor clerical practices changed. In fact, the invaders continued to impress labor and food from the Indians and to interfere in every way possible with Native ceremonies and cultural practices.

This intolerance helped generate the one successful, multitribal revolt that took place in colonial New Mexico, although other factors played parts too. From 1660 to 1680, the Southwest experienced repeated droughts and higher than normal temperatures. For the agricultural Puebloans, this meant crisis, if not disaster. Each year they produced skimpy crops, and each year Spanish demands for labor and food continued. The droughts also affected their nomadic Apachean neighbors. As the aridity continued, their hunting and gathering became less successful, and so they stepped up their raiding of their sedentary neighbors. Responding this, village shamans blamed their troubles on the acceptance of Spanish cultural and religious ideas, and they strove to reenergize the kiva religious ceremonies. Whenever Spanish friars or priests learned of this, they seized sacred items and had the Native priests arrested, frequently whipping some of them publicly and executing several others.

Outraged by this treatment, in 1680 a San Juan Pueblo shaman named Popé persuaded leaders in almost all of the pueblos that they had to join together and annihilate the Spanish or their own gods might destroy them. On August 10, 1680 a concerted attack on the intruders began, with nearly all of the seventeen thousand Puebloans cooperating. In the first few days, fighting broke out in almost every town or village, and the Indians killed hundreds of Spaniards. They focused much of their fury on the churches and clerics, burning buildings and killing priests whenever they could. Those settlers who could flee did so, and early in the fighting over one thousand people straggled south to El Paso. In the days that followed, the Indians drove the rest of the population into Santa Fe. There, after a bitter siege in which the attackers cut off the water supply and burned much of the town, the survivors broke through Indian lines and fled southward. At this point Popé and the other leaders halted the fighting. They wanted to drive the hated invaders out of their pueblos, and once the Spaniards left they had achieved that goal. In the months that followed, they destroyed more of the invaders' property, particularly the churches and any religious objects discarded earlier.

The Spanish considered the Pueblo Revolt of 1680 to be a nativist and anti-Catholic event. In their view, Popé and the other shamans represented Satan, and their fight was just a part of his battle with Christianity. Given the strong ties between church and state in the Spanish empire at the time, the authorities assumed that they had to avenge their military defeat and the desecration of church items. So, twelve years later, in 1692, Diego de Vargas led troops north from El Paso to reassert control over the New Mexico tribes. By this time the Indians' earlier unity had unraveled, and their short-lived freedom ended. Another rebellion, this time in 1696, failed. According to Indian testimony, the priests' actions against Pueblo religious ideas and practices lay at the center of the Puebloans' anti-Christian bitterness. Once they learned this, the clerics wisely chose to ignore many Indian kiva activities, and a sort of standoff between the clerics and the shamans developed. By the end of the seventeenth century, Spanish settlement efforts among the Indians of the Southwest slowed markedly. To colonial leaders in Mexico City, that northern region appeared distant and produced little wealth, and so their interest in expansion waned. As a result, tribal people saw only a slow increase in the number of their oppressors.

During the century after Oñate's invasion the Spaniards' introduction of horses changed the lives of many western tribes drastically. Once they got over their initial shock at seeing these animals, Indians recognized their value. Within a few decades of their seizing, finding, and trading for horses, horse ownership gave them a new mobility that shaped their transportation, hunting, and raiding practices. By the 1650s Apaches got horses from the Pueblos in eastern New Mexico and became mounted hunters. Before the end of the century Rocky Mountain Utes and southern plains Comanches both developed hunting cultures based on their horse herds. The Comanches soon dominated the southern plains trading networks while they became successful buffalo hunters and dreaded raiders. During the eighteenth century Native groups as widely separated as the Nez Perce in the Pacific Northwest and the Lakota Sioux on the northern plains traded and raided to get horses of their own. Well before the United States became independent, horses had become central for many western tribes. A mixed blessing, these animals made life easier for their owners, but the mobility they offered also increased intertribal raiding and warfare.

Encountering the French

The tribes of Florida were first to face intruding Europeans, but within a generation the French followed the Spanish to North America. Although Jacques Cartier and his companions avoided the wanton brutality exhibited by de Soto and his army, Indians along the St. Lawrence Valley of eastern Canada still faced danger when dealing with the strangers. In July 1534, Micmac people fishing along the Atlantic coast saw the explorer's ship near shore. Quickly they launched their canoes hoping to trade, but their eagerness frightened the French, who fired warning shots to keep them at a distance. A day later, by "holding up . . . some furs on sticks," the Indians convinced the French that they only wanted to trade, opening the way for peaceful meetings between the two. Just before they returned to France, the explorers kidnapped two young sons of the chief, Donnacona, hoping that the youths could learn French and serve as translators.

The next summer Cartier returned, sailing his three ships up the St. Lawrence to Stadacona, a village near the site of modern Quebec City. There the captives rejoined their father after promising to lead the French farther upstream. Later they refused to do so and warned the villagers that the explorers could not be trusted. This left Cartier's party to travel farther inland alone. Most of that winter the Indians ignored their unwelcome visitors, until the French became sick with scurvy. Then the Indians taught them how to cure it with a tea made from tree bark and leaves. In the spring of 1536, the treacherous Cartier kidnapped Chief Donnacona and his two sons and sailed back to France. Living there further exposed the captives to common European diseases, and the chief died before he could be returned home. The French explorer came back a third time, in 1541. By then the Indians avoided the strangers whenever they could. Mutual suspicion led to some violence that winter, and in the summer of 1542 the French party gave up and sailed away.

During the next few decades a modest fur trade along the north Atlantic coast began. When the Indians went east to enjoy the warm weather and to fish, they met European fishermen, and by the 1580s they had begun exchanging furs for tools, weapons, cloth, and jewelry. By that time fashions in Europe had changed and the easily workable beaver pelts became central for successful trading. While furs were commonplace for the tribal hunters, metal goods and comfortable fabrics were not, so often the Indians began the trade. Clearly the hunters thought that the trade items they got from the French had at least as much value as the animal skins the strangers welcomed so eagerly, and they traded willingly. In fact, they often thought that they got more from the trade than did their partners. One French cleric reported that his acquaintances laughed about the value the Europeans placed on the furs. They told him that "the Beaver does everything to perfection. He makes for us kettles, axes, swords, knives, and gives us drink and food without the trouble of cultivating the ground." Here the Indians did not consider the trade as exploitation.

The exchange continued and became the economic base for relations by the early seventeenth century, when Samuel de Champlain established the tiny settlement that became Quebec. Both the villagers and the newcomers wanted the trade to continue, so they worked to avoid violence or war that might disrupt it. However, the new alliance that evolved brought warfare anyway, with different groups. In 1609 the five nations of the Iroquois Confederacy in western New York became bitter enemies of the French after Champlain and a few of his men helped the Hurons attack and defeat a Mohawk force that year. The Iroquoians

saw Champlain's friendship with their Huron enemies as a major threat. This relatively minor incident set the stage for more than a century of fighting between the
French and their tribal allies in Canada and the Native people in New York.

For much of the century those tribes dealing with the French came to view
them as trading partners and diplomatic and military allies or as competitors
and enemies. Even though only a few would-be settlers built homes or established farms in the St. Lawrence Valley or south of the eastern Great Lakes, the
newcomers' presence and actions had serious immediate and long-term impacts
on the villagers. Within only a generation after Champlain had founded Quebec,
the Hurons of southern Ontario dominated a trade network that included tribes
living hundreds of miles farther inland. Each spring they brought bundles of beaver pelts down the rivers to the French settlement, and in return they got and
distributed household items such as pots and pans, needles, knives, and textiles
for the women, as well as axes, knives, guns, and traps for the men. Missionaries
moved into some of the larger villages, and Frenchmen crisscrossed the countryside learning the tribal languages, becoming familiar with routes west, and
meeting more and more village leaders.

Over time these contacts changed both Native and European practices and
ideas, but often the tribal people dominated the meetings. For generations the
Indians insisted on gift exchanges, extended speeches, and formal religious ceremonies before agreeing to any trade or diplomatic action. They also enforced
long-standing tribal borders and property. For example, when a canoe convoy
of Huron traders accompanied by a Jesuit priest tried to force its way upstream
past an Algonquian village and refused to pay the toll that was demanded, the
local chief ordered that the priest be hanged "from a tree by the arm-pits" to enforce the customary right of the village leaders to control passage on "their river."
Tribal groups living near the trading posts soon learned how to manipulate the
exchanges to their advantage. They refused to bring in their furs until several
French ships arrived, and then they bargained until they got good prices for their
furs. Experience taught them to be skeptical of the traders' claims and of the
priests' urgings that they accept the European beliefs. Repeatedly they criticized
the French while defending their own customs. At one meeting they rejected a
Jesuit's claims of superiority by assuring him that they were "not thieves, like
you."

During and after the 1630s, when Jesuit missionaries fanned out among the
villages, diseases—usually smallpox, measles, or influenza—swept through each
tribe they visited. Indian leaders blamed the epidemics on the Black Robes, and
the continued French presence caused bitter divisions within some societies. The
shamans considered the Jesuits to be witches and charged that when the priests
administered the last rites to the dying, they were actually killing their patients.
When the clerics carried life-size images of Jesus and the Virgin Mary during
a particularly virulent epidemic, the Indians blamed the images for the sickness
and death. Jesuit efforts to stop Indian torturing of prisoners in one village so

enraged the chiefs that they ordered holes burned in the hands and feet of the victims to mock the crucifixion story. Throughout the seventeenth century, traditionalists strove to keep their French allies from destroying tribal religious, cultural, and economic practices. Often how well they succeeded depended on how far they lived from French settlements and whether or not any missionaries came to their villages.

Over the decades Native peoples living south of the Great Lakes and along the major rivers in the upper Midwest and the Mississippi Valley all met French traders, government officials, or priests. Usually the villagers cooperated by holding councils and negotiating alliances, and frequently they encouraged the strangers to marry young women and become part of the community. As a result, French influence and presence grew as they built tiny trading posts, missions, and forts throughout the region. Not all Indian groups there welcomed the Europeans, but most wanted access to the trade goods that came during times of peace. Others, such as the Iroquois tribes in New York, fought the French and their tribal allies for much of the century. These conflicts, often called the Beaver Wars, brought destruction to many groups. Wide-ranging Mohawk and Seneca war parties moved out of New York, attacking tribes from Pennsylvania west to Illinois and Wisconsin as they tried to smash the French-Huron trading system and the alliances that had evolved. Their assaults forced their tribal enemies to flee or to accept Iroquois domination whenever the French proved unable or unwilling to help defend against the raids.

The experiences of many northeastern tribes, then, differed markedly from that of groups who encountered the Spanish. The Spaniards came to conquer, to exploit, and to convert, by force if necessary, but the French usually came to trade first and to bring Christianity later. For most of the seventeenth century the fur trade dominated relationships between the northern groups, and the Europeans there had to remain mostly peaceful for trade to continue. Certainly the Jesuits brought their full energies and skills to the challenges of converting Indians to Christianity, but they lacked the military support that the Spanish often gave their missionaries. The interethnic contacts in New France brought disease, economic change, village disruption, division, and forced movement. Yet many of the village societies came to terms with the intruders, adapting some European ideas and practices while forcing the French to do many things the Indian way. Richard White, who has studied these relationships extensively, labels the results of the blending of cultures south of the Great Lakes as a "Middle Ground," where the two societies met and each changed by accepting practices of the other.

Encountering the Dutch

For tribal people living along the coasts of present-day New York, New Jersey, and Delaware before the 1660s, the Dutch posed a formidable threat. Although they never invaded in large numbers, their determination, greed, and ethnocentrism caused more than their share of misery. By the early 1620s the Dutch West India Company brought settlers to the Hudson River Valley, and they moved quickly to build Fort Orange, near present-day Albany, New York. More than a century later, one account reported that when they saw the Europeans' ship, the Indians thought that it was "a large canoe or house, in which the great Mannitto [Supreme Being] *himself* was, and that he probably was coming to visit them." Rather than the Supreme Being, the ship carried Dutchmen. Another description noted that "our visitors were white [and we thought that they] must be sick." The Algonquian tribes of the region often competed with or fought each other as well as their Iroquoian neighbors, and so, when the outsiders arrived, the tribes could not unite easily against them. Early trade pleased both sides, but by the 1630s the company directors decided to enlarge their enterprise, and soon they began shipping hundreds of farmers and townspeople to the settlements. This changed relations between the villagers and the colonists quickly. As long as trade drove their contacts, the two sides needed each other. Once Dutch farmers arrived, however, they wanted land, and the Indians' cleared, well-tended plots looked too attractive to resist.

This led to bitter fighting from the 1640s until the English ousted the Dutch authorities two decades later. When colonial farmers spread onto lands being used by Indian families, anger and violence followed. As happened later in New England, the newcomers' unfenced livestock destroyed tribal crops. If Lenape villagers objected or dared to kill the cattle or swine, Governor William Kieft encouraged the settlers to retaliate. Determined to clear the nearby lands of Indians, in 1642 he supplied the farmers with arms and sent them marching through the countryside to intimidate the villagers. The next year he launched a destructive attack on the village of Pavonia, triggering a series of raids and widespread destruction of Native groups. During the negotiations that ended the fighting, tribal leaders protested Dutch aggression vehemently. They reminded the colonial negotiators that the Indians had welcomed the Dutch into their villages, given them young women to marry, and traded with them. "Why," they complained, "did you villainously massacre your own blood?"—clearly thinking that they had created a family relationship with the invaders. The victors could say little in response, but their aggression continued. From 1657 to 1664, raiding and warfare between the Esophus tribe and the Dutch kept the region in turmoil.

The New Netherlands settlement had a broad and long-term impact on tribes of the Northeast that went far beyond the destruction of the coastal groups. Operating out of Fort Orange near Albany, Dutch traders opened a solid trade with the nearby Mohawks. When the Mohawks began their attacks on the French and their Huron trading partners along the St. Lawrence Valley in the 1640s, they needed weapons, and despite company objections to a firearms trade, local officials acquiesced. That relationship remained profitable for businessmen, but more importantly it bound the authorities to a trade and diplomatic alliance with the Iroquois Five Nations Confederacy in what would become New York. For the

Iroquois, that meant a steady supply of arms and other trade goods in the bitter competition with their French and tribal enemies. At the same time, it tied them closely to whichever group controlled the trade at Albany, and during the next century it helped drag them into the imperial wars between the French and the British.

Encountering the English

For American Indians, the English colonists who began arriving in the late sixteenth century eventually became the most important and most dangerous of the invaders. By the time tribal peoples met them, these aggressive outsiders had acquired plenty of experience in attacking and subjugating others. First they had defeated and conquered the Scots. Then they invaded Ireland, where they tried to subdue the "savage" inhabitants and developed ideas and practices used later in North America. In the long run, however, the English movement into North America posed the most serious threat to the aboriginal societies because the English came to settle the land. Although the other invading Europeans may have hoped to do that, only the English ever got large numbers of people to cross the North Atlantic. As a settler society, they needed land, not just furs or hides, and when they took it, their actions brought irreversible changes to the Native societies that faced them.

The British invasion began in the summer of 1584 when the Roanoke and Croatan tribes that lived on the North Carolina coast first encountered English sailors near present-day Roanoke Island. Men from the two ships sent by Sir Walter Raleigh landed, hoping to find a site for a future trading post and settlement. The Algonquian people there welcomed the visitors cautiously, while they traded minor items and tried to make themselves understood. After a few weeks, as the crewmen prepared to leave, they took "two of the savages being lustie men, whose names were Wanchese and Manteo," aboard the ships. Apparently one of the pair volunteered, but it seems likely that the English seized the other man.

Despite that, when Raleigh sent seven ships carrying six hundred men to America in 1585, the Indians remained peaceful. That changed in June of that year, when tribesmen visited one of the newcomers' ships and a silver cup belonging to Sir Richard Grenville turned up missing. The Indians denied having stolen it, but the English decided to punish them for theft. Like the Spanish, Dutch, and later the Russians, they attacked first by destroying the nearby cornfields and then by burning the closest village. The shocked tribesmen took no immediate action, but they soon retaliated. This led to English counterattacks and further Indian raids. Not all of the colonists supported the aggressive tactics their leaders used. In late 1585 one colonist complained that "some of our companie . . . shewed themselves too fierce, in slaying some of the people" over minor matters they should have ignored. During the 1585–86 winter, fears of Indian attacks kept the English worried. When ships expected to bring people and supplies failed to arrive in June 1586, the leaders decided to abandon their settlement. Before giving up, however, Governor William Lane launched another series of attacks, killing and decapitating one chief and scattering the nearby villagers.

The Algonquians had little time to recover or to celebrate their enemies' departure, because just a few weeks later Sir Richard Grenville returned with a new group of settlers. When he learned that the colonists had evacuated the site, he decided to leave only eighteen men to continue the English presence there and then sailed back to Europe. Soon the Indians attacked, killing or driving the men away. In 1587 the last group of colonists arrived, but they needed support from home, and so the governor returned to England to gather more people and supplies. A war between Britain and Spain cut off the colony until 1590, by which time the Roanoke Island settlers had disappeared. Apparently, continuing hostilities with local tribes reduced the settlement, and the survivors migrated north to settle among tribes near the Chesapeake Bay. Whatever happened, this first English colonial venture failed. The experience warned the coastal Indians of the potential dangers the strangers posed.

The Native peoples of coastal Virginia encountered the next English arrivals. In the spring of 1607 three small vessels sailed nearly sixty miles up the James River to what is now Jamestown. After a peaceful meeting with the Paspahegh tribe, the colonists began to build temporary shelters. As soon as they realized that the strangers meant to stay, the villagers "fell to skyrmishing & killed 3" of the newcomers before a volley of English musketry drove them off. The local Indians belonged to a powerful chiefdom of thirty tribes with nearly two hundred villages, all under the direction of a leader the colonists called Powhatan. When he learned about the intruders, Powhatan sent a war party of 160 men to drive them away. Once again the Europeans' small arms, this time aided by cannon fire from the ships in the river, ended the attack.

Having decided that the English offered valuable metal items, Powhatan soon shifted his tactics from military confrontation to diplomacy. Perhaps he hoped to incorporate the newcomers into his confederacy or to become allied with them against his tribal enemies. Despite his efforts, relations remained strained at best, as frequent raids by whites and Indians alike kept the region in turmoil. By 1608, John Smith, a colonial leader, began an aggressive policy of demanding that the villagers stop raiding and also provide corn and other food to the settlers. He led armed bands into nearby villages, often taking food and hostages at gunpoint. Smith infuriated Opechancanough, leader of the powerful Pamunkey tribe and later Powhatan's successor, publicly humiliating him by holding a gun to his head and forcing his followers to fill a boat with corn for the invaders. The young chief's hatred of the English remained hidden for years, but it contributed to two devastating wars against the colonists. Unaware of this threat, Smith boasted that in 1609 the aging Powhatan had begged him for peace, asking "what will it availe you to take that by force you may quickly have by love, or to destroy them that provide you food." Despite such bragging, the sporadic fighting continued.

Pocahontas (Matoaka) c. 1595–1617

Probably the most well-known Indian woman in U.S. history, Pocahontas was the daughter of Chief Powhatan (Wahunsunacock), the leader of a thirty-tribe Indian confederacy in coastal Virginia in 1607 when the first English settlers landed there. As a small child she lived with her mother, one of many temporary wives of the chief. Some years later she rejoined Powhatan's household, being trained in the usual Indian domestic duties assigned to girls and young women. By the time she was about ten she had visited Jamestown several times, at least once carrying messages from her father to the English, as the Indians negotiated for the release of captives they held. Several years later she played a modest role in Indian-white peace negotiations, but it had nothing to do with the later story of her having rescued John Smith from execution. Rather, in 1613 Captain Samuel Argall captured her and the colonists held her hostage at Jamestown. There she learned to speak English and was baptized, taking the name Rebecca. A year later, colonial leaders took her and John Rolfe to Powhatan's village, asking for Powhatan's assent to her marriage to Rolfe. The chief agreed in what both sides considered to be a diplomatic effort to bring peace. In 1615 the couple had a son, Thomas, and a year later the Virginia Company brought Rolfe, Pocahontas, the baby, and several other Indians to London to stimulate interest in the settlement. Apparently the visiting "Indian Princess" impressed her English hosts, but she died as the ship left London to carry her back to Virginia. Her story demonstrates some of the ways that young Indian women could deal with the invaders who wanted to conquer their people.

Source: Helen Rountree, *Pocahontas's People: The Powhatan Indians of Virginia Through Four Centuries* (Norman: University of Oklahoma Press, 1990).

Tired of continued warfare with the English, Powhatan sued for peace in 1614, and the next few years remained calm. Like their European competitors in North America, the Jamestown colonists talked of bringing Christianity to the tribal people. After Pocahontas was baptized, English missionary groups began planning for an Indian college named Henrico, to be supported by contributions from England and by profits made by farming land in Virginia set aside for it. Although the Algonquians had no interest in the foreigners' gods, Opechancanough promised to allow some of his people to listen to missionaries if the whites gave muskets, powder, and lead to some of his men. Soon after that, a few native families moved from their villages into the English settlements, but they stayed only briefly. While there colonial leaders foolishly allowed young Indian men to learn how to use the muskets and to drill with the militia.

While the tribes gained European military equipment, a virtual tobacco craze swept through the colony. With high profits for the crop, English farmers rushed to plant on open land wherever they found it, often on the cleared fields of Native farmers. This increased tensions dramatically. In early 1622, several Englishmen murdered Nemattanew, a charismatic shaman and close associate of Opechancanough. For the angry Indians, this was the last straw, and on March 22, 1622, the Powhatan Confederacy forces overwhelmed outlying settlements and isolated farms. They killed so many colonists that the authorities called the attack the Massacre of 1622. Fighting raged for much of that year, and as late as the spring of 1623 tribal forces annihilated a militia company that had marched out from Jamestown against them. They defended their homeland so stoutly that at one point warriors in sixty canoes attacked the *Tiger*, a small ship in the James River. These actions led the English to recognize Opechancanough as the "Great General of the Savages" but did nothing to end the hostilities. Sporadic warfare continued until 1632, when the confederacy leaders accepted colonial terms for peace.

For the next decade, the Virginia tribes watched as the colonial population grew and whites spread ever farther from Jamestown and into the villagers' home areas. This movement went mostly in one direction, because the colonists built log palisades between the James and York Rivers to keep Indians away from the settlements. Because of the continuing incidents between his people and the pioneers, the aged Chief Opechancanough reinvigorated the Powhatan Confederacy and, although he had to be carried on a litter, in 1644 led it into another all-out war. Once again the tribal forces caught the Virginians by surprise and inflicted heavy casualties, but in the long run the warriors ran out of weapons and ammunition. As the war ended, the English captured the Indian leader and held him briefly at Jamestown. Then they shot him, claiming that he was trying to escape. By the 1670s, when Bacon's Rebellion swept through the Virginia backcountry, the Indians had been reduced to serving as an excuse for pioneer aggression in what became a civil war within the colony. When that conflict ended in 1677, the scattered tribes signed a peace agreement at Williamsburg, which reduced them to dependency on the Virginia authorities.

Tribal experiences in New England varied somewhat from the violence and confrontation in the Chesapeake region. There no major chiefdom stood ready to challenge the intruders. Rather, the tribes had been in competition and conflict for generations. Also, in the years 1616–19 visiting fishermen and traders had introduced epidemic diseases that swept through many coastal villages, severely depopulating some areas. One early observer reported seeing entire towns standing vacant, with once-cleared fields filled with waist-high brush and the "bones and skulls of the dead" lying about where wild animals had left them.

Those same sailors who had carried the plagues kidnapped men from several tribes, and if those individuals ever got home, they spread anti-English stories wherever they went. Thus, even before the English tried to establish colonies, coastal people had reasons to fear and hate them.

Whether the villagers realized this or not, early English colonists certainly feared the New England peoples. Pilgrim leader William Bradford, before he ever got off the *Mayflower*, described the Indians as a "savage people, who are cruel, barbarous and most treacherous." When the coastal Algonquian people saw the English ship offshore, they sent scouts to observe, keeping their distance for weeks. Then, late on December 7, 1620, the villagers came up to the Pilgrims' stockade, making what the terrified whites described as "a great and strange cry" before loosing a rain of arrows into the camp. As in Virginia, the attackers withdrew after the whites replied with musket fire. The Indians ignored the sickly colonists through the winter of 1620–21, except for taking a few tools left in one of the fields and shouting unintelligible words from a nearby hilltop. The Pilgrims responded by placing several of their cannons on the hill.

In March 1621, Samoset, an Abenaki sagamore (chief), walked into Plymouth. Speaking English to his astounded listeners, he described some of the nearby tribes and promised to bring other chiefs to the settlement. On March 22, Chief Massasoit (Yellow Feather) of the Wampanoag tribe led sixty of his men into the settlement. This terrified the Pilgrims, but at that moment the English-speaking Tisquantum (Squanto) stepped forward. He had been kidnapped in 1614, enslaved by the Spanish, and then had worked on an English trading ship, where he had learned the language. Having escaped, in 1621 he lived with Massasoit's people and served as a valued interpreter for several years. Talks between the colonists and their visitors soon led to a formal treaty. The Wampanoag leaders feared the powerful Narragansett tribe just west of them and wanted assurances of help, while the English desperately needed peace and trade. In the agreement the two crafted, the chief agreed to help enforce peace between Indians and whites, end the petty theft of the colonists' tools, and punish those who hurt or robbed the English. John Carver, the colonial governor, agreed that the Pilgrims would aid their tribal allies if anyone else attacked them. This mutual defense pact lasted for the next forty years.

At first the Wampanoag-Pilgrim treaty kept peace, but in 1630 the far more numerous Puritans began their Massachusetts Bay colony at Boston. During the 1630s thousands of Puritans came to Massachusetts, and their arrival strained peaceful dealings with the Indians. Apparently their religious scruples and fears of an Indian war restrained the whites' greed for land at first, because for a time colonial leaders tried to protect the villagers' property and rights. They punished pioneers who ran roughshod over the Indians, and one small community even had to pay for damages English hogs did to tribal crops. As the colonial population grew, white self-confidence replaced wariness, and by mid decade Puritan authorities became more aggressive.

That change in attitude led to a major war in just a couple of years. English entry into the Connecticut River Valley brought the Pequot tribe there face to face with the intruders. They could not have arrived at a worse time for the Indians. By the early 1630s, Chief Uncas had led his Mohegan followers out of the tribe, and the nearby Narragansetts used that move as an excuse to undermine the Pequot intermediary role in trade with the Dutch. In 1633–34 several epidemics swept through the villages, and soon after that, John Stone, a dishonest English trader, appeared. He tried to kidnap some of the villagers to hold for ransom. Enraged, the Indians stormed aboard his ship, killing Stone and eight of the crew. It is not entirely clear that the Pequots carried out the attack, but Massachusetts authorities forced tribal leaders to accept a treaty in which they agreed to capture and turn over the murderers to the English, pay reparations for the killings, and accept colonial settlement in their homeland.

In this first contact with the Puritans, Pequot chiefs recognized that the newcomers threatened their independence, but they had no idea how aggressive and brutal their new neighbors would become. Tribal leaders would not surrender Stone's suspected killers, and they paid only part of the demanded reparations for his death. In 1636, with English settlement moving into the Pequots' homeland, a second incident brought the two sides into conflict. In July that year, Indians on the coast near Block Island attacked and killed another trader, John Oldham. At that point Puritan leaders moved toward war. They demanded that the Pequots surrender those who had killed the two traders and began raiding Indian villages. When the inhabitants fled, the troops burned crops and dwellings. Angry warriors struck back, raiding outlying towns and carrying off isolated farm families as prisoners.

Tribal leaders saw few options and defended their villages vigorously. At the same time, they tried to strengthen ties with neighboring tribes but with little success. Although land hunger rather than genuine piety drove many settlers, the Puritans considered the challenge to their authority at least partly in religious terms. They characterized the tribal actions to block English expansion as the work of the devil, and they called for all-out war. In May 1637 militia leader John Mason led a combined white-Indian army against the largest Pequot village on the Mystic River. Slipping through the palisaded entry in the predawn light, Mason's troops set fire to many of the lodges. When the villagers awoke, they ran out of their burning lodges into a barrage of gunfire and arrows from the force surrounding the village. The Pequots were destroyed. So many died in that morning attack that the slaughter appalled Puritan witnesses. Describing the scene, one of them wrote that "it was a fearful sight to see them thus frying in the fire . . . and horrible was the stinck & sente thereof." When the fighting ended, the victors sold many of their captives into slavery in the West Indies or placed them under the authority of their tribal enemies.

Other tribes avoided that kind of desperate confrontation, but not easily. Although the Wampanoags and other smaller groups had remained at peace since their 1621 treaty with Plymouth, the Puritans wanted to dominate the region. They viewed Indian shamans as spokesmen for the devil, passed laws to control daily activities, and urged whole villages to move into "praying towns" where teachers and missionaries could turn them into good Christians. At the same time, authorities brought the villagers under the colonial legal system. Frontier settlers moved their animals into the forests, often near unfenced Indian fields instead of building fences to keep the livestock from destroying the Natives' crops, and then the whites blamed their tribal neighbors for leaving their fields unprotected. As long as Chief Massasoit remained alive, the two societies avoided war, but in 1661 he died. His son Wamsutta lacked the luck or skills his father had enjoyed, and only a year later Plymouth authorities brought him into town at gunpoint for questioning. They soon released him, but he died before returning home.

While being pressured to accept English political dominance, the New England tribes also faced a cultural offensive led by missionaries and teachers determined to remake them as copies of the English. By the middle of the seventeenth century, John Eliot, Thomas Mayhew, and Mayhew's son (also named Thomas) had brought Christianity to the villagers of Massachusetts and nearby coastal islands. Between 1650 and the 1670s, Eliot established eleven so-called praying towns that drew their populations from some of the most threatened villages. He modeled these communities after Old Testament accounts and developed strict regulations for the new communities. The rules prohibited drunkenness, polygamy, Sabbath breaking, and other activities. English authorities supervised the actions of village magistrates, and so, while the Algonquian towns seemed to have local autonomy, the Puritans supervised almost all aspects of life. In Massachusetts the authorities paid to send at least twenty Indian boys to school, hoping to prepare them for entrance to Harvard. That university established an Indian College in 1658, but it failed. Despite mixed feelings about their Puritan neighbors, some tribal groups participated in these religious and educational activities.

The central dispute between the tribal people and the colonists focused on Indian efforts to retain their culture and independence. Plymouth leaders rejected that idea out of hand, and when young Metacomet (King Philip) succeeded his brother as the tribal chief in 1661, the disputes worsened. Fending off repeated demands for Wampanoag land, Metacomet saw the English as harsh aggressors. Ongoing damage of village crops by the colonists' animals remained a contentious matter as well. As Indian resentment grew, colonial leaders feared that the tribes would unite and attack frontier settlements. To prevent this, English officials demanded that Metacomet surrender his followers' weapons. He objected that this left his people nearly defenseless against their tribal enemies and greatly reduced their hunting abilities. When the magistrates waved such arguments aside, he told them, "I am determined not to live until I have no country." In 1674 a Christian Indian named John Sassamon told the colonists that the Wampanoag chief had begun to prepare for war and to form anti-English alliances. A month later the authorities found Sassamon's body under the ice in a nearby pond. They arrested three men from Philip's band. After being tortured, one of the men confessed to his murder, and all three were executed.

Scattered violence continued for much of the next year, and in 1675 what is now called King Philip's War began. Most of the Rhode Island and Massachusetts tribes joined forces against the English, destroying farms, overrunning entire villages, and killing or capturing hundreds of colonists. The English struck back with an army of one thousand men against the Narragansetts and called on their Mohawk allies from New York to attack Philip's forces too. As usually happened, the Indian soldiers ran out of ammunition and had to resort to using bows, arrows, and lances against colonial troops that were wearing some body armor and using firearms. In the early summer of 1676, colonial militiamen captured Metacomet's wife and son and quickly shipped them off to slavery in the West Indies. On August 11, they surprised and killed the Indian leader. After cutting off his head, they displayed their grisly trophy atop the town gate for years. The war had pitted tribe against tribe as well as tribal groups against the English. When it ended, Indian villages stood vacant and many English towns lay in ashes. The efforts to coexist with the colonists had failed, as the whites smashed all resistance. By the late 1670s, surviving Indians had to accept colonial domination or slip away to join related groups far from the settlements.

For much of the seventeenth century the Carolina tribes had less contact with the English than did groups in either Virginia or New England. The first settlers arrived in 1670, and ten years later they founded what became Charleston. The early outpost resembled French settlement actions in the North, as the pioneers began a trade-based economy. For the coastal tribes this proved advantageous for two reasons. They gained coveted European goods, and they served as intermediaries for the trade between the English and tribes farther from the coast. However, some Indian groups nearby had not settled permanently, and so the English presence disrupted their movements. This resulted in bitter competition among the tribes, particularly in 1674, when the Westos, a group new to the coastal region, opened successful trade relations with the English. In 1680, minor incidents among the Indians and between tribes and whites led the Charleston traders to ally themselves with the Savannahs to defeat and enslave the surviving Westos. Thus, in Carolina, even though few actual settlers contended for tribal land, in a short time Native people there became enmeshed in trade and military alliances with their dangerous neighbors.

As the seventeenth century drew to a close, Indians in many parts of the country had encountered Europeans. Explorers, traders, diplomats, soldiers, and settlers had arrived, forever changing the face of aboriginal America. Some people benefited from the manufactured goods they obtained. Certainly fabric made some clothing more comfortable. Both men and women enjoyed metal implements, the women in the lodge and the field, and the men for hunting, land clearing, or warfare. At the same time, trade relations with whites brought other responsibilities and dangers. Epidemic disease followed the traders' steps closely, and many Native groups also faced unwelcome missionaries. In the Southwest the Spanish brought horses and overcame the Pueblo Revolt. To the northeast the Iroquois and French finally agreed to peace, while in New England and Virginia the local tribes had suffered crushing defeats. Only in the Southeast did most village groups manage to avoid such disasters. Their apparent good fortune resulted from the slowness of European penetration into their home region. In the century that followed, Indians in all of these areas would have to come to terms with vastly altered circumstances. The outsiders who now occupied some of their lands were numerous, dangerous, and here to stay.

Suggested Readings

Axtell, James. *Natives and Newcomers: The Colonial Origins of North America.* New York: Oxford University Press, 2001.

Bourne, Russell. *The Red King's Rebellion: Racial Politics in New England, 1675–1678.* New York: Oxford University Press, 1990.

Calloway, Colin G. *One Vast Winter Count: The Native American West before Lewis and Clark.* Lincoln: University of Nebraska Press, 2003.

Hämäläinen, Pekka. *The Comanche Empire.* New Haven: Yale University Press, 2008.

Merrell, James H. *The Indians' New World: Catawbas and Their Neighbors from European Contact through the Era of Removal.* Chapel Hill: University of North Carolina Press, 1989.

Richter, Daniel K. *Trade, Land, Power: The Struggle for Eastern North America.* Philadelphia: University of Pennsylvania Press, 2013.

Rountree, Helen C. *Pocahontas, Powhatan, Opechancanough: Three Indian Lives Changed by Jamestown.* Charlottesville: University of Virginia Press, 2005.

Weber, David J. *The Spanish Frontier in North America.* New Haven: Yale University Press, 1992.

White, Richard. *The Middle Ground: Indians, Empires, and Republics in the Great Lakes Region, 1650–1815.* New York: Cambridge University Press, 1991.

Witgen, Michael. *An Infinity of Nations: How the Native New World Shaped Early America.* Philadelphia: University of Pennsylvania Press, 2013.

CHAPTER 3

Living with Strangers, 1700–1783

B y 1700, except for Native groups in Alaska and along the Pacific Northwest coast, few people living near the oceans or north of New Spain could escape some contact with the European invaders. The seventeenth-century encounters had brought fundamental changes to North America. Some groups gravitated toward the newcomers for trade, defense, and help against their enemies. Others fled from the disease, warfare, and cultural destruction the whites brought to their villages. Whatever their response, Indians faced new issues. Early plagues reduced their populations, often carrying off leaders, shamans, hunters, and others with special skills. Because of those losses, many small tribes disappeared as their survivors fled, joining nearby villages with a similar culture or language whenever they could. For much of the eighteenth century, Native groups struggled to absorb these refugees. They also developed ways to protect their own social customs, economic practices, and military-diplomatic alliances while dealing with the expanding imperial networks of Britain, France, and Spain.

The European newcomers brought such basic changes that ignoring them became impossible. During the eighteenth century, major wars erupted frequently and brought young Indian men into cooperation and conflict with the English, French, and Spanish. Sometimes tribal soldiers traveled hundreds of miles from home, meeting and working with strangers. Other times, invading armies marched through Indian homelands, depleting game and timber and destroying village dwellings, fields, and even crops stored for the next winter. Honor-bound by diplomatic ties and fur-trade connections, the villagers entered many of these conflicts to defend themselves or to help their allies. In some cases, particular tribes persuaded Europeans to help them fight against their Indian competitors or enemies. More often, however, the imperial conflicts among the invading powers pulled Indians into fights where they had little obvious stake in the outcome. By the time of American independence in 1783, many tribes had experienced drastic and permanent changes in the lives of their members. Their numbers dropped, missionaries ridiculed their religious beliefs and ceremonies, trade and European goods changed their economies, and large-scale warfare had disrupted their worlds. The repeated fighting with both white and Native enemies caused massive destruction in village societies, far more than any other actions by the invaders, and many eastern tribes never entirely recovered from the violence.

Trade and Technology

Often when Indians first met white men, it seemed that they wanted to barter immediately. Certainly exchange was nothing new, because long-standing trade networks had tied far-flung groups together in North America for centuries. Yet what the Europeans often saw as tedious routines and time-wasting speeches had important cultural and diplomatic roles in the village societies. There tribal leaders welcomed the strangers with speeches, prayers, dancing, and feasting, and by smoking the calumet (peace pipe) and exchanging gifts. In these early meetings, Indian ceremonies and customs dominated. Actually they continued well into the nineteenth century. To the villagers, these acts created a relationship as allies, even as distant family, with their guests, and they repeated at least some of the ceremonies each time their new "relatives" visited. It seems to have taken the whites several generations to recognize that their welcome in each village went beyond an eagerness to trade.

Having accepted the newcomers as allies, Indians sought manufactured goods such as metal implements, textiles, weapons, and even paints and dyes, which made an immediate impact on their lives. The men recognized that steel knives and axes cut better and lasted longer than stone ones. Women found that iron and brass cooking pots outlasted stone or ceramic pottery and made food preparation easier. With the colorful fabrics traders brought, it was easier to make comfortable clothing. Much of the time, except for alcohol, firearms, and mirrors, the trade goods coming into the villages offered little that was really new. Rather, the items were better, longer lasting, or easier to use than the Native products they replaced. Because many people wanted the trade goods, the exchange that grew from the early contacts soon included Native groups from the Aleutian Islands in the North Pacific to Hudson's Bay in eastern Canada, and from southern Arizona and New Mexico to the East Coast.

In their efforts to acquire trade goods, villagers became part of a cycle of hunting or trapping, carrying the pelts and hides home and then preparing them for use or sale. Each autumn the hunters left home to gather furs. At first men shot or trapped almost furbearer, but soon beaver pelts became the most desired items except in the Southeast. There the hundreds of thousands of white-tailed deer proved more important than the smaller furbearers. When the hunters returned home, village women cleaned and prepared the hides for trade. Although their work increased, neither the men nor the women were doing things entirely new. Hunters had always left the villages for weeks. Now they might be gone for months. The women had always worked with the hides and furs, but now they had more of them to clean. At the same time, the trade brought important changes to the villages. With many of the men absent for longer periods, the women faced extra duties in the villages beyond just having more furs to work. Also, because the men got their traps, firearms, and ammunition on credit each fall, an unsuccessful hunt might push Indian families or even whole villages into debt that they would never be able to pay. These issues introduced new, long-term pressures to tribal life.

The expanding trade brought new challenges to the Europeans as well. At first they failed to realize that when they shared food and exchanged goods for furs in front of or inside smoky lodges, they were entering into a diplomatic agreement with their trading partners. Indian leaders assumed that they had forged an alliance with the Europeans and expected them to live up to tribal customs. The white traders and diplomats had little understanding of this. Young Indian women chose to marry the newcomers to help strengthen ties between the groups and to improve their family standing. At times village elders encouraged their daughters or other female relatives to live with the visitors. This was to benefit both sides, as the trader would become a member of his wife's clan, gaining access to the leading families in the village, and the Indians would, presumably, gain closer ties to the whites. The practice had a direct impact on trade because although some English traders had Indian wives, their French competitors frequently took village brides. This meant that often even though French goods could not compete with English wares in either price or quality, personal connections within many groups kept the competition between the two nearly even. At times this allowed tribal hunters to play one European power against another.

Much of the time trade brought more violence and misery than benefit to the Native people. For example, in the Southeast bitter competition among the English colonists and between them and the nearby Spanish and French enclaves, as well as fundamental disagreements over Indian policies between the English lords proprietors and colonial leaders, brought disaster to some tribal people. Carolina officials proved so dishonest and brutal that a commission ostensibly set up to help the Indians there did just the opposite, acting for their "oppression [rather] than protection." As a result, warfare racked the area for decades. When several tribes joined them to defeat the Westos in 1680, the English profited by selling the captives into slavery in the Caribbean. Within just a few years traders began to seize women and children in villages where the hunters could not pay their debts. Then they held the captives for ransom or sold them as slaves. The Carolina merchants also encouraged intertribal warfare, urging their allies to capture and enslave other people.

As they tried to keep peace and encourage settlement, the London-based lords proprietors denounced these actions repeatedly. After one of the wars they charged that the Carolina leaders had induced the Savannah tribe "to ravish the wife from the Husband, Kill the father to get the Child and to burne and Destroy the habitations of these poore people into whose Country wee were Ch[e]arefully received by them . . . [and] never have done us hurt." Their words had no impact, and the wars and slave trading continued for another generation. During Queen Anne's War in 1702, Carolina Governor James Moore invaded Spanish Florida. That attack failed, but in 1704 he recruited an army of fifty whites and nearly a thousand Creek and Yamassee fighters to raid Spanish missions in northwest Florida, enticing them with cheap trade goods, arms, ammunition, rum, and loot. These invasions brought vast profits as Moore's army killed or enslaved 325 men and captured 4,000 women and children to be sent to the West Indies as slaves. By 1706 the raids had destroyed the Apalachee missions, and the friars and surviving Indians fled.

The English aggression in Carolina had many parallels elsewhere. For example, far to the northwest the Aleuts, Inuit, and other Indians living in Alaska and along the northern Pacific coast faced invaders at least as greedy and vicious as those from Charleston. There, by the early 1740s, when Russian traders from Siberia reached the Aleutian Islands, the Aleuts launched their boats and frightened the newcomers away temporarily. At a nearby island the Russians met skilled hunting and seafaring people. Their stores of luxurious sea otter pelts attracted the traders' attention, and within just a few months trouble ensued. While camped on the island of Attu, the Europeans abused some of the Native women. When the victims' husbands objected, the traders killed all of the men on the island and then raped and enslaved the women. This incident, at what is still called Massacre Bay, set the tone for relations between the Alaska Native groups and these invaders for generations to come.

The islanders resisted the Russians whenever they could, and between 1762 and 1766 they attacked repeatedly. At Umnak and Unalaska Islands they lured the traders inland away from their ships with stories of vast collections of furs and then killed them. Next they boarded and burned four of the five Russian ships in the harbor. Once news of this reached Siberia, enraged traders smashed their way through the Native settlements, destroying all of the villages on one of the islands and eighteen on the other. This brutal repression worked, as the surviving Aleuts never again dared to retaliate for the ongoing Russian atrocities. Twenty years later Gregory Shelikhov, a leading trader, forced his way ashore on Kodiak Island near the Alaska mainland, where he wanted to set up a permanent base. Knowing what had happened to the Aleuts earlier, the Inuit or Eskimo people there tried to repel Shelikhov's men but failed. He reported that "the savages came down from their rocks in great numbers, and fell upon us with . . . fury." After a bitter fight, the Russian muskets won the day, and they occupied the site.

In the region around the Great Lakes the fur trade brought Indians, English, and French into uneasy relationships that shifted frequently and kept all of the groups off balance from time to time. Prior to the peace negotiated by the French and Iroquois in 1701, tribal remnants from Pennsylvania and western New York had migrated into the Ohio Valley. Algonquians such as the Shawnees, Delawares, Ottawas, and Miamis moved about Ohio, Indiana, and Kentucky, while the Senecas and a few other Iroquoians headed west too. Although they had sought to escape fur-trade violence and competition, the same issues followed them. The Fox Wars, stretching from 1710 into the 1740s, illustrate the disruption and confusion European trade and diplomacy brought to the Native peoples. At one time the Fox or Mesquakie people lived in Ontario, Canada. From there they gradually moved westward, first into lower Michigan and later into Wisconsin and Illinois. Shortly after 1700 they began trading with the French at Detroit, but soon the relationship became strained and then turned violent. By 1712 heavy fighting had broken out, and the French killed more than a thousand members of that tribe. By the end of the 1730s the Mesquakies had almost disappeared, with only remnants living among their relatives, the Sauks, in Illinois and Wisconsin.

Religion and Culture

Even though trade brought Indians and colonists together, other factors also played important roles. At one time or another, most of the European powers talked about bringing Christianity to the heathen in America. This idea sparked an attack on tribal cultures and beliefs that continued for centuries, and some Indian traditionalists insist that this has never stopped. For Native peoples during the eighteenth century it meant being looked down upon by whites as heathen savages. Often village shamans faced ridicule from visiting clerics, who did everything they could to disrupt the tight circle of village life. Missionaries denounced tribal medical practices while offering useless treatments and often bringing diseases that destroyed entire groups. Catholic priests may have brought the most misery to their hosts, because they lived with the villagers more frequently than did the Protestants. Which particular religious groups caused the most damage is hard to judge. Together the missionaries directed generations of cultural destruction from which most Native people have yet to recover. At best their actions present a tragic story of good intentions going terribly wrong.

The Indians considered their own ways clearly superior to the whites'. The Europeans had a more well-developed technology, but the villagers saw their dependence on it as showing both weakness and ignorance. The tribal people practiced rites that differed dramatically from those of the missionaries, and they disliked many things about the Black Robes, as they called Catholic priests, from the start. A proper man took great pride in his hair, but the Jesuits wore theirs cropped short. Their robes caused much rude jesting because they appeared effeminate. Facial hair alienated the villagers too. Travelers, traders, and missionaries reported similar reactions among many tribes. Indians described a beard as "a monstrosity" and "the greatest disfigurement that a face can have," and men wearing them were seen as "very ugly" and "deformed" or looking like dogs. Although only the Catholics had taken vows of poverty, few if any missionaries had much property. In Indian villages, sharing and gift giving were part of everyday life, so the lack of goods created another barrier between the clerics and their intended audience.

The variety of Indian languages protected the villagers from all but the most determined missionaries. Few white men had the time or inclination to learn another dialect for each small group of villages or each tribe; translations therefore remained necessary. Often only the traders could speak tribal languages passably, and they saw little reason to help the meddling clerics disrupt their relationships and business in each village. Few Protestant clergymen lived with the Indians for long, and they had even more difficulties in communication than did their Catholic competitors. When a Yale graduate named John Ogilvie won approval to minister to the Iroquois in New York, one thing in his favor was that he spoke Dutch. His supporters thought that anyone who spoke it could learn Mohawk. Certainly English speakers could never "utter those Barbarous Sounds [of the tribal languages] unless Accustom'd to them from their infancy." A more basic difficulty was that often the tribal languages lacked words for religious ideas that had no place in their belief structures. This frustrated generations of clerics but failed to stop their efforts.

Rarely did many of the villagers accept the new religion. Their shamans attacked it, and often acceptance of the new practices brought personal and family disputes. Indians had their own set of ethnocentric ideas, and these led many to resist the missionaries' teachings. Frequently the colonists demanded that their listeners learn English, but they refused to learn the villagers' tongues. Tribal religious practices remained tied to group welfare and sharing. Protestant teachings tended to emphasize individual actions and decisions. Glaring differences between professed beliefs about how people should act and the colonists' dealings with the Native peoples led some chiefs to suggest that the missionaries first convert their own people before preaching to the Indians. Disputes among competing Christian groups puzzled tribal leaders as well. In one case they sent a missionary on his way, saying that the "Indians could not tell what religion to be of, if they had a mind to be Christians."

Once the tribes had rejected European religion, most colonial powers tried other means to acculturate at least some of the villagers. The Europeans reasoned that if the Indians could speak their language, trade disputes could be reduced and opportunities to make religious converts improved. That meant that local authorities had to educate at least some of the villagers. The 1693 charter for the College of William and Mary in Virginia called on the new school to do just that. However, when it opened in 1700, tribal leaders refused to send any of their children, fearing that the whites might enslave them. Instead they sent young males captured from enemy tribes to the college. Despite this, the Virginians remained optimistic and in 1723 erected Brafferton Hall to house Indians at the college. Village leaders rightly feared that the whites would mistreat their children: during the frequent wars and scares in the Southeast, colonial authorities had held Catawba and the Pamunkey boys hostage at the college. Elsewhere, when local officials urged the Iroquois to send young men to school, Onondaga chief Canasatego refused. He denounced colonial schools because they made the students "absolutely good for nothing." When the Indian boys returned home, he pointed out, they lacked the necessary skills for "killing deer, catching Beaver, or surprising an enemy." Rather than send young Onondagas to the white school, the chief offered to take some English boys and "make men of them," but he got no response from his listeners.

Exchanging young people had been a long-established tribal practice, but usually the Europeans ignored or rejected Indian offers to do so, expecting to acculturate their tribal neighbors instead. As early as 1715, Virginia funded a school at Fort Christanna, where the Quaker missionary Charles Griffin worked with seventy children. Here too, once village chiefs realized that the colonial schools offered only English and some religious instruction, they decided that such education threatened the children's health and culture, so by 1717 they withdrew the students. These earlier meager results seem not to have discouraged the educators, and in 1756 the Reverend Eleazar Wheelock founded Moor's Indian Charity School in eastern Connecticut. He raised money in both England and the northern colonies and then moved the school to New Hampshire, where later it became Dartmouth College. Few Indian young men got past the preparatory school, but Wheelock's efforts demonstrate the continuing pressure Native communities faced over controlling both their children and their future.

Despite their failure to educate many tribal children, some French and English willingly lived among the tribes, absorbing their customs and culture, but often even these bicultural men expected to return someday to their own societies. In places both Indians and some colonials welcomed intermarriage as a way to bridge the cultural gaps between them. While Indians accepted the practice and a few of the invaders talked about the practice, few actively supported it. French religious authorities objected to the irregular nature of Native marriages, while almost all of the English lived in family-dominated settlements that had few unattached men. Nevertheless, some leaders thought that the colonists' aversion to intermarriage caused difficulties with the tribes. William Byrd of Virginia complained that the tribes would never consider the colonists as their friends, because whites had refused to marry Indians even when the settlements lacked enough women. At the same time, few tribal women saw colonials as potential spouses, because they lacked the hunting and other skills necessary to support a family.

Diplomacy and War

During the first century and a half after the Europeans arrived, new diseases, missionary efforts, and economic changes disrupted aboriginal America as it had long existed. Gradually some early traders and government officials became not just economic partners but diplomatic and military allies too. Others became competitors and enemies. Prior to the 1680s, this left tribal leaders facing two kinds of war. They fought against their traditional tribal competitors and enemies, but before the Iroquois wars of the mid-seventeenth century those

conflicts usually had only modest fatalities. However, the entry of aggressive colonial peoples changed that in two ways. First, the intruders encouraged tribal
people to expand their raiding and enslaving the captives they took. As early as
the mid-seventeenth century, Iroquois raiders swept out of western New York
into Ontario and west, south of the Great Lakes, taking hundreds of prisoners
whom they sold as slaves in New France. By the eighteenth century, Comanche
war parties on the southern plains seized hundreds of captives, then selling them
to the Spanish. To the north the Utes did the same, sending a steady stream of
captives from the mountains to other tribes and to colonists in New Mexico. Second, when Native villagers defended themselves against aggressive colonists, the
casualties and level of destruction rose so dramatically that often these conflicts
became desperate struggles for tribal survival.

By the 1680s the situation changed, and from then until the end of the colonial
era villagers living east of the Mississippi River became enmeshed in the new
imperial wars involving Britain, France, and Spain. In some cases this involve-
ment grew out of trading alliances in which they joined their economic partners
against their competitors. In other instances local issues persuaded them to help
one European group against another. Although at times some tribes benefited
from helping the invaders, alliances with them did little more for others than disrupt trade, bring devastation to their villages, or force them to move away from
their home areas. During much of the eighteenth century, violence and warfare
brought by the colonial powers swept across eastern North America repeatedly.
Often these European conflicts gave Native leaders few choices. Indians could
join one of the combatants, try to stay neutral, or move. Whichever path they followed, their lives became more complicated and dangerous than they had been
previously.

Bitter competition between France and Great Britain to gain colonies and expand their economic power led to decades of fighting around the world. While
European dynastic or imperial issues lay behind many of these conflicts, they
engulfed the tribes and colonists alike. Between 1689 and the 1750s these major wars changed Indians' lives dramatically. By choosing to help their trading
partners, Indians fought against both the whites and their own Native enemies.
In King George's War some members of the Iroquois Confederacy renewed
their intermittent war against the French while Abenaki and Wyandot fighters
swept south from Canada into New York. Men on both sides gained little except
the reputation as merciless and bloodthirsty savages. Two decades later, during Queen Anne's War, French and Indian raiders led one hundred people from
Deerfield, Massachusetts, away as captives. In the south, Creeks and Choctaws
attacked traders from Charleston and their Chickasaw allies who had blocked
Creek and Choctaw trade with the French. During the fighting the Chickasaws
begged for English help. "We have not had the liberty of Hunting these [past]
3 years," they complained, "but have had to defend our Lands and prevent our
Women and Children from being Slaves to the French." By the early 1740s, when

King George's War began, most tribes stayed neutral, and some had begun moving west beyond the Appalachians. Bands of Delawares, Shawnees, and small groups of Iroquois who became known as Mingos settled in Ohio and Indiana to escape the continuing flood of colonial pioneers.

They had only a decade to enjoy relative peace in their new homelands, because in 1755 skirmishes leading to the French and Indian War began in western Pennsylvania. Both the British and the French wanted control of what they called the Forks of the Ohio River, the region around Pittsburgh, because from that location they could dominate the fur trade in the entire upper Ohio Valley. When the English learned that French troops were building a fort and trading post there in 1755, the English general Edward Braddock led British troops, Virginia militiamen, and Indian allies west to attack the partially completed Fort Duquesne. The English leader had little respect for his tribal scouts, and the disgusted Cherokees went home while the Delawares and Shawnees left his army to join the French. Without the tribesmen for guides, Braddock led his men into a devastating ambush that destroyed most of his army. He and many of the British officers died in the fighting, leaving young George Washington to direct the retreat to Virginia. The French had many fewer troops than the English, and as the war went on they could not supply or reinforce them effectively because the British fleet controlled the Atlantic. Yet they benefited from the villagers' anger over repeated encroachment on their lands by colonial pioneers. When English negotiators asked the Delawares for help against the French, a tribal spokesman denounced both nations bitterly. "Why do you and the *French* not fight in the old Country . . . ? Why do you come to fight on our land?" he asked. "This makes every body believe, you want to take the land from us by force, and settle it." Obviously the Delawares had no intention of siding with the British. Even without their help, however, by 1760 most of the fighting in America had ended. The 1763 Treaty of Paris removed the French troops and governing officials and turned over present-day eastern Canada to the British. For some tribes in the region, that ushered in another brief time of peace.

Struggles for Independence and Survival

Although these international wars brought frequent destruction and suffering to the Indians, other more local conflicts proved at least as important during the eighteenth century. Whites' cruelty and greed in the fur trade infuriated villagers in many parts of the country, yet most bitterness and violence resulted from pioneers' continuing encroachments on their lands and the colonial governments' unwillingness and inability to police the frontier. Tribal leaders throughout the East complained repeatedly that the colonists never kept their promises. They protested that no matter what the treaty agreements said, the pioneers ignored them and the colonial authorities took no action. The intruders killed the Indians' game, cut their timber, and stole their land. After the Cherokees' defeat in 1777, their chief, Corn Tassel, denounced the American negotiators bitterly. Whenever the tribe parleyed, the whites' "whole cry is *more land!*" "Indeed," he said, for years they demanded "what they know we durst not refuse."

While surrendering their land might appease the whites temporarily, it struck at the heart of tribal culture and identity. For generations Native people had lived in their villages, and when treaty cessions or warfare forced them to move, they lost local religious sites, well-tilled fields, knowledge of usable resources, and some of their shared memories. Village leaders differed over how to deal with these unending invasions of their country. In most communities the elders or peace chiefs tried to negotiate, but that rarely halted the whites' demands for long or ended the disputes. Often the less patient younger men demanded action, calling for war to drive the invaders away. At times, village shamans approved and encouraged the warriors' approach. In fact, from the early seventeenth century through the early twentieth century, tribal religious leaders called on their listeners to avoid all white traders, diplomats, missionaries, or settlers. Frequently these cultural leaders' actions led to direct confrontations when the colonials failed to understand the Indians' religious ideas or practices. In the eighteenth century, tribal people struggled to hold on to their land, but, equally important, they strove to keep their cultures alive and working.

Often their insistence on tribal independence infuriated the colonists, who used any excuse they could to start wars against the Indians. In Carolina the Tuscaroras' experience in 1711 is a clear example. Serving as active intermediaries in the coastal fur trade, that tribe dealt with men from both Virginia and Carolina. These contacts brought prized European goods but also epidemic disease carried by the whites. When smallpox ravaged the tribe in 1708, village leaders correctly blamed the English. The traders further angered the chiefs when they began direct dealings with smaller neighboring tribes. This undermined the Tuscaroras' economy and prestige, so in 1711 Chief Hancock led hundreds of warriors against the colonists. The English responded with an army of nearly five hundred whites and Indian allies, but they had little success. In fact, the colonists fled when the defenders of one fortified village rushed out to attack. As they ran, several Carolinians were "deservedly shot . . . in their arses." Despite that failure, the next year a second army of nearly one thousand men defeated the tribe, killing or enslaving hundreds. At first the survivors agreed to live on a small reservation, but most fled to New York and joined the Iroquois Confederacy as its sixth nation.

Although English destruction of the Tuscaroras frightened other Native groups, the steady encroachments by pioneer farmers caused most of the friction and violence between village farmers and the expanding colonial population. The nearby Yamasee tribe suffered repeatedly from colonial mistreatment and violence. For example, village hunters complained that after they had carried bundles of furs for hundreds of miles for the Charleston traders, the whites often refused to pay their promised wages. They also demanded that English officials prevent criminal whites from raping their wives and enslaving their children during the Yamasee men's absences from the villages. When these abuses continued, Yamasee messengers called for an all-out war against the pioneers and traders. Because several other tribes had similar experiences, in April 1715 they joined the Yamasees and attacked farms and the outlying Carolina settlements. On the first day the raiders killed more than 160 colonists. Within a few weeks they controlled most of the countryside. Catawbas from the North and Apalachees from the South joined in the fighting, and a terrified clergyman wrote that hostile groups "surround us on Every Side but the Sea Side." After bitter fighting for nearly a year, the colonists won, and the Yamasees fled south into Florida rather than face enslavement.

At this same time, the tribes in the Mississippi Valley confronted new challenges from French colonists. Far to the north in New France, few of the Indians were farmers, and so when some settlers took land, few objected. By the early eighteenth century, however, French pioneers in Louisiana encroached on Natchez tribal croplands. Their differing customs led quickly to misunderstandings and then to violence. French leaders there offended Indian sensibilities by ignoring the customary meetings, calumet smoking, and exchanging of gifts, and by not showing proper respect to their chiefs, Great Sun and Tattooed Serpent. Divisions within the tribe also affected relations with the Europeans. Most of the Natchez villages traded with the French, but a few made alliances with English traders from Carolina. This strained their dealings with the intruding whites and provoked isolated violent incidents.

By 1722 more than one hundred French colonists had settled among the Indians, taking some of their best fields. Daily contacts between the two groups led to more trouble. When pioneers gave Indians things such as fabric or pots and pans, their hosts considered them presents. The whites saw the manufactured goods as trade items and demanded something in return. In October that year, in the anti-French Apple Village, a sergeant killed two of the villagers in just such an argument. When the chiefs got word of the murders, they ordered an attack in retaliation. By the time pro-French tribal leaders halted the attacks, angry warriors had killed or wounded a dozen settlers or their slaves and had slaughtered or stolen some of their livestock. Yet because the colonists had built part of their settlement on the sacred land of a worn-down former temple mound, Indian raids continued. In response, the colonial leader Jean-Baptiste Bienville led a six-hundred-man force to the Natchez villages, where they joined their trading partners in destroying the pro-British people at Apple Village.

Peace proved temporary. The pioneer settlers carried smallpox with them, and soon an epidemic struck the villagers. As they recovered from its effects, changes in leadership along with continuing French incursions triggered renewed violence. In 1725, Tattooed Serpent, one of the most cooperative leaders, died. Several years later during the Great Corn Feast, the Indians' most sacred ceremony of the year, the commander of the local French garrison ordered the Natchez to move their villages so that French farmers could use their croplands. This infuriated tribal leaders, and they struck back quickly. Pretending to need weapons and ammunition for hunting, they borrowed these items from the settlers. In November 1729 armed warriors attacked Fort Rosalie, killing its commander and other settlers. In a single day they slew 237 Europeans and placed the victims' severed heads on the fort palisade. Then they took the surviving pioneers off to their villages as slaves. Determined to control the region, French officials opened a war of extermination, and in the next three years they killed, scattered, or enslaved most of the Natchez. This conflict combined issues such as disease, competing trade networks, and quarrels over land, as well as differing cultural practices and religious ideas. Here neither side had any clear understanding of why their strange neighbors acted as they did, so war resulted.

While the southern tribes tried to keep their land and independence, those in the backcountry of New England also experienced English encroachment. There the Eastern Abenaki sought to hold their lands along the Kennebec River in the area between French Quebec and the Maine settlements. Perhaps acting with French encouragement, in 1722 they canoed down the river to attack settlements near Brunswick, Maine, opening hostilities now called Dummer's War. English leaders of the Massachusetts Bay Colony blamed the Jesuit missionary Sébastien Râle for the attack, and in 1724 they sent militiamen to the Indian village where he lived. When the troops stormed into their village, the Abenaki resisted, and in the melee that followed the priest and several Indians died. The whites destroyed the village, scalped their victims, and returned downriver. This incident touched off a series of raids and counterattacks that lasted until 1727, when the fighting ended. For the next several decades the tribe resisted English domination, publicly blaming the colonists for the troubles. "It is you, brother, that always attack us," a tribal spokesman said. "Your mouth is of sugar but your heart [is] of gall." Rejecting English claims to their land, the Abenaki speaker Atiwaneto warned that "we expressly forbid you to kill a single beaver, or to take a single stick of timber [from our territory]." At the same 1752 meeting, he criticized the survey crews then working on tribal land and demanded that they be punished for trespassing.

In the southeast the Cherokees fought for their independence. During the French and Indian War they sent six hundred men north to help the English in Pennsylvania. While the Cherokees campaigned there in 1757, English authorities built two new military outposts: Fort Prince George among the Lower Cherokee villages and Fort Loudoun among the Overhill groups. When colonists learned of the new forts, they flooded onto lands still owned by the tribe. Then, when the men who had gone north to join the war against the French started for home, pioneers in western Virginia attacked, killing forty of them, apparently to collect the scalp bounty the colony paid. Tribal customs about clan retribution demanded that the families of the victims attack the English. To settle the continuing disputes, Carolina governor William Lyttelton met a Cherokee delegation at Charleston. When talks bogged down he seized Chief Oconostota and several more men as hostages until other tribal leaders captured and surrendered those accused of killing pioneers.

Indian customs prevented their turning over any more warriors to the governor, and eventually he released some of the hostages, including Oconostota. Governor Lyttleton's taking hostages had so enraged the chief that soon after his release he led an ambush against the soldiers at Fort Loudoun. In response the garrison commander murdered the prisoners still being held there, setting off what the colonists called the Cherokee War of 1760–61. At this point, raiding parties swept across the southern frontiers, killing, burning, and routing the pioneers. They forced troops at Fort Loudoun to surrender and later killed most of them in retribution. In 1760 English authorities sent an army of thirteen hundred regulars, supported by colonial rangers and Indian allies, smashing into the Cherokee homeland, where they destroyed crops, burned villages, and drove the fleeing Indians into the wilderness. This failed to end the raiding, however, as the villagers fought to retain their land and to retaliate for this latest colonial invasion. That in turn led the British commander, Sir Jeffrey Amherst, to send another expedition of some three thousand men through the Cherokee country, where they destroyed fifteen villages completely and damaged many others. Lacking enough guns and ammunition to resist effectively, tribal leaders sued for peace, and in late 1761 the Cherokee War ended. At that point many villages lay in ruins, and the victorious colonial leaders extracted a harsh treaty. It included new British forts in the Indians' country and a major land cession. Thus, for the tribal people, their alliance with the colonists against the French had failed completely. Not only did they get nothing positive for their help, by the time the French and Indian War ended they had also tasted bitter defeat at the hands of their allies.

In each of the disputes that led to Indian wars for independence, tribes lost at least in part because their traditional competitors or enemies sided with the Europeans against them. Although intertribal conflict continued for more than another century, by the middle decades of the eighteenth century chiefs, war leaders, and shamans began calling for cooperation against the invading whites. As early as the 1740s, refugees from villages that French, British, or colonial forces had attacked came together in the Ohio Valley. There Delawares, Miamis, Mingos, and Shawnees struggled to bring some order to their communities. They had few options. They could agree to a single set of leaders in each village and promise to support them. They could also find ways to cooperate with people in other villages. Even as early as the late 1730s, shamans had called for tribal people to pull back from their contacts with the colonists. Local prophets came onto the scene, denounced the whites as witches and as representatives of evil who contaminated Indian life, and then disappeared. At first they had little impact, but gradually their ideas began taking hold.

By the 1750s, Indian leaders focused most of their attention on the British and on the American colonists, pointing out that these people brought disease, introduced alcohol, and encouraged hunters to become dependent on trade goods. At a meeting that same decade, the Catawba leader Hagler attacked the whites for the rum trade. The liquor, he said, "Causes our men to get very sick and many of our people has Lately Died by the Effects of that Strong Drink." A few years later the Delaware shaman Neolin also preached against alcohol, and by 1760 his ideas had spread through the disgruntled tribal societies. He reported that the spirits told him that the Native people could only restore order in their villages if they returned to traditional practices and accepted his teachings. They had to abandon their use of white trade goods and even most of their contacts with the newcomers. By this time some Indians saw their world as having two irreconcilable civilizations, theirs and that of the invaders, and even though many eastern villagers never saw Neolin, knowledge of his ideas spread rapidly. Yet even here, tribal divisions and competition limited the impact of his teachings. Shamans who represented other beliefs or who saw Neolin as an interloper objected to his calls for change whenever they could. Ultimately, his effort to develop a multitribal or pan-Indian movement failed, but it represented something new.

Neolin's preaching became important when the Ottawa war leader Pontiac used them in his calls for war. Whereas other prophets had denounced the impact of trade goods, Neolin's distinctly anti-English rhetoric gave Pontiac phrases that helped him to mobilize anti-British feelings among the groups near Detroit. In 1763 the British and French had signed the Treaty of Paris, which surrendered French claims to North America. More important to the Indians, the agreement left them at the mercy of the British and their colonial allies, the very people who posed the biggest threats to tribal survival. So, early that year the Ottawa warrior spread Neolin's idea that the tribes had to join forces against the invading whites. According to Pontiac, the Master of Life described the English as people "who have come to trouble your country," and he ordered the Indians to "drive them out, make war on them!" If they did that, the spirits would help them to regain what they had lost in the preceding generations as they dealt with the English. That summer, as traders fanned out across the frontier with the news that their French brothers had left, many tribes joined in the fighting that came to be called Pontiac's Rebellion. Fort after fort fell to attacking war parties, until only Detroit and Pittsburgh remained. As usual, in just over a year the Indians' individualism and the need to feed their families caused many to return home, and by 1765 the British and their colonial allies had won. Yet almost for the first time, Neolin and Pontiac succeeded in getting differing tribal groups to cooperate as they sought to blunt the English encroachments and destruction of their village societies.

Unfortunately, the pioneers ignored tribal complaints in their violent and unrelenting movement west. Their repeated incursions onto tribal lands, destruction of game, and frequent mistreatment of Indians increased tribal bitterness along the frontier. At the same time, shamans reported visions in which voices from the spirit world urged them to break off all contacts with whites. These anti-

English and anti-American teachings rarely called for war but did nothing to ease tensions. An Assinsink prophet named Wangoment urged villagers to avoid the pioneers, to quit trading animal skins for alcohol, and to return to more traditional customs. Joining other shamans, he taught that the spirits had punished the Indians for allowing the corruption of tribal society through contact with the whites. These nativist ideas divided many tribes. Often local chiefs and shamans had come to terms with the whites, and some owed their influence and power to the very trade being denounced. So the prophets encouraging a return to aboriginal values further divided their own societies at a time of renewed stresses.

By the 1770s, Indians had come to see most pioneers as their enemies, so violent incidents and raids continued. As whites surged into Kentucky, the Delawares, Mingos, Shawnees, and Cherokees all objected, and in 1774 Cherokees attacked traders on the Ohio River. The Virginia authorities retaliated, indiscriminately attacking innocent as well as guilty people. In April 1774, frontiersmen welcomed a small Mingo party into their camp, got them drunk, and slaughtered them. The Mingos' Shawnee neighbors took up arms, and this set off a major war scare. Terrified pioneers hurried to fortified villages or fled. Virginia governor Lord Dunmore sent three militia forces into Ohio and Kentucky, where they burned crops and destroyed villages. After early victories, Shawnee leader Cornstalk sued for peace. In the Treaty of Camp Charlotte, signed later that year, the Indians surrendered their Kentucky hunting grounds, and hundreds of frontier families hurried to the newly opened region. Angry anti-American feelings remained, and during a meeting at Fort Pitt in western Pennsylvania one tribal spokesman denounced the colonists' actions. "You have feloniously taken possession of part of our country," he charged. Therefore, he threatened, "we now tell you in a peaceful manner to quit our lands . . . or blame yourselves for whatever may happen."

While many eastern tribes had grown increasingly anti-American, those in the Southwest had continued to trade with and fight against the Spanish there for generations. By the middle of the eighteenth century their distance from Mexico City and continuing hostility had blunted the invaders' efforts repeatedly. Despite that, by the 1770s Spanish determination to control the West Coast and renewed interest in Indian missions brought Franciscan friars into California. Within just a few years they established missions along the coast from San Diego north to present-day San Francisco. They got off to a good start and in 1784 reported having 4,650 "neophytes," as they called their converts. For most of these Indians the friars brought misery and death. Forced to live in crowded buildings, eat unbalanced diets, and endure harsh treatment, they had terrible lives. A local official described their fate as "worse than that of slaves." One of the Franciscans observed that the Indians "live well [when] free but as soon as we reduce them to a Christian and community life . . . they fatten, sicken, and die." Bad diet and wretched living conditions weakened many as epidemic disease swept through the mission populations repeatedly. Even without frequent war as faced by tribes in the East, the Native population on the West Coast, estimated at sixty thousand in 1769, fell to about thirty-five thousand by 1784. That decline continued through 1821 when a newly independent Mexico took control of the region.

In the American Revolution

News that the colonists had declared their independence from Britain did little to change relations between the frontier peoples. The long knives, as Indians called the Virginia pioneers, had made it clear that they considered all Indians their enemies. As a result, when the American Revolution began, most eastern tribes remained neutral or joined the British as a way to fight for their own continued independence. In the Southeast the pioneers in the Watauga region of eastern Tennessee encroached steadily on Cherokee land. When most established tribal leaders took no action, Chief Dragging Canoe labeled them Virginians, not real Cherokees, and in April 1776 he led an attack that set off another vicious frontier war. His men fought alongside Choctaw and Muscogee (Creek) allies, but they could not turn back the tide of settlement. Rather, militia armies from Virginia, as well as from North and South Carolina, invaded Cherokee country, destroying villages, burning crops, and taking hundreds of prisoners. With their shelter and food supply gone, tribal leaders asked for peace. At the 1777 negotiations Chief Corn Tassel objected to the colonists' demands. "It seems misterious to me why you should ask [for] so much land near me," he remarked, at first refusing to cede more land. Yet the chiefs had no choice and signed the Treaties of DeWitt's Corner and Long Island, surrendering their lands east of the Blue Ridge Mountains as well as the areas already occupied by the aggressive pioneers. Despite this defeat, later, when it looked as if the British would defeat the colonists, Chief Dragging Canoe launched new attacks along the frontier. Response came quickly, as militia forces smashed through the Cherokee country again. They destroyed crops and villages, leaving the Overhill towns in shambles. In 1781 the discouraged chiefs had to sign a second Treaty of Long Island, surrendering more of their home territory.

Molly (Mary) Brant, 1736–1796

In New York the Six Nations Iroquois Confederacy had a central role in events during the last half of the eighteenth century similar to that held by the Powhatan people in early Virginia. Molly (Mary) Brant and her younger brother Joseph became influential in those circumstances. Born in 1736, the daughter of Peter and Margaret, a Christian Mohawk family, Molly and her parents lived at the village of Canajoharie in western New York. After her father died, her mother married a Mohawk sachem whose first name was Brant, and Molly took that as her family name. She lived in a fine house, was a member of the Church of England, and spoke both Mohawk and English. During the 1750s Molly met Sir William Johnson, the British diplomat charged with overseeing Iroquois relations, and in 1759 she had the first of their nine children. Johnson installed her as his "housekeeper" and she served as his hostess at diplomatic meetings, took charge of the servants and slaves, and oversaw affairs during his absences. Her close relationships with some Iroquois leaders helped Johnson keep them as British allies, and at the same time his prominence boosted her status within the tribes. Johnson died in 1774, and left his land, money, and slaves to her but the home to his eldest son, so she returned to her home village. During the American Revolution she was a strong loyalist, viewing the colonists as a threat to Iroquois independence. By 1777 she had to flee and moved north into Canada. There she settled on land from the British at present-day Kingston, Ontario, where she lived until her death in 1796. She served as an important link between the Mohawks and the English and after Johnson's death had an influential role in Iroquois affairs.

Source: Earle Thomas, *The Three Faces of Molly Brant* (Kingston, Ont.: Quarry Press, 1996).

Most northern tribes either sided with the British or remained neutral. Like villagers in the South, they faced constant pressure to cede their land even when that was the last thing they wanted to do. Many wished only to be left alone, but they could not escape the whites' demands for land. The Iroquois Confederacy in New York split when the revolution began, as the Oneidas and Tuscaroras sided with the colonists and the Senecas and Mohawks joined the British. Under Mohawk leader Joseph Brant, tribesmen ambushed and defeated Gen. Nicholas Herkimer. In May 1778, Brant led his force along the Mohawk River, while other tribesmen joined Colonel John Butler in raiding across the Wyoming Valley region in Pennsylvania. Later that same year the British and Indians swept through the nearby Cherry Valley, driving terrified pioneers away. The colonists responded with new invasions of the Iroquois home territory. In those campaigns the Americans burned or destroyed whatever Indian property and crops they could, leaving the northern tribes nearly destitute. Some fled west to the Ohio Valley, and many Mohawks joined Brant when he moved to Canada.

Farther south the Shawnee, Delaware, Mingo, and Wyandot raiders swept through Kentucky and the Ohio Valley. Their attacks kept followers of frontiersman and militia leader Daniel Boone penned in their small palisaded villages for months. In 1777 the Shawnee chief Blackfish attacked the Kentucky settlements, disrupting the pioneers' farming and hunting and reducing their winter food supplies to dangerous levels. Early the next year, a Shawnee war party captured Boone and about thirty other Kentuckians as they were gathering salt. The Shawnees took their prisoners back into Ohio and Indiana, where they adopted Boone and several others. Despite their precautions, in June 1778 Boone escaped and raced back to Boonesborough to warn of another attack. Fortunately for the settlers, the Shawnee and their allies delayed until September 1778, when they besieged the village. This attack failed, but for the next several years parties of Delawares, Wyandots, Shawnees, and others raided settlements beyond the mountains. Fighting there continued into 1782, when the warriors defeated a colonial force under William Crawford. Seeking vengeance for the murders of peaceful Christian Indians by Pennsylvania pioneers, the victors burned Crawford to death slowly.

By the time rebellious colonists gained their independence, tribal groups within the borders of the new United States saw little to celebrate. When the Iroquois learned that the British had abandoned them in signing the 1783 Treaty of Paris that formally ended the war, they complained bitterly. "Brother . . . we were greatly alarmed and cast down when we heard the news," Mohawk leader Joseph Brant wrote. His people had good reason to feel betrayed and angry. Their experiences with the Anglo-American governments and people of the late colonial era offered them little hope for the future. The victors represented everything that had brought misery to the villagers. Whiskey peddlers, violent and land-grabbing pioneers, and a new government whose officers treated tribal people as defeated enemies presented only bleak prospects for peaceful relations. Even the most optimistic chiefs had to feel some uncertainty, perhaps even dread. Encroachments on their lands continued, alcohol-induced violence disrupted most villages, and divided leadership and religious confusion undermined village unity. The preceding two centuries of living with the intruding Europeans had brought many changes, but few of those had positive results for the Indians. Instead, now they faced a self-confident and aggressive government whose citizens feared or hated them.

Suggested Readings

Axtell, James. *The Indians' New South: Cultural Change in the Colonial Southeast.* Baton Rouge: Louisiana State University Press, 1997.

Dixon, David. *Never Come to Peace Again: Pontiac's Uprising and the Fate of the British Empire in North America.* Norman: University of Oklahoma Press, 2005.

Dowd, Gregory E. *A Spirited Resistance: The North American Indian Struggle for Unity, 1745–1815.* Baltimore: Johns Hopkins University Press, 1992.

Hämäläinen, Pekka. *The Comanche Empire.* New Haven: Yale University Press, 2008.

Naske, Claus M., and Herman E. Slotnick. *Alaska: A History of the 49th State.* Norman: University of Oklahoma Press, 1987.

Perdue, Theda. *Cherokee Women: Gender and Culture Change, 1700–1835.* Lincoln: University of Nebraska Press, 1999.

Richter, Daniel K. *Trade, Land, Power: The Struggle for Eastern North America.* Philadelphia: University of Pennsylvania Press, 2013.

Santos, James A. *Converting California: Indians and Franciscans in the Missions.* New Haven: Yale University Press, 2004.

Shannon, Timothy J. *Iroquois Diplomacy on the Early American Frontier.* New York: Penguin Books, 2008.

Weber, David J. *The Spanish Frontier in North America.* New Haven: Yale University Press, 1992.

White, Richard. *The Middle Ground: Indians, Empires, and Republics in the Great Lakes Region, 1680–1815.* New York: Cambridge University Press, 1991.

PART III

Facing the United States

CHAPTER 4

Villagers versus the United States, 1783–1840s

The Postwar Era

The 1783 Treaty of Paris that ended the war between the British and their American colonies granted the rebels independence. Because the English negotiators ignored their tribal allies when negotiating the treaty, they left the Indians facing angry pioneers and a new government that viewed them as dangerous, but defeated, enemies. By this time the tribes and colonists had fought each other on and off for nearly two centuries, and they had come to fear and hate each other. When American officials could not keep the pioneers from pushing onto tribal lands, wartime violence continued. Sensing its own weakness, the new government acted as if it owned all the territory between the Appalachians and the Mississippi River by right of conquest. For the Native villagers this meant immediate confrontation with the new nation. They asserted their independence, rejected American claims of victory over them, and demanded that the pioneers leave their country. This put them in direct conflict with the United States. For the next half-century tribal leaders negotiated, prayed, fought, and relocated as they struggled to keep their identities, customs, and homelands while facing ever more aggressive frontier neighbors.

The issues that brought Indian-white conflict before and during the War for Independence remained, as hunting parties of villagers and pioneers clashed repeatedly in an area that stretched from western New York, west into the Ohio Valley, and south into Tennessee and Georgia. Tribal chiefs wanted peace and hoped that the commissioners they met would agree to keep intruders out of their territory. At the same time, the American government needed the funds it got from selling western land to survive, so it wanted to seize the region from the Indians. With each side wanting what the other could not or would not give, the situation remained chaotic for the next ten or twelve years. At the time village leaders tried to protect themselves by using multitribal confederacies, negotiations with the Americans, religious and cultural revivals, diplomacy with the British and Spanish, and, when those failed, warfare. Some of these tactics succeeded for a time, but even with these options chiefs struggled to keep their people from being overrun and destroyed by the advancing frontier population.

Struggles in the Ohio Valley

In the first few years after American independence, the Native people west of Pittsburgh failed to deal effectively with government agents. Those negotiators extracted harsh treaty concessions from the Iroquois at Fort Stanwix in 1784, from the Delawares, Wyandots, and Ojibwas at Fort McIntosh in 1785, and from the Shawnees at Fort Finney the next year. Tribal leaders denounced government attempts to treat them as conquered enemies, because many of the groups had not been defeated. They considered themselves British allies, not subjects, and scoffed at the idea that diplomats in Europe could deed away their lands. Their bitter objections persuaded officials in Canada to offer some help and encouragement. After promising to support Indian land claims, they refused to move their troops out of forts that now stood within the United States. From those posts, English military and civilian officers assured their Native allies of continued support and urged them to resist any American settlement in their territory.

Some chiefs ignored the British effort because they feared that their allies would not live up to these new promises, but others sought to use any help they could get. Still, rather than depend on the Europeans, Mohawk leader Joseph Brant soon became the leading Native spokesman as Indians worked to create a multitribal alliance against the Americans. In December 1786, representatives of at least nine tribes met on the Detroit River to plan a unified approach. When the discussions ended, they sent a message to Congress, promising to work for peace. However, they insisted that all negotiations about land be held in public and that any treaties with the United States require that all tribes of the confederation agree. Any other negotiations they would consider "null and void." Having said that, they prepared to defend their lands and homes, as runners traveled south to forge new ties between the confederation and the Muscogees and Chickamaugas there.

By 1787, while the Constitutional Convention debated how a new government should operate, young Indian men raided isolated settlements and attacked travelers. Mingos and Miamis now joined the Delawares, Wyandots, and Shawnees in the fighting against pioneers in Kentucky and West Virginia and along the Ohio River. The frontiersmen retaliated, raiding north into Ohio and Indiana, burning crops and leveling villages. While pioneers denounced their government for not destroying the tribes, Indian leaders asked the British for continued support. Officials in Canada urged the Ohio Valley groups to defend their homeland and supplied them with trade goods and weapons. By 1789, when George Washington became president, the region west of Pittsburgh had become a war zone.

Pioneers in western Pennsylvania and in Kentucky begged the new government to help them against the Indians because the raids had brought their settlement almost to a stop. The president ordered Gen. Josiah Harmar to mobilize frontier militia units and then attack the villages in Ohio and Indiana. In September 1790, his force of about 1,450 men marched north from present-day Cincinnati, burning crops and villages. Miami chief Little Turtle and Shawnee leader Blue Jacket had their men drop trinkets along the trail to persuade the pursuing whites that their people were in full retreat. The ruse worked, and on October 17 Harmar's force blundered into an ambush while trying to cross the Eel River. The terrified militiamen broke ranks, threw down their weapons, and fled. When reinforcements stopped them, one soldier cried out, as it was recounted, "For God's Sake retreat—you will Be all killed—there is Indians enough to Eat you all up." Four days later, the reorganized troops launched a second attack on the Miami village of Kekionga, but the tribesmen defeated them again in heavy fighting. Despite Harmar's report of success, the Indians had killed more than 10 percent of his men. The two victories persuaded the tribesmen that they could resist the Americans.

Once the federal officials realized how thoroughly the warriors had defeated Harmar, they planned a follow-up expedition for the next summer. Arthur St. Clair, the territorial governor, received command and led a force of about twenty-three hundred, mostly militiamen, north into the Indian country. The Miami victory the preceding summer encouraged resistance, and fighting men from at least ten tribes united against the Americans. By October 1791, the army had moved north, building several forts as it made its way slowly into Indian country. Military historians suggest that General St. Clair posted his men with care, but that made little difference. The warriors surprised them anyway. Attacking at dawn on November 4, the warriors stormed into the camp focusing their heaviest fire on the clearly marked officers and the artillerymen. Caught almost entirely by surprise, the cowardly militiamen broke ranks and fled, leaving the small units of regular troops to face overwhelming numbers of attackers. The retreat turned into a rout as soldiers abandoned most of their equipment and weapons, leaving their wounded comrades behind. When Chief Little Turtle halted the slaughter, more than six hundred soldiers lay dead and hundreds more had been wounded. What the Miamis called "The Battle of a Thousand Slain" was the worst defeat that Indians inflicted on U.S. forces in American history.

This stunning victory elated tribal leaders, who had now twice defeated American armies in little more than a year. At this point the British urged them to demand that the Ohio River become the boundary between their lands and those of the pioneers. Some of the chiefs had already decided to make this their goal, so they rejected government efforts to reach a peace agreement. In fact, they became so confident that in 1792 they murdered two American negotiators who had traveled west to meet them. The next year confederation spokesmen again insisted on the Ohio River as the only boundary they would accept. At a council they assured the visiting diplomats that they wanted peace but also told them, "We have therefore resolved to leave our bones in this small place to which we are confined" rather than surrender more land to the United States. Their clearly stated determination to resist persuaded the government to halt the negotiations. It had to have the land and to protect the settlers there, so President Washington and his advisors decided to rebuild the army and take the region by force.

While he persuaded Congress to create a new army, confederation leaders met with British officials who urged them to continue their demands for all of Ohio as Indian country. U.S. officials rejected that out of hand. Instead, Gen. Anthony Wayne trained the new army and in the summer of 1794 led his troops north along the Ohio-Indiana border. Blue Jacket and Little Turtle gathered between fifteen hundred and two thousand men to oppose the Americans, but this time they faced well-led and well-trained regular troops, not just pioneer militiamen out to shoot a few Indians. General Wayne knew that Indian fighting men fasted for at least twenty-four hours before going into battle, so he announced the day he expected to fight. Rather than attacking as promised, however, he waited several days until the hungry warriors scattered to get food. Then he moved, assaulting the Indian force on August 21 at a place called Fallen Timbers near present-day Toledo. Because of Wayne's delaying tactics, only about eight hundred Indians remained to oppose his troops, and this time they, not the advancing whites, had to flee. When the retreating warriors reached the nearby British fort, its officers closed the gates and refused to protect or help them, and chiefs realized that they stood alone. Their resistance broken, the next summer they signed the Treaty of Greenville, ceding much of Ohio and parts of Indiana as well.

Southeastern Disputes

In the South, the Cherokees and Muscogees (Creeks), faced the encroaching pioneers in Tennessee, Georgia, and Alabama. These Native groups struggled to keep their lands and independence as the northern tribes had, but their long-standing rivalries made it difficult to form defensive alliances against the Americans. Instead they tried a combination of negotiations and violence to gain their objectives. Federal officials gave the region little attention because some of the states still claimed land there, and often this left the tribes facing the pioneers alone. When squatters in east Tennessee settled illegally on Cherokee land, they created the state of Franklin to protect their territorial claims. Then in 1785 they persuaded a few minor village chiefs to sign the Treaty of Dumplin Creek, an agreement that ceded the disputed area. Most Cherokee leaders objected, and later that year U.S. officials wrote a new compact, the Treaty of Hopewell, which repudiated the earlier cession and recognized tribal independence. Both the Indians and federal officials hoped this would slow pioneer intrusions, but that did not happen.

Whites continued using the rivers flowing through tribal lands and settling illegally beyond the new borders. When minor incidents continued, the Cherokees called for another treaty. In 1791 some forty chiefs met with U.S. negotiators at Knoxville. There they agreed to the Treaty of Holston, which surrendered more land and allowed pioneers to travel through tribal territory. In return, the federal government sent troops to remove squatters who had refused to leave the region. These actions infuriated frontier citizens, and soon white volunteers began raiding Cherokee settlements, looting and burning crops and buildings, and shooting peaceful villagers. For the next several years Indians and whites attacked each other, until news spread of Anthony Wayne's victory over the Ohio Valley tribes at the Battle of Fallen Timbers. Once Cherokee leaders understood the determination of federal officials to impose their will in the frontier regions, they decided that they had to make peace. In 1798, at Tellico in Tennessee, they signed yet another agreement, ending their raids.

While the Cherokees tried to hold off the aggressive pioneers in east Tennessee, the Muscogees in what is now Georgia and Alabama faced demands from aggressive Georgia officials for ever more land cessions. When chiefs from a few villages signed several agreements, those from other towns objected. They repudiated these treaties and asked the Spanish, who then controlled Florida and the Gulf Coast, for help. In 1784 Alexander McGillivray, a mixed-race spokesman for the villagers, asked the nearby Chickasaws and Choctaws to join the Creeks in signing the 1784 Treaty of Pensacola with Spain. The Spanish promised to supply trade goods and to help the Indians protect themselves. They also paid McGillivray to keep them informed of American moves in the region. Bitter divisions among the Creeks led some other village leaders to oppose him and to reopen talks with the Georgians. Agreements they signed in 1785 and 1786 surrendered most of the tribal land near that state's border. Objecting to the new cessions, McGillivray rallied his supporters and struggled to gain control of the tribal government. His followers formed a vigilante-like group of constables to suppress his Creek rivals and then began raiding outlying frontier settlements.

The war parties drove the invaders from their eastern lands in 1787, and their success brought at least the possibility that the United States might intervene. This frightened Spanish officials in Florida, who tried to persuade McGillivray to end the raids. When he ignored their requests, they cut off the supply of arms and ammunition as well as other trade goods the tribe depended on, and the violence diminished. The new U.S. government began operations in 1789, and soon American negotiators visited the Creeks. When they told their hosts that the United States expected to enforce the earlier treaties between Georgia and the tribe, an infuriated McGillivray disrupted the council meeting. "By God I would not have such a Treaty cram'd down my throat," he shouted, shutting down the talks abruptly. The next year President Washington invited Creek leaders to reopen negotiations in New York; McGillivray and Hopoithle Miko agreed to work together there. That summer they concluded the Treaty of New York, which recognized some tribal claims to the disputed lands and allowed the Creeks to expel illegal settlers from their territory. In return, the Indian negotiators agreed that their lands lay within the United States. To get the treaty, the leaders surrendered over half of the disputed area near the Georgia border, and that caused continuing disputes within the tribe for several decades. Yet this agreement eased relations between the villagers and their greedy neighbors for a time and averted major wars like those in the Ohio Valley.

Pacific Coast Tribes

Although the United States reached only as far as the Mississippi River, groups west of that boundary could not escape the expanding European presence in their homeland regions. By 1790 the czar had granted the Russian-American Company an exclusive charter to trade in Alaska and along the Pacific coast. That same year, company traders began moving south. There they met the Tlingit Indians, who were already trading successfully with the British and the Americans. Ignoring the villagers' objections, company leaders founded Sitka as their headquarters. After just a few years of mistreatment by the high-handed intruders, the Indians attacked. In 1802 they killed at least 150 Russians and their Aleut workers. When it appeared that neither side could win, the two negotiated a truce. Ten years later the Russians decided that they needed an agricultural settlement in California in order to obtain food for their Alaska trading posts. They sent 175 men to build what became Fort Ross, about ninety miles north of San Francisco. As elsewhere, the local villagers attacked when the traders took land for their crops and demanded that the nearby Pomo tribe give them labor, women, and food. The raids limited the Russians' crop yields, but the Europeans' violence and the diseases they carried caused sharp population declines among the Indians in just a decade or two.

Decades earlier, Spanish authorities had grown alarmed at the Russian activities along the California coast, and in 1769 they began a countermove from the south, meant to discourage other powers from claiming much of the Pacific Coast region. By early that year, two small ships and an overland expedition reached San Diego. The invaders set up camp near a village of Kumeyaay people there. Father Junípero Serra led a small party of Franciscans, while the accompanying soldiers and workers set about building permanent quarters. Their plan included bringing Christianity to as many of the coastal tribes as possible and solidifying Spanish economic and political control over the region. The local villagers watched the invaders' activities for a little more than a month. By then they realized that the strangers intended to remain, so they attacked but failed to drive the newcomers away. Resistance continued, and in 1775 a larger revolt occurred at San Diego. Within less than a decade soldiers, settlers, and friars marched up the coast, founding twenty-one missions accompanied by presidios or forts along the way. By the late 1770s they had extended their occupation of the coast as far north as San Francisco Bay.

For California tribes, the Spanish missions brought disaster. Although at first the mission fathers worked with volunteers, within a couple of years the soldiers rode out into the countryside to "recruit" Indian laborers. They rounded up people and herded them from their villages to the missions, where the clerics forced them to change every aspect of their cultures. New food, work, clothing, and strange religious practices disrupted their lives. The Spanish segregated men and women, often crowding them into cramped buildings, a practice that fostered the spread of disease. As a result, within the next two decades the mortality rates shot up, with many more people dying each year than were born. Within just a few years, most of the missions became virtual prisons where the priests forced their Indian converts to work as laborers, herders, and builders with little compensation. When small numbers of the boldest or most desperate people fled, soldiers returned them forcibly. Once back, they faced beatings and reductions in food as punishment. The missionaries justified such treatment as the only way they had to bring such barbarous and ignorant people to Christianity. Seventy-five years later, when the West Coast became part of the United States, the Native population in California had fallen by at least 75 percent.

Religious and Political Visions

Tribal groups in the path of the expanding U.S. frontier also dealt with missionaries, but their experiences varied widely from those of the coastal peoples. In fact, their own shamans often incorporated Christian ideas and occasionally even Anglo-American practices into their teachings. Other prophets, such as Neolin, who preached as early as 1760, called for their listeners to abandon trade with the whites and return to using traditional skills, tools, and goods. Forty years later, the situation had changed dramatically for many tribes. They had been on the losing side in the revolution, thousands of pioneers poured onto their lands, and alcohol and disease ate at the heart of many villages. Traditional teachings seemed powerless to turn back the clock or to offer protection from the ongoing difficulties people faced. Healers could not prevent or end epidemics, political leaders signed away tribal lands, and military action brought only more death and destruction. In these circumstances Protestant missionaries offered to help individuals who had given up their tribal beliefs and those so thoroughly defeated that they saw acceptance of the white man's way as the only road to survival.

Indian prophets responded to the situation too, leading movements of religious and cultural reawakening during much of the nineteenth century. Just a year before it began, a Seneca girl reported having visions in which the spirits called for villagers to reject the religious ideas of the Society of Friends, or Quakers, then active along the U.S.-Canada border. In New York the Mohawks heard calls for abstinence from alcohol and for a return to the white dog sacrifice, which had long been abandoned. Then in 1799 a little-regarded Seneca shaman named Caneodiyo or Handsome Lake began to offer new teachings. Apparently he suffered from serious depression, and at one point his family thought that he had died. When they began to prepare his corpse for burial, he revived from what had been a deep trance or coma. He told of his experiences in the spirit world and preached that four evils had to be cleansed from Iroquois society if it were to survive: witchcraft, alcohol, "love magic" (promiscuity), and abortion. Handsome Lake had other visions that also became part of his teachings. Adapting some ideas gained from Christian missionary teachings, he suggested that the world faced destruction and called for personal repentance of individual and group sins.

His teachings included distinctly Seneca ideas as well. Tribal ceremonies needed careful observance. At the same time, Handsome Lake urged leaders of the secret medicine societies to open their rites, and he made anti-alcohol efforts central in his preaching. Traditional mourning periods often lasted for months, which he thought placed too much emphasis on death. A pacifist, he urged his listeners to renounce warfare as an option for dealing with the whites. During his years as a shaman, he encouraged the Iroquois to combine what he saw as the best elements of their culture with those of their neighbors. He stressed that agriculture, pacifism, and individual family actions had to be combined with clan and village practices if the Senecas hoped to survive. His followers brought his ideas together as the Code of Handsome Lake or the Long House Religion, and some have followed these beliefs down to the present.

At about the same time, a Shawnee prophet began preaching a new message in Ohio and Indiana. A local shaman whose heavy drinking and excessive talking earned him the title of "Rattle" or "Noise Maker" from other villagers, he soon became the leader of a multitribal religious and cultural revival. In 1805 he fell into a trance, and, as had happened with Handsome Lake, his family thought that he had died. When he awoke, he claimed to have visited the spirit world, where the Master of Life instructed him what to say when he returned to earth. Changing his name to Tenskwatawa or Open Door, he quit using alcohol and began to travel from village to village with his new teachings. He encouraged his listeners to end their contacts with all whites, to stop the fur trade, and, in particular, to stop drinking alcohol. At this point his message focused on bringing stability to family and village life, yet he also denounced the American pioneers as causing most Indian suffering. When other shamans questioned his teachings, he accused them of ignorance or even witchcraft.

Soon people from nearby tribes responded to the new prophet's teachings, sending groups to hear his ideas firsthand. Within a year his influence grew, and he took part in the ceremonial burning of witches in several Delaware villages. When Indiana Territorial governor William Henry Harrison heard about the Shawnee's spiritual claims, he scoffed. "If he really is a prophet," Harrison challenged, ask him to "cause the sun to stand still—the moon to alter its course—the rivers to cease to flow—or the dead to rise from their graves. If he does these things, you may then believe that he has been sent from God." Unwittingly, the governor boosted Tenskwatawa's credibility, because the shaman had learned about an upcoming eclipse of the sun. Using that knowledge, he responded to Harrison by telling villagers who doubted his teachings that the Master of Life would soon blot out the sun as a sign that the Prophet spoke the truth. On June 6, 1808, the eclipse took place, and Tenskwatawa's credibility rose quickly as his followers carried news of his "miracle" and spread his teachings from one village to another, increasing his prestige and gaining new converts.

The Prophet's success in persuading his adherents they should move to his village led him to relocate the community to northwestern Indiana. There he established a new settlement on Tippecanoe Creek that soon came to be called Prophetstown. Some nearby villagers objected to the new town, but Tenskwatawa claimed that the Master of Life had commanded him to move and that mere mortals had no right to interfere. From this village runners fanned out, spreading his teachings and recruiting others. When threatened by food shortages, he sent his brother Tecumseh north to seek help from William Claus in Canada. Tecumseh told Claus that the Indians wanted no part of any quarrel between the British and the Americans. Still, the villagers refused to accept the pioneers as close neighbors, and the warrior told his host that the Shawnees and their allies expected to drive the intruders from their lands. Tecumseh also promised that if the United States and Britain did go to war, the Ohio Valley tribes would join the British against the frontiersmen. Not satisfied with having sent a delegation to Canada, the Prophet led another to visit Governor Harrison. While there, he pledged to remain at peace and succeeded in getting the governor to feed several hundred Indians for more than two weeks.

That support failed to help the villagers make it through the 1808–1809 winter unscathed. Food shortages left many malnourished, and disease swept through Prophetstown. Chiefs and shamans who considered Tenskwatawa's plan to unite the tribes a threat to their status accused him of having poisoned those who died. As some tribes struggled with these internal divisions, Governor Harrison renewed his efforts to browbeat the villagers in Ohio and Indiana into surrendering more land. At Fort Wayne in October 1809, he persuaded some Miami, Delaware, and Potawatomi leaders to sign another treaty of cession. In that agreement Little Turtle, Beaver, and Five Medals sold three million acres of Ohio and Indiana land for just a few pennies an acre. Their action infuriated both Tenskwatawa and his brother Tecumseh. The two threatened to kill other chiefs who dared sign any new treaties that surrendered more territory to the Americans. Tecumseh said that the land belonged to all Indians and that no one tribe or group had the right to sell it without getting the consent of the others. At this point the leaders' attention shifted from cultural and religious issues to politics, economics, and possible military actions, as Tecumseh worked feverishly to unite all of the tribes beyond the Appalachians against the United States.

Farther south, the groups in the Creek confederation had not succeeded in settling their disputes either with the Georgia pioneers or among their own political elite. Treaty signings with Benjamin Hawkins, the government negotiator there, divided these villagers as well. By the early nineteenth century, the Muscogees tended to retain more of their religious and cultural practices than did many other tribes. They rejected missionary efforts, saying that they knew God without the Bible, and still used traditional practices such as the Black Drink Ritual and the Green Corn Ceremony. However, the villagers could not agree in either their individual towns or the confederation. Many leaders accepted the need for peace and accommodation with the white settlers. During the 1790s, Alexander McGillivray had urged the Creeks to accept livestock and a more sedentary life. While some followed that path, others wanted to direct the cultural changes rather than just accept everything from white society. Nativist leader Hillis Hadjo, or Josiah Francis, was one who took this approach.

Some Creeks traveled north to Prophetstown to hear Tenskwatawa's teachings, and during the winter of 1811–12 others flocked to hear Tecumseh when he visited the southern tribes looking for allies against the Americans. His message showed Indian frustration and anger. "War now. War forever. War upon the living. War upon the dead," he raged. "Dig their very corpses from the grave, our country must give no rest to a white man's bones." This rallying cry brought the bitter internal divisions in Muscogee society to the fore, as the villagers debated whether or not to support the northern militants. As leaders in the Upper Creek villages who favored partial assimilation expanded their authority through the Creek National Council, more traditional Creeks objected. The messianic teachings of the Shawnee Prophet and the often similar ideas of Muscogean shamans attracted hundreds of followers, who came to be called the Red Sticks because of ceremonial staves they carried. Their disputes usually centered on religious and diplomatic issues, but often the militants objected to the growing personal property and greed exhibited by some tribal leaders. In response, they killed domesticated animals whenever they could, because livestock represented a clear acceptance of Anglo-American lifestyles. They also may well have objected to the animals because of the destruction they wrought on family cornfields.

When the traditionalists charged their opponents with witchcraft, they brought about division and violence. Several times they burned leaders whom they saw as too pro-American. Their opponents then used the authority of the Creek National Council and armed force to protect some of the accused while killing several nativist leaders. In February 1813, Little Warrior led a group of Creeks sympathetic to Tecumseh's plans for intertribal unity on a raid in which they killed several white pioneers. This action brought his expulsion from the National Council and its decision in April that year to execute him and his followers. With a contingent of between fifty and one hundred men, the council forces surrounded the dissidents and attacked their cabin. When the defenders ran out of ammunition, the attackers set the cabin afire, killing all but one of Little Warrior's group as they scrambled out of the burning building. This conflict tore the tribe apart, and during the War of 1812, Red Sticks fought their fellow tribesmen as well as the frontier armies sent against them, keeping the southeastern frontier in turmoil for years.

Diplomacy and Warfare

The teachings of Tenskwatawa and other prophets called for rejecting the goods and customs of the whites, but by themselves such teachings had only a modest impact. During the first decade of the nineteenth century, the map of the region west of the Appalachians had changed drastically because of exploding pioneer settlement. In 1800 three territories—Northwest, Indiana, and Mississippi—joined two states there, Kentucky and Tennessee. A decade later, Ohio had become a state, and the Michigan, Illinois, and Louisiana Territories encompassed nearly the entire area between the Mississippi and the Appalachians. These developments brought frontier settlers and Indians into ever more frequent contact with each other. By 1810 the Shawnee Prophet's brother Tecumseh began repeating earlier calls for an alliance of all the tribes beyond the Appalachians and an end to any further land cessions to the United States. News of his efforts terrified frontier settlers and upset government plans for signing more treaties of cession. The movement he led also split many tribes, with older established chiefs striving to keep peace and younger ones demanding warfare.

While villagers debated how to deal with the Americans, international issues brought the United States into the War of 1812 against the British. This conflict encouraged dissidents in many tribes to renew or continue their negotiations with the British in Canada and the Spanish along the Gulf Coast. Such groups as the Winnebagos (Ho-Chunks), Sauks, Mesquakies, Shawnees, and Delawares traveled regularly to Malden, just across the Canadian border from Detroit. There British officials encouraged tribal resistance to American advances and promised supplies and weapons. Despite the inconsistency of past British support, Indians saw few alternatives to asking them for help. In the South, Creeks, Choctaws, and Seminoles negotiated with local Spanish officials for assistance. As a result, well before the United States declared war in June 1812, Indian raiding had begun in the West.

The incessant demands for land cessions angered tribal leaders regardless of what stance they took toward their expanding neighbor. However, the efforts of agents like Benjamin Hawkins among the southern tribes outraged militants everywhere. Frontier officers encouraged the adoption of American attitudes toward private property and the keeping of livestock, both issues that struck at the heart of village social networks. In addition, the whites' ideas about gender roles, particularly in farming, upset many. In most of the eastern tribes the women did the majority of the actual fieldwork, tending and harvesting the crops, while the men performed other duties. Government officers denounced this division of labor, encouraging a change that put Indian women inside their lodges while the men conducted business, did the farming, and negotiated with whites. These efforts disrupted village life and angered many who otherwise might have remained at peace. As a result, when actual war broke out, Indians felt that they had legitimate reasons to enter it, usually against the United States.

In the North most tribes divided, as some villages or bands sided with the British and others tried to stay neutral. Fighting began there well before any declaration of war. William Henry Harrison led an attack on Prophetstown in November 1811, as Tecumseh traveled across the South trying to recruit support for an anti-American confederation. Furious at his brother Tenskwatawa for having failed to avert war, the Shawnee leader allied his followers with the British and persuaded large numbers of Ohio and Mississippi Valley warriors to fight against the pioneers in Michigan, Ohio, Indiana, and Ontario. They won some limited victories, but in the end American numbers turned the tide. In late 1813, Harrison led American forces into Canada north of Lake Erie. There the British commander Col. Henry Proctor retreated until he reached the Thames River. When Harrison's troops attacked, the small British force fled, leaving Tecumseh and the Indians unsupported and outgunned. After suffering heavy losses, the warriors retreated. When Tecumseh died in the fighting, many of his discouraged followers returned to their villages. In the upper Mississippi Valley, fighting continued into 1815, as Winnebago, Kickapoo, Sauk, and Mesquakie raids kept the frontier in turmoil for another year and a half, until the British stopped supplying munitions and weapons.

Fewer tribes opposed the American settlers in the South, because the Spanish there chose not to supply them as fully as the British had done in the North. Some Choctaws, Creeks, and Seminoles fought repeatedly, but to no avail. Most of the fighting grew out of the Red Stick War that resulted from the intense struggle among the Creeks over how they should deal with the Americans. The National Council denounced the minority Red Sticks as a threat to tribal survival and helped the pioneer armies from Georgia and Tennessee against their fellow tribesmen. Led by William Weatherford (Red Feather) and Peter McQueen, the dissidents attacked Fort Mims, a stockade that protected many of their tribal enemies and their mixed-race families. Some 250 defenders died in the fighting, as did fifty or more of the Red Stick attackers. During the winter of 1813–14, Andrew Jackson led a militia army south into Alabama, attacking Red Stick forces repeatedly. On March 27, 1814, his forces trapped the main Creek force at what is called Horseshoe Bend on the Tallapoosa River and destroyed some eight hundred of the outnumbered defenders. This reduced Creek resistance, but nearly two thousand of the Red Stick survivors fled southeastward into Florida, where they joined the Seminoles and their black allies there. Their frequent raids across the Spanish border into the United States kept the frontier situation confused until Andrew Jackson's 1817–18 invasion of Florida halted most of the violence.

While Native groups in the East scrambled to deal with the onrushing Americans, the tribes to the west had few of the same problems. Those living beyond the Missouri River encountered few American pioneers before the massive 1849 gold rush to California. Instead they met and worked with small numbers of fur traders from St. Louis, Montreal, or Hudson's Bay in Canada. These men wanted furs, not land, and seemed to benefit Native life instead of threaten it. At first their presence had only a modest impact on Native economic patterns, but by the early nineteenth century that changed. Tribal competition and rivalry brought increasing violence as hunters from each group tried to dominate the local trade. Growing numbers of mounted Sioux tried to block whites from moving up the Missouri with trade goods for people living farther upriver. After the War of 1812 ended, repeated intertribal raiding and attacks on traders along the Missouri River persuaded some whites to send trappers directly to the Rocky Mountains, bypassing their unpredictable Indian partners entirely. By the 1840s this flood of white and Indian hunters destroyed most of the furbearers in the Rockies and along many western streams. The fur trade also introduced epidemic diseases that reduced some tribes drastically. For example, in 1837 smallpox epidemic tore through groups living along the Missouri, and the Mandan villagers in North Dakota lost all but 138 out of nearly 2,000 people that summer. With their numbers reduced and their resources depleted, the smaller western groups could not resist effectively when advancing pioneers arrived.

Eroding Tribal Identity and Landholdings

American victory in the War of 1812 ended military resistance as an option for most tribes east of the Mississippi. It also brought them face-to-face again with angry federal officials who saw the villagers as defeated enemies. In some ways the situation resembled that of a generation earlier when the victorious Americans dealt with tribal people after the War for Independence. Now they forced village leaders to negotiate, and in 1815 and 1816 Indians signed a series of new treaties. In these they accepted U.S. supremacy, promised to remain at peace, and agreed to end their ties with foreign governments. By now the Indians had lost the options of warfare and foreign alliances, and they needed to find new ways to deal with the United States and its advancing frontier population. They could leave the country, and some did, moving to Canada, Florida, or to the West. Few chose that option, however, because they wanted to keep what was left of their ancestral homelands. Others, particularly in Illinois and Wisconsin, avoided the pioneers whenever they could. This worked for another decade, but then expanding frontier settlements brought thousands of whites into the region.

The largest tribes remained in the Southeast, and they faced increasing pressures from citizens as well as from state and federal governments in the decade after the War of 1812 to change their way of life. In 1819, Congress established the Indian Civilization Fund, an annual appropriation of $10,000 to be spent in addition to existing treaty annuities for a program that focused on acculturation.

In theory the villagers would learn to read, would accept Protestant Christianity, and then would become sedentary farmers. The plan aimed at breaking down tribal communal landholding and adopting private property. If each family had its own farm, the theory ran, they would remain there and would need less land than if they continued hunting and trading. When that happened they could be persuaded to wear white people's clothing, speak English, and become part of the expanding American society. In theory, the program promoted peace on the frontier. Its supporters reminded those who opposed spending money on "the savages" that this effort cost far less than war and was less dangerous too. Congress ignored evidence that nearly all of the eastern Natives had been successful large-scale farmers for generations. It also overlooked many examples of individual Indians fully integrated into the cash economy with their white neighbors. Some kept large herds of cattle, while others had plantations using slave labor, operated river ferries, or owned roadside inns and taverns.

The Civilization Fund offered little new, but it focused both attention and cash on acculturation. A few clergymen, teachers, and government officials had visited and lived among some of the villagers for years. They hoped to undermine Indian clan obligations to share food, clothing, or tools with each other. To do that the intruders encouraged villagers to adopt personal private property, sedentary agriculture, and to learn to English. To change gender roles they urged women to quit tending crops, learn to spin and weave, and take care of their house and family. They encouraged the men to stop hunting and take over the women's duties in the fields. In their efforts to convert the villagers to a new religion, somehow the missionaries missed the irony of linking Christianity with their hope to make Indians more selfish than their Native customs allowed. These demands struck at the heart of clan and family duties and gradually created new divisions in tribal societies. For example, whites living with the Creeks asked village leaders to give their National Council new powers. This eroded local independence as Council leaders began to criticize chiefs who challenged their actions, and it angered local shamans who upheld traditional village ceremonies. Soon they began to oppose the changes sweeping through tribal life. Class divisions showed clearly as wealthy leaders began fencing their land to keep their livestock in and claim the property as theirs. They acquired slaves who herded hundreds of cattle for them, often despite bitter objections from their own people.

Others continued to hunt, trap, and trade for manufactured goods that often worked better than their traditional tools or weapons. By this time their role in the fur and hide trades had reduced the numbers of game animals drastically, and often the men invaded the territory of tribal competitors or enemies. For example, when the Sauks and Mesquakies from Illinois or the Winnebagos from Wisconsin crossed the Mississippi into Iowa they risked attacks by Dakota Sioux who tried to defend their hunting area.

Some federal officers saw the Indians' persistent trade debts as a way to get the villagers' land as payment for what they owed. Using this process prior to the War of 1812, William Henry Harrison got eastern tribes to surrender about forty-five million acres between the Appalachians and the Mississippi. Clearly his tactics had persuaded some angry chiefs to join the British in that conflict. After the war the land grabbing continued and some villagers retreated across the Mississippi to escape the American negotiators and pioneers.

Others chose to adopt the parts of the acculturation program they considered useful. As early as 1804, Cherokee leaders had welcomed the Rev. Gideon Blackburn, who came to build a Presbyterian school among them. Shortly after that, Chickasaw chiefs asked to have farmers and blacksmiths sent to their villages. They expected that these men would make and repair equipment for them and also teach young men the skills to do those things themselves. Such signs of tribal interest encouraged churches and missionary societies to support educational, vocational, and religious work among some groups. They cooperated with federal officials, who saw the mission groups as doing the work of "civilization" less expensively than others would. By 1823, one mission board called for support of its efforts because "the American Savage is capable of being both civilized and Christianized." Many village leaders in the South were the mixed-race offspring of British traders and Indian mothers, and often they saw their future differently from their less acculturated relatives. They adopted slavery, large-scale agriculture, ranching, businesses, mills, and ferries, and sent their children north to secondary schools for their education. Such individuals hardly needed to be civilized. The issues that came to divide tribal groups went far beyond the leaders' parentage, however. Sometimes quarrels broke out between the traditionalists and those who chose to accept Anglo-American practices. At other times family, clan, and tribal political disputes divided tribal groups. Whatever the causes of such splits in village societies, the disunity weakened efforts to retain both tribal culture and lands.

Voluntary Removal

By the 1820s, the eastern tribes had few options left. They could try to acculturate and hope that their pioneer neighbors would accept them or that the government might actually live up to its promises and protect their land titles. This rarely happened, and so as early as the late eighteenth century some village leaders had chosen to move away from their white neighbors. The Stockbridge and Munsee people of Wisconsin provide a good example of this. A combination of eastern Algonquian groups including Mahicans and Delawares, they lived originally in Massachusetts and New Jersey. By the 1780s, white settlers overran the mission settlement of Stockbridge, and the villagers accepted an invitation to live with the Oneida tribe in New York. Shortly after the War of 1812 ended, some of them chose to join groups of Delawares near the White River in Indiana. There hatreds resulting from wartime campaigning a few years earlier persuaded them to look farther west for a permanent home. In 1821 they negotiated a purchase of land along the Fox River in Wisconsin, and a year later they began moving. From 1822 until 1831 they cleared land, planted crops, and built several new villages in Wisconsin. Then, about the time they had finished the difficult work of settlement, white pioneers filtered into the area and federal negotiators persuaded the Indians to move to new land east of Lake Winnebago, where they remained until 1856, when they had to move again, this time to a small reservation next to the Menominee tribe. Some of their descendants live there today. During the 1820s and early 1830s, groups of the Oneida and Brotherton Indians from New York also migrated to Wisconsin.

Other tribal groups began to consider moving away from the ever-present pioneers. From 1815 to 1830 at least a million people had settled beyond the Appalachians. This left the villagers there with ever less land for hunting or farming, because the pioneers demanded all of the resources. Facing almost constant trouble with their white neighbors, some chiefs decided that to survive they had to move west beyond the Mississippi. Earlier, during Thomas Jefferson's administration, federal officials had urged the eastern groups to abandon hunting and become sedentary farmers. The president persuaded Congress to let Indians exchange their eastern lands for areas in the new Louisiana Territory. Then he tried to pressure the Cherokee to relocate. Some village leaders among the Chickamaugas decided that they should resettle, and most of them moved to Arkansas. Others went west without selling their village sites, so that by 1811 at least two thousand Cherokees had left their homes in Tennessee or Georgia. However, many of the rest had become partially acculturated, wanted to keep their lands, and refused to negotiate any new cessions.

Two things happened in the decade after the War of 1812 that persuaded federal officials to step up their efforts at encouraging voluntary migration. First, a continuing flood of new settlers surged west, pouring into the new states of Indiana, Illinois, Alabama, Mississippi, and Louisiana. Their presence left only Florida in the South and Michigan Territory (including what is now Wisconsin and part of Minnesota) in the North with enough space for Indians trying to live in traditional ways. Pioneers moving into newly opened regions proved no more willing to live alongside Native people than had others on earlier frontiers. Native leaders recognized the growing pressures for them to acculturate or move. Some welcomed missionaries, teachers, and mechanics to their towns, but others urged their people to migrate. In 1817, Cherokee leaders Charles Hicks, George Lowry, and Going Snake signed a treaty that gave the United States nearly one-third of their remaining tribal lands. Under that agreement, they had the option of crossing the Mississippi, and by the 1830s at least six thousand of them had done so. Clearly, whether Indians liked it or not, by the 1820s they saw their freedom slipping away. They faced a rapidly growing white population and increasing demands that their lands and other resources be thrown open for the settlers.

When Secretary of War John Calhoun commissioned the Rev. Jedediah Morse to investigate conditions among the tribes east of the Mississippi, village chiefs cooperated, presenting two distinct views. For some, the onrushing pioneers brought disaster, and they sought some means of escape. Others, such as the Cherokees, Creeks, and Choctaws, had acculturated leaders, and many of these bilingual men had adopted white economic practices entirely. Their teenaged sons went to secondary school in New England, while the fathers operated mills, ferries, ranches, and plantations. The Cherokees supported eighteen schools, often staffed by white missionary teachers. In the mid-1820s Sequoyah developed an easy-to-learn Cherokee syllabary that spread "through the nation like a fire among the leaves," bringing literacy in their own language to almost the entire tribe in less than a single decade. Clearly these people could not be labeled "naked savages." With educated leaders, growing economic strength, and widespread literacy, the tribe posed a major challenge to frontier politicians and land-hungry pioneers. When they realized that many Indians had no intention of moving west, Georgia politicians increased their clamor for some way to force the tribes out of the state. Their angry demands, and the desires of some federal officials to solve what they called the "Indian problem," led to calls for a formal removal program to do just that.

Sequoyah (George Giss or Guess) c. 1770–1843

Born in 1770 or soon after, Sequoyah was the son of a white father and a Cherokee woman, Wut-the, and spent his early life with his mother's family. The boy never went to school, and he spoke Cherokee but no English. At home he tended the garden and herded cattle while his mother operated a small trading post. Apparently he was injured or slightly crippled, and so he did not become a successful hunter or warrior, although he did serve in the Cherokee regiment that fought against the Creeks in the Red Stick War of 1813–14. He became a skilled silversmith and a self-taught blacksmith. As a young man he ran the trading post and, impressed by what he called the whites' "talking leaves," by 1809 he began working to develop a Cherokee alphabet. His family and friends thought this was useless and some feared that writing was a sign of witchcraft. After much work he decided to use symbols for Cherokee sounds rather than words, and he developed the eighty-six characters in the Cherokee syllabary. When no one took this seriously, he taught it to his six-year-old daughter. In 1822 he traveled to the Cherokees then living in western Arkansas, and after persuading them of its value he returned east and began teaching his people to read. The syllabary spread literacy quickly and by 1825 the tribe adopted it as the official written language. In 1828 the bilingual *Cherokee Phoenix* began publishing, using the syllabary. The next year Sequoyah moved to Oklahoma and there worked toward tribal reunification. He died in 1843. His syllabary gave traditional Cherokees a way to record cultural practices and ideas and gave that tribe the first written Indian language.

Sources: Margaret Bender, *Signs of Cherokee Culture: Sequoyah's Syllabary in Eastern Cherokee Life* (Chapel Hill: University of North Carolina Press, 2002); William G. McLoughlin, *After the Trail of Tears: The Cherokee's Struggle for Sovereignty, 1839–1880* (Norman: University of Oklahoma Press, 1993).

Forced Removal

Tribes and the U.S. government were on a collision course. Few Indians wanted to move from their ancestral homes, particularly when other tribes already occupied the lands farther west. At the same time, many voting citizens demanded that they leave. So from the mid-1820s through the mid-1840s, removal—at first voluntary, later forced—became national policy. Tribal groups devised a variety of tactics to deal with the crisis. Some signed treaties and moved despite their objections. Some stalled and hoped that they could avoid having to move. A few small groups hid or were overlooked and so retained some of their lands. Others enlisted white supporters and fought government actions through the courts. In two cases, the Sauks and Mesquakies in Illinois, and the Seminoles in Florida, groups resisted, subsequently suffering through the Black Hawk War of 1832 and the Second Seminole War from 1835 into the early 1840s. Whichever tactics Indian groups tried, they faced increasingly hostile public opinion and impatient federal officers. As a result, the removal process, whether peaceful or violent, brought as much suffering and misery to many tribes as had the wars and intermittent raiding earlier in the century.

During the administrations of Presidents James Monroe and John Quincy Adams, federal negotiators fanned out across the frontier, securing treaties by any means possible. Coercion, bribery, and threats of force all came into play, as tribes and bands saw their lands shrink year by year. Bitter debates over how to deal with American demands pushed some tribal societies to the brink of civil war and made it all but impossible to halt the land losses. The nontraditional Cherokee leaders encouraged wider acculturation, hoping this would gain their acceptance by white neighbors. They established a national council and in 1827 wrote a constitution. This move brought immediate objections from some of the older and less acculturated chiefs. Led by White Path, they held an unofficial

Indian removal, 1820s–1840s

council to voice their displeasure with earlier laws that struck at traditional practices such as clan revenge, infanticide, matrilineal inheritance, and polygamy. At the same time, they denounced efforts to force Christian morality and practices on the tribe.

White Path and his fellow traditionalists had several goals. For one, they hoped to slow or even reverse the growing centralization within Cherokee society. The national council had reduced the number of chiefs by nearly two-thirds and also had cut back on the autonomy of the village councils. Cherokee shamans added to the confusion, objecting to what they thought was a movement to proclaim Christianity as the official tribal religion. At that point missionaries and Indian converts referred to the majority of the tribe that still practiced some of the customary tribal dances and other ceremonies as "backward," "ignorant," and "polluted." Clearly, the traditionalists felt threatened by such attacks on their cultural practices. They struggled to avoid the unwanted changes in their society, but the contest rarely went beyond angry debates. In May 1827, one of the missionaries reported that "the whole [Cherokee] Nation here is in the greatest turmoil. The greater part wants to have . . . the missions dissolved." Meeting into the middle of the summer, the two sides failed to settle their differences, but before the year ended acculturated leaders wrote a national constitution patterned on that of the United States. This led directly to the decade-long removal crisis that overwhelmed the tribe. State authorities in Georgia reacted angrily to the new tribal constitution and in 1828 passed anti-Cherokee laws that abolished the new government, jailed chiefs if they tried to carry out their duties, and set up a state lottery to sell tribal land. That same year Andrew Jackson won the presidential election, bringing strongly held ideas about Indian affairs to Washington. Many of his congressional supporters came from the South and the West, and in 1830 they passed the Indian Removal Act, which soon forced most eastern Indians west beyond the Mississippi River. Although divisions continued among the Cherokees, both sides rejected leaving their homeland. The acculturated tribal leaders hired William Wirt, former U.S. attorney general, to represent them in a suit against the state of Georgia. This resulted in the 1831 *Cherokee Nation v. Georgia* Supreme Court decision that described the Indians as "domestic, dependent nations." Although the Cherokees lost that case, the decision laid the foundation for the legal status of Indian tribes from that day to the present. It declared that they were not independent, but it recognized that they had land claims and other rights. The next year, in *Worcester v. Georgia*, the Court found the tribes to be entirely beyond any state authority and subject only to the federal government.

During the mid 1830s the Cherokees often appeared divided and uncertain about how to deal with the United States. Nevertheless, most rejected the idea of leaving their native lands and moving west. As early as 1819, their chiefs had rejected any more land cessions, and now both the assimilated and the more traditional leaders saw no reason to change that stance. However, the Georgians' continuing assaults and the realization that the federal government now refused to protect them persuaded some to accept the need for removal. A small group that came to be called the Treaty Party formed around Major Ridge, his son John, and Elias Boudinot, a nephew who edited and published the *Cherokee Phoenix,* the bilingual tribal newspaper. Experienced, well educated, and economically successful, these men saw their less-acculturated tribal neighbors as having little chance to resist the greedy Georgia pioneers, so they supported the Ridges and forced Boudinot to resign his editorial post. In this case the dispute divided the acculturated leaders rather than separating them from more traditional Cherokees.

Having lost their positions of influence, Treaty Party leaders decided that the tribe had few options. It had to accept removal or be destroyed, so they took direct action. In 1835 John Ridge led a delegation to Washington for talks, but opponents blocked acceptance of the agreement Ridge had signed. In December 1835, American negotiators came south, met the pro-removal leaders at New Echota, and negotiated another treaty. This one surrendered Cherokee title to all tribal lands and accepted the need for prompt removal. Despite clear objections from the majority of Cherokees, the U.S. Senate ratified the treaty in 1836 and gave the tribe another two years to start west. Few did so, and in early 1838 U.S. Army units began rounding up the unwilling Indians. As they waited in open stockades, many fell ill, whereupon Chief John Ross persuaded federal authorities to let the tribal government supervise the removal. By 1840 the Indians had walked and ridden west on what they called the Trail of Tears because of the suffering and fatalities experienced along the way. Removal pushed most eastern tribes west, as the tide of pioneer settlement continued to bring thousands of new inhabitants into the region between the Appalachians and the Mississippi River.

The Cherokees had tried to use their level of acculturation to gain public support. When that failed they turned to legal maneuvers to ensure that they would retain their homelands, but this too failed. A few small groups tried to fade into the woods, hills, or swamps to avoid being pushed west, and at times they succeeded. Others simply refused to move and soon found themselves in a military struggle to retain their homelands. In the long run, that worked no better than acculturation or avoidance, but during the 1830s and early 1840s it spread terror across several frontier regions. By the removal era, bitter divisions frequently weakened village unity. The Sauks and Mesquakies of Illinois and Iowa offer a good example of how this led to unexpected conflict. These two tribes were closely related, often shared village sites, and frequently intermarried, yet their intra-tribal divisions helped bring about the 1832 Black Hawk War. American negotiations had planted the seeds for this conflict in 1804 when William Henry Harrison persuaded a handful of Sauk leaders to sign a treaty that surrendered their lands east of the Mississippi. The agreement allowed the villagers to stay in Illinois until the government sold the land, and it took until 1829 for this to happen.

By that time Sauk and Mesquakie leaders disagreed among themselves about removal. Some of the villagers had been living in Missouri and Iowa for several decades, while others returned to Illinois each spring to plant their corn crops. Black Hawk, an aging warrior, led the anti-removal group, while Keokuk persuaded a majority of both tribes that safety lay beyond the Mississippi. In 1831 U.S. troops forced Black Hawk's followers west into Iowa. Once there the women complained that they could not break through the matted soil to clear land for new crops, and they begged the leaders to recross the Mississippi so that they could use their traditional fields. In April 1832 after a miserable winter in Iowa, nearly two thousand people followed Black Hawk back into Illinois. This "Indian invasion" by what was known as "the British Band" spread panic through frontier settlements there. Governor John Reynolds called out the state militia, and Gen. Henry Atkinson led a force of U.S. regulars after the Indians. Sauk attempts to parley failed, because the militia had no interpreters. From May through August the Indians managed to avoid their pursuers, but the U.S. troops caught them trying to cross the Mississippi at the mouth of the Bad Axe River. When the fighting ended on August 2, the British Band included only a few hundred survivors of the nearly two thousand people who had dared to "invade" Illinois that year.

In Florida the longer Seminole War began in 1835. It ended in 1842 with a similar result. Most of the tribe relocated west to Oklahoma, with only a few scattered remnants remaining in Florida.

By the 1840s, U.S. officials were congratulating themselves for having solved the "Indian question." They had relocated tribes, and virtually all federal lands lay available for pioneer purchase and occupation. However, events quickly undercut their satisfaction. Not all of the targeted tribes moved west. Today, large numbers of Cherokees remain in North Carolina, as do Choctaws in Mississippi and Seminoles in Florida. At the same time, for the Indians removal had brought misery and bitter regrets. A traveler in frontier Wisconsin reported hearing an aging Winnebago grieving. "A few short years and our nation will be unknown," the elder lamented. "Then, when the stranger . . . shall call out upon every hill, *where is the Winnebago?* Echo alone shall answer from the west—*where is the Winnebago?*" Native refugees faced dissension and violence as they occupied new regions not always similar to their eastern homelands. Some western tribes attacked them, and the divisions and controversies that existed at removal continued to disrupt them in their new homes. What neither federal officials nor the Indians could have predicted—the growth of the United States from the Rocky Mountains to the Pacific coast during the 1840s—quickly destroyed any hope for long-term peace and harmony in the West. Instead, by mid-century Indians faced an aggressive and powerful United States, eager to occupy the West and to exploit its resources, often at Indian expense.

Suggested Readings

Anderson, Gary C. *The Indian Southwest, 1580–1830: Ethnogenesis and Reinvention.* Norman: University of Oklahoma Press, 1999.

Blackhawk, Ned. *Violence Over the Land: Indians and Empires in the Early American West.* Cambridge: Harvard University Press, 2006.

Brooks, James F. *Captives and Cousins: Slavery, Kinship, and Community in the Southwest Borderlands.* Chapel Hill: University of North Carolina Press, 2001.

Cave, Alfred A. *Prophets of the Great Spirit: Native American Revitalization Movements in Eastern North America.* Lincoln: University of Nebraska Press, 2006.

Edmunds, R. David. *The Shawnee Prophet.* Lincoln: University of Nebraska Press, 1983.

———. *Tecumseh and the Quest for Indian Leadership.* Boston: Little, Brown, 1984.

Martin, Joel. *Sacred Revolt: The Muskogees' Struggle for a New World.* Boston: Beacon Press, 1991.

Meyer, Roy. *The Village Indians of the Upper Missouri Valley.* Lincoln: University of Nebraska Press, 1977.

Murphy, Lucy E. *A Gathering of Rivers: Indians, Métis, and Mining in the Western Great Lakes, 1737–1832.* Lincoln: University of Nebraska Press, 2000.

Nichols, Roger L. *Black Hawk and the Warrior's Path.* Arlington Heights, Ill.: Harlan Davidson, 1992.

Perdue, Theda. *Cherokee Women: Gender and Culture Change, 1700–1835.* Lincoln: University of Nebraska Press, 1998.

Wishart, David J. *The Fur Trade of the American West, 1807–1840.* Lincoln: University of Nebraska Press, 1979.

Illustrations

Cahokia town plaza. Courtesy of Cahokia Mounds Historical Society.

Ætatis suæ 21 Aº 1616.

Matoaks als Rebecka daughter to the mighty Prince
Powhatan Emperour of Attanoughkomouck als Virginia
converted and baptized in the Christian faith and
Wife to the worᵗ Mʳ Tho: Rolff.

(Above) Pocahontas, from a portrait by William Sheppard.
Courtesy of Library of Congress, LC-DIG-det-4a26409.

(Opposite, above) The Indian Fort Sasquehanok, 1720.
A European depiction of an Atlantic coast village.
Courtesy of the National Archives of Canada, C36345.

(Opposite, below) Mandan earthen lodge, from Edward
S. Curtis, *The North American Indian* vol. 5 (1908).
Courtesy of Library of Congress, LC-USZ62-1114582.

750.   Lieutenant Taylor and seven of his Indian scouts, Pine Ridge Agency, Jan. 19th, 1891

(Above) Carved totem poles at Alert Bay, British Columbia, 1900. Courtesy of Library of Congress, LC-USZ62-47016.

(Opposite, above) Monument to the largest group hanging in American history, at the end of the Minnesota Sioux War, in Mankato. Courtesy of the Library of Congress.

(Opposite, below) Lt. Charles W. Taylor and seven of his Sioux scouts, Pine Ridge Agency, 1891. Courtesy of Library of Congress, LC-USZ62-43683.

(*Above*) Teenage Indian students at Carlisle Indian School in Pennsylvania, 1904. Courtesy of the Library of Congress.

(*Opposite, above*) Seminole family in traditional clothing, Florida, 1910. Courtesy of the Library of Congress.

(*Opposite, below*) New Mexico Pueblo leaders' 1923 protest against land-title changes. They hold canes given to them by President Lincoln as a promise of fair treatment. Courtesy of the Library of Congress.

(Above) Cherokee activist Ruth Muskrat presents President Calvin Coolidge with a copy of *The Red Man in the United States*, December 1923. Courtesy of Library of Congress, LC-USZ62-107775.

(Opposite, above) American Indian Movement (AIM) protest poster, 1970s. Courtesy of the Library of Congress, LC-USZ 62-3685.

(Opposite, below) Participants in the "Longest Walk," sponsored by the American Indian Movement in 1978. Courtesy of the Library of Congress, LC-U9-36364.

The Struggle for the West, 1840–1890

Regional and Tribal Varieties

T he western tribes differed widely. Along the Pacific Northwest coast, they lived in long cedar plank houses with elaborately carved totem poles nearby. They hunted whales and other sea mammals in large canoes capable of holding thirty or forty men. In the desert Southwest, Puebloan groups built multistory apartment buildings from rock or sun-dried adobe blocks. On the plains, hunters mounted on fast horses tracked the vast buffalo herds and lived in leather tepees. Still farther east along the Missouri River and between that stream and the Mississippi, agricultural villagers lived in large earthen lodges and hunted to complete their diets. At the beginning of the nineteenth century most of these people had mastered their physical environments. Their cultures flourished and they stood at the height of their social, military, and economic powers. Many possessed horses and almost all of the groups had firearms. These gave them both the mobility and the weaponry they needed for protection against enemies, whether Indian or white. So the large tribes of the plains—Lakota Sioux, Cheyenne, Arapaho, Pawnee, Comanche, and Kiowa—stood between the advancing Americans and the resources and wealth they sought. Yet the Indians' very strength and success, as well as their lack of knowledge of the threat posed by the United States, may have led many into a near-fatal overconfidence.

Between the 1804 Louisiana Purchase and the 1848 Treaty of Guadalupe Hidalgo, the United States acquired the land stretching from the Mississippi River to the Pacific Ocean. This action brought the western tribes into increasing contact with American leaders who were determined to attach the new regions firmly to the United States. These leaders cared no more for the claims of Indians there than for those of the eastern tribes then being forced west beyond the Mississippi. American exploration and gradual occupation of tribal homelands would change the country and its people forever. At first only small parties of explorers, fur traders, and trappers arrived, but within a few decades hordes of miners, farmers, and other settlers poured west, carrying with them disease, bigotry, and violence. This brought large, fiercely independent, and often mobile tribes into direct contact, competition, and conflict with pioneers who feared and despised the Native peoples. Indian efforts to retain their independence, cultural practices, and homelands included diplomacy, trade, religion, flight, and warfare, with only modest success. These actions stood at the center of their dealings with the United States for most of the nineteenth century.

Early Meetings

Many western tribes lacked experience with Americans, but that changed quickly. During early March 1804, a few Sauks stopped at St. Louis to visit the Spanish governor of upper Louisiana, Charles Delassus, whom they considered a friend. Years later Black Hawk, who was in the group, remembered learning that the United States would take over the region that same day, and that their "Spanish father" would leave. "We were sad," he said, "because we had always heard bad accounts of the Americans from Indians who had lived near them!" Later that summer, as the Lewis and Clark expedition worked its way slowly up the Missouri Valley, it only narrowly avoided disaster when encountering the Teton Lakota (Sioux). On September 25, 1804, the expedition halted in South Dakota to meet the Sioux, who came down to the river. When William Clark and a few men rowed to shore, the Indians there grabbed the bow cable of the boat and surrounded him. Thinking that the explorers were really traders, they threatened to drive them back downstream unless the Americans gave them more presents. When the leaders refused, the young men jostled Clark, who drew his sword, signaled his companions on the larger keelboat to prepare their weapons, and had a shouting match with the chiefs. The incident, though ending peacefully, offered an example of the conflicting goals and actions of the two sides. The Lakota wanted the newcomers to stay out of their country, except on Sioux terms, and the explorers expressed the government's determination to enter it.

For the next generation the Lakota people saw their goal of a free West nearly come true. Although modest numbers of traders, mountain men, and government explorers crisscrossed the region, the idea that the plains were desert and that the region beyond them lay outside the nation's borders kept all but the most hardy or foolish from venturing there. Yet the relative isolation most tribes enjoyed began to crumble after 1821, when Mexico achieved its independence. A brisk trade between the border merchants and Santa Fe developed, and in 1822, farther to the north, fur traders William Ashley and Andrew Henry sent the first of their hired trappers west to become mountain men. Within just two or three years these intruders began drifting onto the southern plains, the upper reaches of the Missouri River, and the northern Rockies. This brought them into frequent and often violent contact with tribes living in those regions. Still, the outsiders' numbers remained small for the next several decades, as few nontrappers or nontraders ventured west from the US or north from Mexico.

During that time the tribes of the Missouri Valley region, the northern and central plains, and the Rockies played active roles in the fur and hide trade that dominated those regions. Hunters killed game and women prepared pelts and hides for market. In a few villages white trappers and traders acquired Indian wives who then played central roles in the growing trade. In many cases, however, Native people considered the trappers interlopers, even thieves, who killed the beaver and other furbearers, took food from Indian hunters' families, and left fewer pelts for the villagers to use or trade for manufactured goods. Even more disastrous than the increased environmental stresses they introduced, the whites accidently brought diseases that raced through tribal camps, killing thousands of their own customers and suppliers. In the summer of 1837 traders carried smallpox to the people of the upper Missouri Valley and the northern Rockies, nearly destroying entire communities. Among the Mandans, one village of six hundred lost all but fifteen people in only three months. Terrified and angry, infected people fled, only to spread the contagion. In despair, Four Bears, a dying Mandan chief, reminded his listeners, "I do not fear Death my friends. You know it, but to die with my face rotten, [so] that even the Wolves will shrink in horror at seeing Me," that was too much. He urged the warriors to kill every white man they could find; but of the estimated 1,800 members of the tribe, only 138 survived the disaster, and they lacked the numbers to accept his challenge.

Although the Mandan example appears to be the most dramatic, smallpox and other diseases swept across the West repeatedly in the nineteenth century, greatly weakening many tribes. The Blackfeet, for example, encountered smallpox while attacking a Shoshone camp shortly before the opening of the nineteenth century. As they pushed their way into the enemy tents, one warrior recalled being "appalled with terror." "There was no one to fight," he stated; only "the dead and the dying" remained, "each a mass of corruption!" Two days later the pox began its march through the attackers' ranks, killing at least a third of that particular band. Other tribes reported similar terror and destruction when this disease first swept through their camps.

During the mid-1840s the situation in the West changed almost overnight. In 1845 the United States annexed Texas, and the next year it negotiated a border settlement with Great Britain for the Oregon Country. Just two years later, American officials tore California and the Southwest from the grasp of Mexico. Within just five years the nation had expanded to the Pacific, and this changed the Indians' circumstances immediately. Now, instead of having only occasional meetings with settlers, they encountered them repeatedly, as thousands of pioneers headed west to the fertile Oregon Country and California. When workers discovered gold at the Sutter's Mill site in 1848, tens of thousands of gold-maddened would-be miners raced to California. The less spectacular, but steadier, movement of pioneer farmers that began during the 1840s continued to lure settlers west as well. These miners, farmers, and townsfolk demanded territorial government and later statehood. By the time the removal program forcing most eastern tribes west of the Mississippi ended in the 1840s, white pioneers had begun to arrive throughout much of the same area. This meant that the western tribes and those newly pushed there by the government could not escape increasing contacts with whites and their insistence that the land and its resources be taken from the Indians.

When tribal people encountered overland pioneers traveling to Oregon in the 1840s, they had no way of knowing that these people were only the advance party for the hundreds of thousands soon to follow. However, as they watched the wagon trains and livestock frighten the buffalo, destroy the grass along the Overland Trail route, and foul the water holes, the plains tribes objected. At first no major violence occurred, but Indian leaders complained about white incursions. At the same time, the pioneers asked for protection from the "Indian threat" they faced traveling west, and federal officials provided funds for mounted troops and for building forts along the trail. By 1849 the army had taken over the trading posts that became Fort Kearny in Nebraska, Fort Laramie in Wyoming, and Fort Hall in southern Idaho. Although small, often isolated, and too weak to protect westward-moving emigrants, these outposts became centers for the American invasion of Indian homelands. At each of them the western tribes met agents, soldiers, traders, and other whites, and almost from the start those encounters led to tension and occasional violence. Nevertheless, despite how it would later be presented by Hollywood, of the nearly quarter of a million pioneers who trekked west before 1860, fewer than four hundred died during Indian raids. Most of the rest never encountered any hostile warriors. That remained true for the Indians too, as few of the villagers met any individual Anglo-Americans.

Negotiations and Conflicts

Not anticipating major conflicts with the tribes, in 1849 Congress moved the Office of Indian Affairs from the War Department to the newly created Department of the Interior. In the Senate debate over this measure, Sen. Jefferson Davis remarked that although "wars and rumors of wars came annually" in the past, by that time peace rather than war symbolized the normal relations between the United States and the tribes. This noble sentiment proved incorrect time and again over the next forty years, as Indians and whites clashed repeatedly. Hoping to protect the travelers crossing the northern plains, in 1851 the government hired former mountain man Thomas Fitzpatrick to negotiate a peace treaty with tribes from that region at Fort Laramie. Most of the groups responded, and in the treaty they agreed to stay at peace with each other, to allow the United States to build roads and forts through their country, and to make restitution for any later raids on pioneers moving west. In turn, the treaty called for the United States to protect the Indians from the pioneers and to pay them annuities for at least the next ten years. Once the Senate ratified this agreement, many felt that it had set a pattern for peaceful relations with the western tribes, but unfortunately peace became a rare commodity.

Following the ratification of this agreement, the expected annuity payments drew thousands of Brulé, Oglala, and Miniconjou Lakotas to Fort Laramie each summer. Their camps stretched along the major migrant trails west, and violent incidents happened repeatedly. In June 1853, while the Lakotas drifted in for their payments, one of the young men shot at a soldier operating the ferry across the

Platte River. Rather than working to calm the situation, the post commander sent a young second lieutenant with twenty-three men to the Miniconjou village. There he seized the offender, and when fighting broke out, his men killed six Indians and then hurried back to the fort. The angry chiefs confronted Fitzpatrick when he arrived with the annuities, insisting that the fort be closed because "the soldiers of the Great Father . . . [had made] the ground bloody," but the authorities ignored their demand.

Having learned nothing from this rash behavior, the soldiers at Fort Laramie repeated it the next summer when hungry Indians killed and ate a cow that had strayed from one of the wagon trains. On August 19, 1854, Lt. John L. Grattan led thirty-one men with two artillery pieces to the camp of the Brulé chief Conquering Bear, where he insisted that the village leaders surrender the man who had killed the animal. When the band's leaders refused, Grattan ordered his men to begin firing. The chief died immediately, and mounted warriors killed all but one of the soldiers on the spot. Wounded, the lone survivor escaped to the fort but soon died there. The attack on their village so infuriated the Lakotas that they sacked the local trader's building and took many of his goods. Then they rode north to avoid other contacts with Americans. Although the soldiers were to blame for the so-called massacre, the War Department ordered U.S. forces west to punish the Indians. This led to Gen. William S. Harney's 1855 campaign, which culminated in a costly defeat for the Brulé at Ash Hollow.

These events on the plains represented the cycle of violence that occurred there for the next several decades. Often wild rumors, raids, retaliation, and flight became part of frontier life for Indians and whites alike. By the 1850s this was true in both the Pacific Northwest and California, as miners and farmers swarmed into those areas. Miners seemed particularly eager to exterminate nearby Indians. They formed local units of a group they called the California Volunteer Militia and marched from one mountain valley to another hunting their human prey. These actions reduced the tribal population of California from about one hundred fifty thousand in 1848, when the United States acquired the area, to only thirty thousand by 1861. While the miners diverted water and stole timber from them, the tribes suffered even more as farmers and ranchers took their land and drove them into the hills. Hoping to keep peace and gain control of most California land, the government sent negotiators to persuade the California Indians to accept reservations. These groups signed eighteen treaties setting aside about 7.5 million acres, but because Anglo and Spanish-speaking Californians objected, the U.S. Senate refused to ratify the agreements. In 1853 Edward F. Beale became the superintendent of Indian affairs for California, and he managed to set up five small reservations that protected at least a remnant of the tribes there.

To the north in Oregon, settlers treated the Indians nearly as badly as in California, so that by the mid-1850s raiding and warfare began there too. As they had on the plains, government negotiators sought to herd the tribes into out-of-the-way places and to keep them out of the settlers' path. Pioneers entering the Northwest heard lurid tales of the 1847 Cayuse War and the massacre of the Rev. Marcus Whitman and his family in that conflict, and they demanded that Indians be moved. In 1854–55, Washington territorial governor Isaac I. Stevens pressured many of the tribes to accept three treaties reducing their land base and opening much of the region for settlement. Tribal divisions and treaty provisions that forced groups with widely differing languages and customs to share reservations led to violence, and in 1855 war broke out. For the next three years the Yakima or Plateau Indian War brought many Native groups together against the whites. By late 1858 the hostilities had ended, but the disputes over land, the location of reservations, and constant white encroachments on the Indians' home territories kept relations between tribes and pioneers on edge for another generation.

As the tribes of the Far West lost their lands and much of their independence through warfare and increasing white population, those farther east faced similar pressures. From Minnesota in the North to present-day Oklahoma, tribal and village leaders heard a steady drumbeat of demands that they surrender some of their land and move to smaller holdings or to new locations. In 1844, prior to the U.S. war with Mexico, frontier leaders began calling for the opening of parts of the Indian country in present-day Kansas, lands newly settled by eastern tribes. With the U.S. seizure of California and the Southwest in 1848, demands for railroad connections to the West Coast and for territorial government for the regions between the Missouri Valley and California brought renewed pressures on the tribes living in eastern Kansas and Nebraska. In 1854, as Congress created the new Kansas and Nebraska Territories, federal agents negotiated treaties with local groups such as the Kansas, Osages, and Pawnees, as well as with eastern refugees like the Kickapoos, Miamis, and Delawares, that stripped millions of acres from them. In Kansas, territorial officers openly speculated in Indian lands while squatters pushed their way into areas that still belonged to the tribes.

Diplomacy and Warfare

The years from 1860 to the 1880s brought repeated negotiations and clashes between Indians and other Americans as village leaders tried to protect their homelands. For groups living in the new territories, near mining camps or along the major trails, each passing year brought more difficulties. The small army garrisons scattered across the West offered little help in halting incursions by pioneers, and when the regular troops headed east during the Civil War, sporadic violence broke out. In August 1862, conflict between the Dakota (Eastern Sioux) and the settlers began in Minnesota when annuities owed to the Indians failed to arrive during a particularly hot, dry summer. Although the local agent and several traders there had plenty of supplies, they refused to issue any to the Dakotas before the actual payments from the government came. When Chief Little

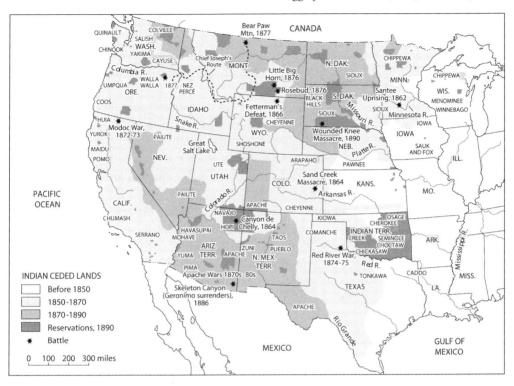

The Indian frontier and major conflicts

Crow asked for food, Andrew Myrick, one of the traders, reputedly said that if the Indians were hungry, "Let them eat grass or their own dung."

Outraged Dakotas stormed out of the meeting, and two days later four young Indian hunters arguing about their personal bravery killed two farm families. At that point Little Crow, who had worked for peaceful relations with the whites for years, decided he had little choice. His people could flee, they could fight, or they could remain and be destroyed. He decided to fight, and that summer more than a thousand settlers and perhaps an equal number of Indians died. The trader Myrick was among the first victims; the warriors left his corpse on the prairie, its mouth stuffed with grass. By autumn the Dakotas had run out of ammunition and the war ended. The army confined seventeen hundred Indian prisoners to a stockade at Fort Snelling, in present-day Minneapolis. There military courts sentenced three hundred of the warriors to death, but President Abraham Lincoln pardoned most of them. Still, on December 26 at Mankato, Minnesota, the army executed thirty-eight of the men in the largest public hanging in American history. When the fighting there ended, Little Crow led several hundred Sioux north into Canada. Other angry Dakotas fled westward, often joining relatives on the plains and spreading anti-American feelings.

Other plains tribes responded violently to American incursions and mistreatment as well. In Colorado prospectors found gold by the end of the 1850s. As thousands of miners trekked to Denver, they infuriated the Cheyennes and Arapahos of the central plains, and sporadic raiding kept tensions high for several years. In 1864, Colorado governor John Evans demanded that all of the villagers return to their permanent camps. Those who refused to do so he considered hostile, although groups hunting on the plains had no way to hear about the governor's proclamation. In November, Southern Cheyenne leader Black Kettle camped near Fort Lyon on Sand Creek in southeastern Colorado, where he thought the local commander had promised him safety. There he and his followers fell victim to a brutal, unprovoked attack led by Col. John M. Chivington of the Colorado Volunteers. At daybreak on November 29, 1864, some seven hundred militiamen stormed into the Indian camp and by day's end had killed more than seventy of the villagers, mostly women and children. In an orgy of violence, the Indians "were scalped. Their brains knocked out; the [militia]men used their knives, ripped open women, clubbed little children," a trader present at the scene testified later. Soldiers "knocked them in the head with their guns, beat their brains out, [and] mutilated their bodies in every sense of the word." Their brutality, which earned the event the name "Sand Creek Massacre," outraged many Americans and led to a congressional investigation that denounced Colonel Chivington and his men. This incident stands as one of only a few white actions against Indians to be called a massacre. Usually that term was reserved for Indian victories.

The Civil War years brought little but violence to other Indian communities as well. In Indian Territory—present-day Oklahoma—the major southern tribes suffered badly after the 1861 withdrawal of federal troops. Because some of the tribes still identified with the South, their leaders joined with the Confederacy hoping for better treatment than they had received from the U.S. government. They organized four regiments of Indian troops numbering nearly five thousand men, and these units served throughout the Civil War. Not all of the members of each tribe backed the South, however, and Creek leader Opothle Yoholo led a mixed group of Creeks and others wishing to remain neutral north into Kansas. One of the Cherokee regiments followed and by the end of 1861 had defeated and scattered this group. For the rest of the war, Indian detachments raided Union forces, and as the Confederacy wore down, U.S. troops raided tribal communities. By 1865 more than ten thousand people in Indian Territory lived in refugee camps, and all of the major tribal groups had seen their governments and economies destroyed. When the war ended that year, tribal support for the Confederacy gave the United States another excuse to demand land cessions, this time as reparations for wartime damages supposedly inflicted by the Indians.

Tribes in other areas suffered as well. As U.S. regular troops moved east to fight the Confederacy, hastily recruited regiments of volunteers replaced them in much of the West. Often composed of pioneers or men from newly settled areas, these units had little respect for the Indians, as their actions at Sand Creek demonstrated. In the Southwest the frequent raiding between the citizens of New Mexico Territory and their Navajo neighbors led to demands that the tribe be punished. Responding in 1864, Gen. James H. Carleton ordered Christopher (Kit) Carson to invade the heart of Navajo country. Leading units of the California Volunteers, Carson destroyed livestock, orchards, and villages in a scorched-earth campaign that ultimately forced the Navajos to surrender. The victors then marched their prisoners on what became known as the "Long Walk" to a reservation at the Bosque Redondo in southeastern New Mexico. There they got sick from bad water, watched their crops die in the dry infertile soil, and had to defend themselves from Apache attacks. Soon they took the initiative, slipping away to hunt or raid their enemies, forging ration tickets to get enough food, and holding their cultural and religious ceremonies secretly. By 1868 the federal officials there recognized that the relocation had failed, so they allowed the exiles to return to their homeland.

Once the Civil War ended, pioneers surged west again, plunging the plains into sporadic violence for another dozen years. Gold discoveries in Montana during the war had led suppliers of camps to open the Bozeman or Powder River Trail north from the Platte River to the mines. This route cut directly through the heart of the best hunting territory of the Lakotas, who raided travelers there repeatedly. Responding to the miners' calls for protection, the army built three forts to guard the route, but Lakota warriors under Oglala leader Red Cloud kept the troops penned up in their forts. On December 21, 1867, the Sioux lured the boastful Capt. William J. Fetterman and his eighty-man command into an ambush, killing them all. The Indians called their victory "The Battle of the Hundred Slain" and demanded that the United States remove its troops from the region.

Even before these events, many Americans had grown tired of reading about battles and warfare, and in 1867 the government established a peace commission to negotiate the movement of the tribes onto reservations throughout the plains. At Fort Laramie in what is now eastern Wyoming and Medicine Lodge Creek in Kansas, commissioners met Indians from the major tribes of each region. By this time many tribal leaders had come to accept the need for peace and a few moved grudgingly to the new reservations. At first Red Cloud refused to sign the treaty until the government agreed to abandon the forts on the Bozeman Trail. It did so to avoid more fighting, and as the soldiers marched and rode south, Indians burned each of the three hated military posts to the ground. For the moment, that ended major problems on the northern plains, as the tribes moved reluctantly toward their new homes. Yet the 1868 Treaty of Fort Laramie included provisions that led to future conflict. It placed the Sioux reservation on the Missouri River, although tribal leaders wanted it farther west. By allowing Sioux hunters to follow buffalo herds beyond reservation boundaries, it encouraged frequent movement, particularly by those who refused to stop hunting, accept land, and become farmers.

When the peace commissioners traveled southeast from Fort Laramie to Medicine Lodge Creek, the assembled tribes they met proved even less enthusiastic about accepting reservations and becoming farmers than those to the north. After listening to American negotiators, the Kiowa chief White Bear, or Satanta, reminded his listeners that his people had not been at war and that they had no desire to settle on any particular part of their land. "I love to roam over the wide prairie," he said, "and when I do it I feel free and happy." The Comanche chief Ten Bears echoed these ideas. He chided the commissioners, claiming that American soldiers had begun hostilities against his people. Then he said, "I want to live and die as I was brought up. I love the open prairie, and I wish you would not insist on putting us on a reservation." At the same meeting Satank, or Sitting Bear, of the Kiowa expressed different ideas. He saw the new treaty as generous and ensuring peace. "You know what is best for us," he told the whites. "Do for us what is best. Teach us the road to travel, and we will not depart from it forever." Such divisions among tribal leaders appeared frequently in treaty negotiations and help explain why lasting settlements and sustained peace remained so difficult to achieve.

Agreements with the United States often did not remove the existing points of conflict. For example, in the treaties signed at Medicine Lodge Creek in 1867, federal negotiators promised that the government would prohibit commercial buffalo hunting in areas claimed by the Southern Cheyennes, Kiowas, and Comanches, yet the slaughter continued. After complaining in vain, tribal leaders including Quanah Parker (Comanche), Lone Wolf (Kiowa), and Stone Wolf (Cheyenne) agreed to a coordinated attack on the hunters at a camp called Adobe Walls in the Texas Panhandle. Their cooperation showed that the chiefs recognized clearly the threat the hide business posed to their food supply, and they put aside their differences long enough to carry out the attack. What they failed to anticipate was that they had no weapons to counter the whites' long-range rifles, and despite repeated charges, they could not overrun the hunters' defenses. This June 1874 fight opened the Red River War, bringing several columns of cavalry into the region. By August the army considered many of the bands on the southern plains hostile, and a month later Col. Ranald Mackenzie led an attack at Palo Duro Canyon. Most of the Indians escaped, but the troops destroyed all of the food, camp items, and lodges and also captured over fourteen hundred horses. After taking the best mounts for his men, Mackenzie ordered the destruction of over one thousand of the animals. As a result of continued pursuit, frequent small-scale battles, and wretched late-autumn weather, most of the southern tribes drifted back to their assigned reservations. By 1875 the region largely had been pacified.

Tribes on the northern plains had been rather quiet following the 1867–68 treaty signings at Fort Laramie, but continuing white incursions angered the Indians. Work on the transcontinental railroad had begun in 1864, and within just a few years buffalo hunters had killed large numbers of bison to feed construction crews. Still, aside from minor clashes, the people in that region remained at peace. In 1870, Red Cloud, Spotted Tail, and several other Sioux chiefs who had signed the Fort Laramie Treaty traveled to Washington hoping to get better treatment of Indians from the government. The reservation agent had told the leaders that they needed to change their way of life. Rather than living by hunting, now they had to become farmers, like the white men. Red Cloud, in particular, had other ideas. He had agreed to surrender much land to the United States but not to become a farmer. Rather, he told federal officials, "The Great Spirit did not make us to work. The white man owes us a living for the lands he has taken from us." He insisted that their reservation should be near Fort Laramie, but he got no new concession to do more than hunt there temporarily.

While Red Cloud tried persuasion, other Sioux leaders led their men on raids against nearby tribes and whites alike. Then in 1874 the government broke its promise to keep pioneers out of South Dakota's Black Hills, a region the Lakota people considered sacred. That summer Lt. Col. George Armstrong Custer led more than a thousand soldiers accompanied by prospectors and newspaper correspondents north into the area. The newsmen reported that the region contained rich farmland, grazing land, and good timber, and one wrote that miners had found gold as well. This set off a rush of prospectors that the army had to keep out of the Indian lands. Despite the turning away of hundreds of gold-seekers, by the summer of 1875 at least eight hundred men were panning for gold there. Unable to keep the intruders out, federal officials moved to purchase the Black Hills that same year. They brought the subject up when Red Cloud and Spotted Tail visited Washington again and in September 1875 sent the Allison Commission west to the Red Cloud Agency to negotiate the sale. The commissioners got nowhere. Tribal leaders realized that the government wanted their land, and many of them had no intention of selling it. Red Cloud asked sarcastically why the Great Father did not put wheels under the Indians so that he could move them whenever he chose? On the other hand, chiefs such as Spotted Bear demanded far more than the $6 million the negotiators offered. "Our Great Father has a big safe, and so do we," he said. "This hill [the Black Hills] is our safe." With that, he and others rejected both the $6 million and a substantial annuity in exchange for ceding the Black Hills.

When the talks broke down, the commissioners returned to Washington and many of the Lakotas resumed their raiding across the northern plains. Some of the bands had attacked white travelers and railroad crews repeatedly over the preceding several years, and their actions created anger and frustration that led to frequent calls for unilateral action by the government. The commander of the U.S. Army, Gen. William T. Sherman, called upon Congress to abrogate the Treaty of 1868 "inasmuch as the Sioux have not lived in peace." His civilian counterparts went further. When they received the report of Inspector E. C. Watkins describing the actions of "certain wild and hostile bands" of Sioux and his recommendation that the army should "send troops against them in the winter . . . and *whip* them into subjection," they agreed. Together, Commissioner of Indian Affairs Edward Smith and Secretary of War William Belknap ordered the Sioux agents to tell their charges that they had to return to the reservation or be considered hostile. Some of the hunting bands had stayed out on the plains and so did not hear of the agents' demands. Others simply ignored the orders. Their inaction led directly to what became known as "Sitting Bull's War."

In the spring and summer of 1876, while many Americans celebrated the national centennial, army columns moved into the northern plains, hoping to force the tribes there onto reservations. Indians who remained on the plains included large numbers of Lakotas and Cheyennes, determined to keep their nomadic hunting lifestyle. In addition, almost all of the young men who had wintered on the reservation left to join their friends and relatives on the plains once spring arrived. As a result, that summer the Native people had plenty of fighting men and defended their country skillfully. To end the violence, the army sent three columns of troops into the northern plains. Coming from Montana, Dakota, and the southern plains, they hoped to converge on the tribal people. Responding to this invasion of their homeland, in mid-June Crazy Horse defeated Gen. George Crook's forces at the Battle of the Rosebud.

Just one week later, on June 25, 1876, the most famous battle of the Indian wars took place. The Battle of the Little Bighorn, fought near the stream the Indians called the Greasy Grass, occurred when Lt. Col. George Armstrong Custer led most of the Seventh Cavalry in an attack on the summer encampment of the Sioux and Cheyenne. Ignoring warnings from his Indian scouts about the size of the camp, Custer divided his force of 650–700 men into three units and attacked. A storm of shot and arrows killed all of those under his immediate command. The disaster shocked the nation, and the army redoubled its efforts to corral the plains peoples that fall and winter. Soldiers tracked the scattered bands, defeating some and making it nearly impossible for the rest to survive. By spring 1877, most of the Indians had drifted back onto their reservations. Sitting Bull fled to Canada with his followers, but they were to return five years later.

The defeat of the plains tribes was part of a larger story. When clerks at the U.S. Census Bureau reported that the frontier had ended in 1894, they also noted that the nation had fought more than forty wars against Native people since the War for Independence. In almost every one of those conflicts Indians had fought against other tribal people as well as the whites. In 1866 Congress had created the Indian Scouting Service, and both Pawnees and Apaches regularly served in specific units to help the army. Others, including Arikaras and Crows, volunteered to guide military columns against the Lakotas, their hated, long-time enemies.

The scouts got uniforms, horses, and weapons—all things they lacked on the new reservations. At the same time they helped their own people while hurting their tribal rivals. Crow chief Plenty Coups described how the tribal leaders decided to help the whites, because "we had always fought the three tribes, Sioux, Cheyenne, and Arapahoe, anyway, and might as well [continue to do that]." He remembered that the Crows helped the Americans "because we plainly saw that this course [of action] was the only one which might save our beautiful country for us." In other cases Indians wanted revenge for past defeats, hoped to defend their homeland from powerful tribal invaders, or expected to get personal recognition as successful warriors and leaders. These motivations made sense to each indigenous group, but clearly they reduced any chance to hold back the invading whites.

Migration or Flight

Many tribal groups lacked the numbers and mobility the plains people had used in their struggles to defend their homelands, so they turned to migration, even flight, to avoid the grasping pioneers and their government. By 1800 the Kickapoos began migrating to the West from Indiana and Illinois. Some went as far as northern Mexico, but most halted in Missouri and Kansas. Despite several treaties giving them land there in the early 1830s, many later fled, joining their relatives in Mexico. Their migrations back and forth across the border brought accusations that they committed depredations on frontier citizens, and in 1874 U.S. troops pursued them into Mexico. Shortly after that, some of them moved north to settle in Oklahoma. Facing repeated demands from agents there to assimilate, they returned to Mexico twenty years later. Since then Kickapoos have lived in both countries.

Far to the northwest, many of the Nez Perce people, who lived in Washington, Oregon, and Idaho, also chose flight rather than resettlement on a reservation away from their traditional homeland. In November 1876, while discussing the tribe's reluctance to move to an established reservation, Chief Joseph told negotiators, "We will not give up the land. We love the land; it is our home." Gen. Oliver O. Howard, a federal commissioner, threatened to use force if the chiefs refused to lead their people onto the reservation. In Washington, officials gave the tribe until April 1, 1877, to move to the reservation, setting up a situation remarkably similar to that of a year earlier, which had set off the Sioux War and led to Custer's destruction. In June 1877, a small group of young Nez Perce men killed nineteen settlers, terrorizing the frontier. Fearing indiscriminate retaliation, the leaders decided to flee. Led by Chief Joseph, Looking Glass, and Ollokot, some eight hundred of the non-reservation Nez Perce fled south into the mountains. They outrode and outfought the army, traveling hundreds of miles while seeking shelter from other tribal peoples. Finally, realizing that no one wanted to help them, they set out for Canada, but this tactic failed. When the refugees got within fifty miles of the border in Montana, Gen. Nelson Miles intercepted them, and after some difficult fighting in an early autumn snowstorm, on October 5, 1877, Chief Joseph surrendered.

Another clear example of flight occurred in Arizona Territory during the Apache Wars there. The situation in the Southwest resembled that of the Lakota and Nez Perce people. The Indians were ordered by the government to move to a reservation, but they refused. In this case, the destination was the San Carlos Reservation, where, the Apache complained, "there is no grass, there is no game." Years later another Apache cynically described San Carlos as "a good place for the Apaches—a good place for them to die." In 1877, as American troops pursued the Nez Perce in the Northwest, Apache chief Victorio and his Warm Springs band left the Arizona reservation, saying that "it is better to die fighting than to starve." After eluding pursuit for three years, the fugitives migrated south into Mexico, where Victorio died at the hands of Mexican forces. Several times during the mid-1880s, Geronimo and other Chiricahua Apache leaders led small groups of their people south of the border to escape what they saw as virtual imprisonment on the reservation. Using Apache scouts to help locate Geronimo's band in 1886, the army talked the weary fugitives into surrendering and returning to the United States. Once the captives were back in the country, federal officials ordered them shipped east to prison in Florida, and few ever got back to their homelands.

Cultural Initiatives

As they experienced continuing disruptions of their lives, many tribes looked to their cultural and religious rites for assurance. Existing tribal or village shamans continued to direct ceremonies such as the Green Corn Dance, the Sun Dance, and the Buffalo Dance. Modifications of these activities and new practices were introduced as well. Among the Vermillion band of the Kickapoos, the shaman Kenekuk offered a combination of traditional ceremonies and new ideas by the 1830s, when his group moved from Illinois to Kansas. His teachings included a rejection of alcohol, an end to the usage of the old clan medicine bundles, considered to have spiritual powers, and a flat prohibition on selling any more tribal land to the whites. Surprisingly, while most of the tribe migrated into Mexico, the Vermillion band managed to retain their small Kansas landholdings.

In the Pacific Northwest a Wanapam shaman known as Smohalla came to the fore as pioneers flooded into the region. A hunchback with a large head and short legs, he often had visions. As many other shamans had done, he claimed that his teachings came from his visits to the spirit world. Skilled at predicting earthquakes and the start of the annual salmon runs, as well as at locating good hunting spots, he led tribal resistance to accepting the whites' ways. During the wars of the Columbia Plateau in the 1850s he urged his followers to remain neutral but also attacked many of the Americans' practices. His teachings, named the Washani Creed, spoke to traditional practices and values. Indians should avoid the white people's farming techniques and should accept the natural forces around them. He claimed that "men who work [like the whites] cannot dream" and taught that visions brought knowledge from the spirit world. Smohalla also preached against signing treaties and selling tribal lands to the whites. Those who ignored this, he predicted, would be cheated and "be punished by God's anger." His so-called Dreamer Religion gathered adherents throughout the area, and despite persecution by local Indian agents he remained a strong force for tribal rights in the region until his death in 1895.

The shamans already mentioned used dreams, traditional rites, and prophecies to protect their followers and to help them cope with pressures for assimilation. Wovoka, a Northern Paiute from western Nevada, brought about something rather different. His visions led to the Ghost Dance movement that swept across the northern plains in 1889–90 and brought death and destruction to the Lakota Sioux in the 1890 massacre at Wounded Knee. Sick with fever, in 1889 Wovoka experienced visions that became the basis for his teachings. He preached that by returning to their old ways, tribal people could bring back their ancestors as well as the buffalo. Urging his listeners to reject alcohol and live in peace, he gave them a new rite, the Ghost Dance. If done correctly, he promised, this ceremony would bring a return to the old days when Indians lived happily without any white neighbors. When the Lakotas heard of Wovoka's preaching, they sent observers, who accepted the shaman's new ideas. Among other things, he promised that "when the time comes there will be no more sickness and everyone will be young again." His teachings found ready acceptance, and soon the sound of the new dance echoed across the Lakota reservation. When Sitting Bull seemed to encourage his followers to join the dancing, agency officials became frightened and called for his arrest. That effort turned violent, as his adherents tried to prevent Sitting Bull from being taken to jail. In the melee that followed, Indian police shot and killed the aging leader. Fearing that the government meant to kill them too, hundreds of Ghost Dancers, led by Chief Big Foot, fled, only to be overtaken by the Seventh Cavalry, Custer's old command. While soldiers disarmed the Lakotas, firing broke out and by the time the fighting ended, nearly 250 Indians lay dead, most of them women and children.

Losing Freedom

Although tribal leaders had used diplomacy, military action, migration, and cultural tactics to deflect the onrushing American pioneers, by 1890 these efforts had failed. That left the survivors facing reservation life and continuing pressures from federal agents to acculturate. Government officials demanded that all of the tribes abandon their traditions and join the white American mainstream. Indians had encountered such insistence for generations, often deflecting or avoiding the most damaging results. However, once a group lost its independence and moved onto a reservation, its options shrank quickly. The government's long-standing policy of using the church, the school, and the plow now became central in its program of forcing plains Indians to abandon their traditional culture. Farming proved particularly ill suited to many of the western reservations, where poor soil, lack of water, and great distances from any possible markets hampered even the most ambitious efforts. In addition, a series of harsh winters and devastating summer droughts in the 1880s and 1890s destroyed much of western agriculture. Ironically, the official policy demanding that Indians become small-scale farmers came at a time when thousands of white American homesteaders on the plains failed, gave up farming, and streamed into cities and towns as the nation changed from being one of small farmers to one of people living in an urban, industrial society. This meant that the tribes continued to remain outside of the mainstream because of reformers' misguided and out-of-date ideas about how to solve "the Indian Problem," because of Indians' physical isolation from the rest of society, and because of growing racial antagonism and discrimination throughout the West.

As the reservation evolved in the last third of the nineteenth century, reformers and officials alike saw it as an essential training ground where tribal people could gain the knowledge and skills they needed to become part of white American society. Some reformers who had worked toward the abolition of slavery, such as Lydia Maria Child and Wendell Phillips, turned their attention to Indian affairs once the Civil War ended. Others had dealt with tribal groups through earlier church- or government-sponsored programs for decades. Whatever their background, these supposed reformers expected to destroy the tribal cultures and to recast Indians in the image of other Americans. By the late 1860s these people and their ideas became central, as federal authorities sought to make the West safe for settlement, to end the sporadic fighting there, and to cut spending on Indian affairs. Few whites expected any objections from the reservation dwellers. Even fewer proved willing to listen when they complained. This left tribal and band leaders few options. Their resistance to the advancing whites had failed, and they had little hope of protecting their people or their cultures.

A certainty that Indians might disappear entirely if the whites failed to step in with help and supervision drove those efforts to shape Indian policy following the Civil War. The 1867–68 peace commission–led negotiations at Fort Laramie in Wyoming and Medicine Lodge Creek in Arkansas demonstrated this. Each of the treaties resulting from those meetings called on Native Americans to adopt farming, live in white-built homes, and send their children to school. To help achieve those goals, in 1869 newly elected president Ulysses S. Grant signed legislation creating the nonpartisan Board of Indian Commissioners, a group of unpaid volunteers, to oversee government-Indian relations. Then he accepted the suggestion that to deal honestly with the tribes, the government needed to appoint Christian gentlemen as agents for the reservations. In theory, they would avoid the greed and self-interest demonstrated by so many of the political appointees then holding Indian Office positions. Westerners in particular dubbed what they saw as a misguided effort to save the Indians from extinction as Grant's "Quaker Policy," because it relied on religious groups for nominations to fill reservation jobs. Unfortunately for the tribes, many of the new appointees lacked the experience, personal skills, and good sense to serve effectively. They came and went as often as their predecessors, usually having accomplished little except to confirm Indian fears that these religious bigots wanted to destroy tribal rites and customs.

As more pioneers moved west, pressure on the government to open more Indian lands for whites continued. This led to continuing efforts to shrink reservations and a sort of latter-day removal policy that saw tribes such as the Northern Cheyennes and the Poncas being pushed into present-day Oklahoma, or the scattered bands of Western Apaches having to move onto the hated San Carlos Reservation. Once there, the tribal people faced dreary prospects. Rarely did Indians find themselves residing in their traditional homeland or having access to valuable land, timber, or water. Instead, they encountered agents who struggled to impose federal mandates on them. Agency personnel rarely understood tribal languages, and virtually none of them could speak one. They made few efforts to get to know the band or tribal leaders. Implementing federal policy meant trying to force Indian men to cut their hair, wear white men's clothing, have only one wife, speak English, live in a regular house, and practice small-scale farming on often infertile land that lacked sufficient water.

Sarah Winnemucca, c. 1844–1891

Daughter of Old Winnemucca, headman of a small Northern Paiute band, Sarah Winnemucca was born in about 1844 near the Humboldt Sink in western Nevada. Her grandfather, Truckee, had served as a guide for explorer John C. Fremont and fought in the war with Mexico. Those experiences persuaded him that his granddaughter should learn about the whites. In 1857 Sarah and her sister went to live with the family of William and Margaret Ormsby, in Carson City, Nevada. For a year the two girls worked as servants and playmates for the Ormsbys' daughter. While there Sarah learned to read, write, and speak English. During the 1870s she lived on the Malheur Reservation in eastern Oregon and on the Yakama Reservation in Washington. At both places she worked as an interpreter for the government. In 1879 she and her father traveled to Washington to see Secretary of the Interior Carl Schurz, pleading for a return to their homeland, but that failed and they returned to the Yakama Reservation. After marrying a white soldier, Lewis Hopkins, in 1883 the couple traveled east where reformers helped her give a series of three hundred public lectures about Indian rights and mistreatment. In her talks she also supported the allotment of tribal land then being debated in Congress. That same year she published an "as told to" book, *Life among the Paiutes*, with her editor Mary Mann. Based on material from her experiences and speeches, the book may have been the first written and published by an American Indian woman. Sarah returned to Nevada and ran an elementary school for Indian children that stressed tribal culture. Her husband died and she ran out of money, so in 1887 the school closed. Four years later she died of tuberculosis.

Source: Sally Zanjani, *Sarah Winnemucca* (Lincoln: University of Nebraska Press, 2001).

The agents' actions combined with Indian attitudes toward their own forced acculturation brought despair to most reservation dwellers. The Ghost Dance that swept through some Lakota camps resulted from the desperation that gripped some tribes. Often agents reported little success in persuading Indians to become farmers. The chiefs had predicted just such results even before the government forced them to abandon their traditional lifestyles. During the treaty negotiations at Medicine Lodge Creek in 1867, Kiowa leader Satanta had objected to moving to a reservation. "I don't want to settle there," he told the commissioners, because "when we settle down, we grow pale and die." The Lakota chief Red Cloud expressed similar sentiments in his 1870 discussions with federal officials in Washington. He described the Sioux reservation and nearby hunting lands as "nothing but an island. When we first had this land we were strong," he said; "now we are melting like snow on the hillside." These statements certainly described the situation on many reservations. While westerners cheered as the Indian population plummeted, reformers and government officials alike wrung their hands in despair. They wanted to destroy tribal cultures but did not expect to kill the people. By the late nineteenth century, new efforts to transform reservation life became central to federal efforts at dealing with Indian peoples for the next fifty years.

Suggested Readings

Anderson, Gary. *Little Crow: Spokesperson for the Sioux.* St. Paul: Minnesota Historical Society Press, 1986.

Dunlay, Thomas. *Wolves for the Blue Soldiers: Indian Scouts and Auxiliaries with the United States Army, 1860–90.* Lincoln: University of Nebraska Press, 1982.

Hurtado, Albert L. *Indian Survival on the California Frontier.* New Haven: Yale University Press, 1988.

Iverson, Peter. *Díne: A History of the Navajos.* Albuquerque: University of New Mexico Press, 2002.

Jacoby, Karl. *Shadows at Dawn: An Apache Massacre and the Violence of History.* New York: Penguin Books, 2008.

Kehoe, Alice B. *The Ghost Dance: Ethnohistory and Revitalization.* Longview, Ill.: Waveland Press, 2006.

McLaughlin, William G. *After the Trail of Tears: The Cherokee Struggle for Sovereignty, 1839–1880.* Chapel Hill: University of North Carolina Press, 1993.

Nichols, Roger L. *Warrior Nations: The United States and Indian Peoples.* Norman: University of Oklahoma Press, 2013.

Prucha, Francis P. *American Indian Policy in Crisis.* Norman: University of Oklahoma Press, 1976.

Trennert, Robert A. *Alternative to Extinction: Federal Indian Policy and the Beginnings of the Reservation System, 1846–1851.* Philadelphia: Temple University Press, 1975.

Utley, Robert M. *The Indian Frontier of the American West, 1846–1890.* Albuquerque: University of New Mexico Press, 1984.

West, Elliott. *The Contested Plains: Goldseekers and the Rush to Colorado.* Lawrence: University Press of Kansas, 1998.

———. *The Last Indian War: The Nez Perce Story.* New York: Oxford University Press, 2009.

The Twentieth Century and Beyond

CHAPTER 6

Survival and Adaptation, 1890–1930

Changing Worlds

For many Indian groups, forced relocation onto reservations proved at least as traumatic as crossing the Atlantic Ocean did for European immigrants during the nineteenth century. They confronted new surroundings, language, clothing, food, religion, and limitations on their personal freedom, while being forced to abandon many traditional practices and ideas. At times the tribes faced situations as dangerous as their earlier military conflicts with the U.S. government, including malnutrition, poor housing, and disease at their new locations. They also encountered westerners who feared or despised them, and newspaper editors who attacked them regularly in print. One Arizona newsman claimed that accurate portraits of Indians showed their "low brows, the flat heads, the sunken eyes [and] the large mis-shaped mouths." In 1876, when news of Custer's disaster at the Little Bighorn spread, a Laramie, Wyoming, editor demanded that "a bounty [be] placed on Indian scalps." Attitudes of this sort made tribal people's adjustment to their new situations difficult and forced them to focus all of their skills on surviving.

Even before the plains wars ended, some of the chiefs had objected to moving onto the new reservations. Lakota chief Red Cloud stated, "I do not want my reservation on the Missouri; this is the fourth time I have said so. . . . Our people are dying off like sheep; the country does not suit them." His complaints, like those of many others, produced no response. By the late 1860s, federal policies focused on settling the tribes on specific reservations, away from the main immigrant trails and mining areas. Usually this meant shifting people south into Indian Territory—present-day Oklahoma—or north into Dakota. For those who followed the buffalo herds, such moves limited their food supply and came at a time when commercial hunting had begun to push the vast herds toward extinction. Grieving over what some called war between the whites and the buffalo, people reported seeing hundreds of skinned animal corpses left on the ground to rot. The hide hunters killed so many at one time that Indians who traveled through the Judith Basin in Montana recalled, "The whole country there smelled of rotting meat. Even the flowers could not put down the bad smell." The Indians thought that to escape the slaughter, the buffalo fled, entering an opening in one of the mountains and leaving the plains peoples to plead for food rations from the government.

For some, moving to the new reservations meant abandoning the scenes of victories over their tribal enemies, being unable to use their accustomed locales for traditional rites, or seeing others invade and despoil their sacred places. The Lakotas experienced this when they lost the Black Hills, as did the Chiricahua Apaches when federal actions forced them out of their mountain homes in southeastern Arizona. The idea of leaving family grave sites caused much unhappiness and unwillingness to migrate. Many tribes from the North or West, such as the Nez Perce from Washington and the Northern Cheyenne from Montana, sickened and died in what they called the "Warm Land," present-day Oklahoma, and the Chiricahuas from Arizona had a similar experience after being imprisoned in Florida and then Alabama. The reservation system itself proved equally demoralizing. As a bureaucracy whose goal was to remake Indians in the image of other nineteenth-century Americans, the Office of Indian Affairs was staffed by employees who rarely had much sympathy for the people they oversaw. Its agents acted on orders from the commissioner of Indian affairs and held little autonomy. Most considered Indians to be a doomed race and lacked any sensitivity toward or understanding of tribal cultures. As a result, the agents imposed their own ideas about how to prevent the extinction of Native Americans. To achieve that goal, they thought it essential to attack everything that identified Indians as different from the rest of society. As the system developed after the late 1860s, agents' actions brought them into direct conflict with traditional leaders such as chiefs, shamans, healers, and military men on the reservation, leading to decades of misery and bitterness, some of which remain even today.

Attacks on Tribal Cultures

Government officials and Indians alike faced continuing pressures from reform-minded individuals and groups. Usually affiliated with Protestant churches and missionary societies, these so-called friends of the Indian played important roles in shaping and implementing federal policies. Beginning with the creation of the nonpartisan Board of Indian Commissioners in 1869, the reformers quickly built networks of concerned citizens. By the early 1880s they helped found such groups as the Women's National Indian Association and the Indian Rights Association. In 1883 these people held the first annual Lake Mohonk Conference of the Friends of the Indian at a posh resort in New York State. That meeting attracted the major groups and many prominent individuals then working toward better treatment for Native Americans. Unfortunately for the Indians, the reformers shared the goals of federal policy. They wanted the reservation dwellers to relinquish their culture and to look, act, and speak like other Americans. Often the only disputes they had with the government focused on dishonest federal employees and the tactics used to bring about the goal of cultural transformation. On the assumption that Indians needed to speak, read, and write English in order to survive, education quickly became a cornerstone of the reformers' efforts.

Some tribes had operated their own schools or had cooperated with church or mission-society groups for decades. In Indian Territory, present-day Oklahoma, the Cherokees developed a broad educational system of their own. By 1868 they operated sixty-four schools, including separate female and male seminaries for secondary school instruction. The tribal curriculum reflected the interests of the largely acculturated leaders who dominated the Cherokee national council at the time. They directed the schools to hire tribal members as teachers whenever possible, supervised course contents, and encouraged instruction in Cherokee. Still, the students received little more training than basic literacy and almost nothing to help them retain tribal culture. These schools differed from their government-run counterparts in two ways. They gave the students almost no vocational training, but, more important, they did not attack Cherokee customs and avoided the harsh treatment so common in white-run schools.

Despite the Cherokee example that showed that tribes could educate their own children, the government turned its attention to Indian schools. At first, teachers moved to the reservations, but by the late 1870s the beginnings of a boarding-school system had developed. Capt. Richard H. Pratt convinced his superiors that it made more sense to educate Indian captives then incarcerated in Florida and Alabama than to keep them imprisoned. In November 1879 he opened what became the Carlisle Indian School to work with students from Dakota and Indian Territories. Using former army buildings in Pennsylvania as dormitories and classrooms, he dressed the students in cast-off army uniforms, cut their hair, changed their names, and addressed them in English. Students marched to and from their activities in formation, faced inspections, and received whatever benefits came from a military-school experience. Pratt expected that his graduates would move into white society, and so began what he described as an "outing" system, in which he sent the older students to work in white homes, factories, and businesses. In theory, this equipped them to become integrated into the national economy. In fact, often they became low-wage laborers for local citizens.

Pratt became a sort of one-man advertisement for off-reservation boarding-school education, and by 1885, although the government had established 86 day schools on reservations, it had built another 114 boarding schools. The Indian Office also contracted with church groups to operate a few other schools, but these played only a small part in the evolving system because in 1894 the government ended its financial support of church-operated institutions. Whichever variety of school—government- or church-run, day or boarding—their faculties worked to disrupt the cultural bonds that held tribal societies together. First they separated the children from their families, by taking them far from home and keeping them at school for years to help achieve that goal. As a result, after years of being forced to speak English, many of the young people could not understand their own languages when they left school. Next the reformers sought to break down "the degrading communism of the tribal" people and to replace it with individualism. Essentially, the missionaries, teachers, and agents wanted each child to be like most other Americans and have a "desire for property of his own."

At first, reservation officials encouraged parents to send their children to the boarding schools, but once the families realized that the children might remain away from the reservation for years, they objected. Some hid their sons and daughters, while others simply refused to cooperate. By 1891, Congress passed legislation that required all Indian children to attend classes either at home or at one of the boarding schools. When this failed, federal agents began to use the Indian police or even detachments of soldiers from nearby forts to round up potential students. Years later, one of the participants remembered that the "proceeding created quite an outcry. The men were sullen and muttering, the women loud in their lamentations, and the children [were] almost out of their wits with fright." Even these tactics failed to produce enough students, and soon agency personnel cut off the weekly food rations to force uncooperative families to surrender their children.

At that point officers loaded the would-be students onto trains and sent them to distant towns, often in the East. To begin the cultural change, the school staff supervised the bathing of each newcomer and the exchanging of Indian blankets and moccasins for mass-manufactured clothing. Next at Carlisle, each boy received two suits while the girls got dresses. All of them received underwear and boots as well. Then the school officials focused on cutting the new students' long hair. One young boy remembered crying because we "were all 'bald-headed.' None of us slept well that night; we felt so queer." In fact, for children from tribes such as the Lakota, who prized long hair, losing their braids proved one of their most traumatic school experiences. Having changed their charges' appearance, the teachers then turned to giving each incoming student a new, non-Indian name. Occasionally the children chose their own names from a list on the chalkboard, but this happened before they could read so they had no idea how the names sounded or what they meant. At other times the school personnel just assigned the students new names. The teachers had no idea how to pronounce the tribal names, so English names made their jobs easier. In addition, federal officials thought that giving Indians surnames would help them fit into the legal system and protect their property years later.

Despite being lonely, frightened, and homesick much of the time, some of the children found certain aspects of living away from home interesting, even fun at times. They enjoyed playing musical instruments, marching in school bands, and trying out their new clothes. Luther Standing Bear, a Lakota, remembered that at first some of the boys had no idea whether they should button their pants in the front or the rear. He commented that his first pair of boots was too large, but he liked "the noise they made" when they squeaked as he walked. Along with other boys in his group, he remembered spending much of the first night after getting the clothing walking the floor. Some of them even went to bed still wearing their new clothes. For a few children, school presented challenges to be overcome. Years later Charles Eastman reported that when he went east to school, his father told him, "Remember, my boy, it is the same as if I sent you on your first war-path. I shall expect you to conquer." Despite the hardships and the educators' often cruel efforts to stamp out all things Indian in them, some of the children came to terms with their alien surroundings, creating their own "underground" society under the noses of the school employees, while making lifelong friends.

Although few agents and teachers found much positive in the cultures they worked to destroy, some federal officials disagreed. When Francis E. Leupp became commissioner of Indian affairs shortly after 1900, recognizing the tribal societies' strong communal traditions, he thought that efforts to acculturate the Indians should move less rapidly than school leaders considered necessary. He suggested that students might learn more effectively if their classes were moved outside when pleasant weather made this possible. His efforts to dismantle the worst elements in the boarding-school system faded when he left office. Others accepted his critique of the schools, but for different reasons. By the early twentieth century, some reformers had become discouraged because many graduates "returned to the blanket" when they got home, because they had no chance to practice their newly acquired skills on the reservation. Refusing to accept this situation as simply a lack of opportunity, whites explained it as the result of low-level intellectual capabilities. For example, an official at the Hampton Institute, a Virginia school that taught both blacks and Indians, described the tribal groups as belonging to one of the childlike races. "We should teach them to labor," he wrote, "in order that they may be brought to manhood." Many of the skills the schools imparted had little use once the young people returned home, but Indians benefited in some unexpected ways. Being forced to speak English allowed them to make friends with young people from other tribes, and by the end of the nineteenth century a new generation of articulate, poised, and educated tribal members wanted to use their new skills to help their people. Thomas Wildcat Alford, a Shawnee student from Carlisle, remembered leaving school ready "to use the club of white man's wisdom against him in defense of our customs . . . as given to us by our people."

The effort to destroy Indian communities went far beyond education. Various Christian churches had sent missionaries to work among the tribal people for generations, and once the government began to develop the reservations, the religious groups wanted to continue their efforts there. Following the Civil War, Baptists, Episcopalians, Presbyterians, Quakers, and Roman Catholics all sent clergy and lay representatives to do just that. Indians had mixed responses to the missionaries. Some wanted nothing to do with the intruding clerics and repeated the same arguments that tribal leaders had used for generations. Watching the often bitter denominational fights over both doctrine and jurisdiction, they wanted no part of learning how to "quarrel about God." Others accused the whites of acting hypocritically by not practicing what they taught. After all, they pointed out, it was the supposedly Christian Americans who brought liquor into the villages and who corrupted the young women. More than one chief or shaman suggested that the churchmen get their own society to act according to its beliefs before trying to push them onto the Indians.

Some of their objections stemmed from the continuing missionary efforts to stamp out traditional sacred dances and other ceremonies. When they witnessed the self-torture used as a central part of the Sun Dance on the plains, whites denounced the rite as a relic of barbarism and as something that needed to be halted. In the Pacific Northwest, the giveaway or potlatch ceremonies horrified local white observers, because some individuals or families nearly bankrupted themselves in these ritual demonstrations of generosity. Their willingness to give their property away just to impress people in other clans and villages proved their lack of civilization. Clearly they had to learn the value of personal property. By the 1880s the reformers had persuaded federal authorities to outlaw both the potlatch and the Sun Dance. Yet some missionaries identified with their charges, serving them honestly and faithfully for years. They recorded meetings with the agents, wrote letters to Washington, translated the speeches of visiting officials, and denounced corrupt and incompetent federal employees. For example, in Minnesota the Sioux called Episcopal bishop Henry Whipple "Straight Tongue" because of his efforts to help them and his obvious honesty. Yet to accept the missionaries' teachings meant abandoning or modifying their own beliefs. For some, the Christian God seemed more powerful than the spirits of their Native religious systems, but acceptance of the new religion came slowly, unevenly, and often without full understanding of its central doctrines.

Cooperation and Resistance

On many reservations the agents decided that they needed to reduce the chiefs' authority in order to enforce the regulations so many Indians hated. Prior to being pushed onto reservations, villagers had used ridicule, social pressure, and clan customs to direct people's actions. Now as the chiefs and shamans lost some of their influence, the agents tried to dominate reservation life. By the early 1870s a few of them began recruiting men to serve as Indian police, not only to help keep the peace but also to enforce the government's demands. On the San Carlos Apache reservation in Arizona, agent John Clum organized a tribal police force within days of his arrival. He told tribal leaders that he wanted "to appoint some Indians as police-men" who would help him keep order among the groups sharing that reservation. Clum publicized his recruitment efforts shamelessly, and soon the commissioner of Indian affairs at the time, Ezra Hayt, learned of them. In 1877, he asked for money to recruit reservation police throughout the West, and a year later Congress appropriated the funds. The new officers were "to be employed in maintaining order and prohibiting illegal traffic in liquor" on the reservations. Initially, up to 480 men could be hired. This program became so successful that in 1879 Congress doubled the size of the force, and by 1890, fifty-nine reservations had their own Indian police.

On the reservations young Indians joined the tribal police for many reasons. For some, it helped break the monotony and alleviate the lack of employment opportunities available to them. Others used police duty as a way to avoid the backbreaking labor needed to start farms. Particularly in societies with strong warrior traditions, having a uniform and firearms made reservation life bearable. However, those looking for excitement or adventure soon found that police duties included mostly routine and minor tasks. They served at the pleasure of the local agent and so became a sort of enforcement arm for his office. In that capacity their work entailed such tasks as carrying messages, helping with the monthly ration handouts, and building roads. They helped keep intruders off Indian lands, investigated horse thefts, tracked down children who fled their schools, and kept order by arresting drunks or others who angered or refused to cooperate with the agent.

Not all agency police performed effectively, and their actions had the potential to shatter local communities. In order to get and keep their jobs, the officers had to serve as models of acculturation. They cut their hair, wore white men's clothing, and followed orders not to participate in outlawed tribal ceremonies. In fact, their orders required them to report it when people on the reservation held traditional dances, but often they avoided doing this. Their efforts at enforcing anti-liquor laws, breaking up family fights, and arresting people earned them little popularity. One agent reported that "the police are looked upon as a common foe, and the multitude are bitterly opposed to them." This became clear in the incident that led to Sitting Bull's death. In December 1890 Standing Rock agent James McLaughlin feared that the Lakota leader was about to leave the reservation and join the Ghost Dancers, so he asked the police to arrest Sitting Bull. Lieutenant Bullhead, who led the police detachment, told the chief that he needed to visit the agent and then could return to his home. When Sitting Bull resisted, the police tried to pull him outside and get him on his horse for the ride to the agency headquarters. As soon as the chief's followers realized that he was being arrested, they rushed to protect him, and one of them shot Lieutenant Bullhead. At that, the other officers shot Sitting Bull, and pandemonium broke out. When the firing ended, Sitting Bull and seven of his supporters lay dead. Four of the policemen were killed immediately and two more died soon after the fight.

In early 1883 Congress established a system of courts for Indian offenses as another tool for bringing reservation dwellers into the general society. Headed by respected leaders, the new courts could be used to enforce regulations against holding traditional ceremonies, as well as to deal with other minor offenses. They focused their attention on polygamy, shamans' anti-Christian activities, the use of alcohol, and other actions the agents wanted to end. These courts relied on the reservation police to enforce the agents' rulings and to gather and present evidence. Men who served as judges also had to practice white cultural norms: cutting their hair, avoiding liquor (not that all whites did this), and having only one wife. Although the decisions handed down in these tribal courts needed the agents' approval, often the judges used their positions as a way to protect tribal customs. For example, when the Cheyenne judge Wooden Leg heard of old men who had multiple wives living separately on different parts of the reservation, he "just listened, said nothing, and did nothing." Quanah Parker, Comanche leader, managed to ignore all of the rules and still retain his judgeship for a time. He wore his hair long, kept all of his wives, and later worked toward the legalization of peyote in Oklahoma. When he refused to give up his polygamous ways, he lost his court office, but in the meantime he personified resistance to the hated federal policies.

While the agents used the Indian scouts, police, and courts to bring local order, some of the chiefs simply defied federal authorities and moved off their assigned reservations. In 1877, when the Northern Cheyennes heard that they might be sent to live on the Southern Cheyenne reservation in Oklahoma, they objected. "Our people did not like this talk," one chief remembered; "all of us wanted to stay in this country near the Black Hills." Despite their protests, officials forced them to move, and for three months that summer the more than nine hundred Indians trekked south. On August 5, 1877, they reached their destination. From the start things went badly. In just a few days the newcomers learned that the agent had almost no food for them and that the infertile soil and poor hunting meant that they might face starvation. Even worse, after only a few months they started to die from fevers and malaria. Chief Little Wolf told the agent that his people had come south to visit, and that before moving south they had been promised that if they did not like the new country, they could return north. Either they had misunderstood what the agent had told them, or the officials had lied to them. In either case they could not return home but had to remain in Oklahoma.

That winter the Northern Cheyennes suffered from poor housing, bad diet, and disease, and in 1878 they faced a summer worse than the previous one. By August, continuing disease persuaded some of the chiefs to return north regardless of what the agent or the soldiers said. Their agent urged them to remain for another year, but Little Wolf replied, "We cannot stay another year, we want to go now." After more meetings, some of the chiefs chose to return north. They told the agent of their plans, but apparently he did not believe them. In September, Little Wolf and Dull Knife led some 297 people away from the reservation. They moved north quickly, but army units followed with orders to force them to return. On September 13, the soldiers attacked, but they had to retreat when the Cheyennes drove them off. From then on, the small band moved through Kansas and then Nebraska, often only hours ahead of pursuing army units or civilian vigilante groups. By October, the group had split. Those wanting to return to their traditional homeland in the Tongue River country left with Little Wolf. The rest traveled toward the Red Cloud Agency at Fort Robinson in Nebraska, when the cavalry overtook them. In January 1879, orders came from Washington that the Cheyennes had to return south. They refused, and the local commander ordered them locked in unheated barracks without food for five days. At the end of that time they still refused and then broke out of the barracks, only to be pursued and, in most cases, killed by the soldiers. Little Wolf managed to surrender his band without more fighting and described the end of the trek with some bitterness: "Dull Knife took one-half of the band and surrendered near Fort Robinson. . . . They gave up their guns, and then the whites killed them all."

The Ponca people of Nebraska also tried to ignore reservation assignments, but with less-disastrous results. After bitter objections, they too had moved south from their homeland to Oklahoma with an army "escort." In 1878 when they arrived the government offered them a new reservation, but the Poncas had to walk another 150 miles to get there. Lacking implements and food, many fell ill and died. As the last son of Chief Standing Bear lay dying, he made his father promise to bury him in their Nebraska homeland. So, in January 1879, a party of sixty-six Poncas headed north with the body to carry out the promise. When they reached the Omaha Reservation, troops arrested them, under orders to return them to Indian Territory. This time a different result lay ahead. General George Crook gave the story of Standing Bear's action to an Omaha newspaperman named Henry Tibbles, and he in turn recruited a sympathetic lawyer who pleaded the Indians' case. At the end of a widely publicized trial, the federal district court judge ruled in *Standing Bear v. Crook* that the Poncas were not prisoners but a free people and that they could act independently from the wishes of the federal government. This decision weakened the legal basis for many restrictive federal actions toward the tribes, but unfortunately it failed to bring any immediate changes in Indian policy implementation.

Facing Allotment

Reformers and bureaucrats almost all supported the work of the schools and churches and service as scouts, police, or judges, but these efforts paled when compared to the allotment policy as a way to destroy tribalism. The idea of giving individuals or families their own land for farms had been around at least since the days of Thomas Jefferson, and by the 1880s it became the central component in the government's acculturation program. Speakers at the Lake Mohonk conferences, members of the nonpartisan Board of Indian Commissioners, and popular authors such as Helen Hunt Jackson all joined their voices with those of missionaries, educators, and politicians to support this idea, which grew out of the realization that the reservations kept Indians isolated from the rest of society. Government officials and reformers alike objected to communal landholding as somehow un-American and suspect as socialistic. One reformer echoed missionary ideas from an earlier generation when he denounced the reservations as "hopelessly wrong," calling for actions to make Indians "more intelligently selfish" by persuading them to accept land as personal property. Allotment seemed one of the most effective means to do that and dismantle the reservations at the same time.

A policy of cutting the reservations into small family farms attracted support from promoters, business groups, and pioneers. Local politicians complained that large reservations blocked local economic development and discouraged population growth. One governor complained about the "enormous tracts occupied by tribes" which he thought could bring prosperity to the region once the government reduced the Indians' land base to a reasonable size. Miners, farmers, timbermen, and others joined the chorus, hoping to exploit resources that lay on tribal lands. Local boosters used newspapers effectively to claim that taking Indian lands would be "the impetus of the development" of their particular region. Throughout much of the West, they or their local representatives sent a steady stream of complaints, petitions, and requests to Washington, demanding that reservation lands be opened for use by white Americans. This campaign persuaded Congress to take action, and in 1887 it passed the General Allotment or Dawes Act.

This legislation incorporated the reformers' ideas and at the same time met the desires of westerners seeking access to tribal lands and resources. It called upon the president to order the survey and division of reservations into family farms with allotments or land parcels of 160 acres for heads of families, 80 acres for single adults, and smaller portions for minor children. Each person or family had to select their own land, but if they refused to do that, the local agent chose a plot for them. Agents conducted a reservation-wide census, prepared tribal rolls, and, using those rolls, made the land assignments. When an Indian accepted a tract, the federal government held title to it for the next twenty-five years, ostensibly to protect the Indian from losing the land until having time to learn its value. Reformers saw this policy as the way to solve the "Indian problem." Once individual families gave up tribal practices and became self-supporting farmers, they could gain American citizenship, and that would demonstrate that the government plan to dismantle the tribes had succeeded. When all tribal members received their allotments, the unassigned acreage or "surplus" land, could be sold to nearby whites. In passing this legislation, Congress overlooked one significant detail that has haunted tribes ever since. The law made no provision for any population growth. Children born after officials recorded the allotments and sold the "surplus" had no chance to receive any acreage, but at the time no one questioned this because decision-makers assumed that the policy would erase the tribes.

Both during the debate over severalty and after passage of the 1887 act, some people urged caution or raised questions about the future. For example, during the debates over the bill Senator Henry Teller predicted that in less than a single lifetime the allotment policy would cost Indians much of their reservation land. "The real aim of this bill," he charged, "is to get at the Indian lands and open them up for settlement." He said that the wide variety among the tribes made chances for success of any single policy unlikely, and he recommended that the reformers work to get the Indians acculturated before giving individual Indians their own land. Even Senator Henry Dawes, whose name was tied to the bill, lost his enthusiasm prior to its passage. When President Grover Cleveland signed the bill into law, Dawes foresaw trouble ahead and commented about "the hunger and thirst of the white man for the Indians' land." By 1881, Ohio senator George Pendleton joined those who predicted problems, saying that the Indians needed "to change their modes of life or they will be exterminated." Yet, beyond raising that note of concern, he offered little constructive advice. Less than twenty years later, one of the reformers described severalty as "a mighty pulverizing engine for breaking up the tribal mass." This proved wrong, but while the tribes remained, much of their reservation land base did not.

On the reservations themselves Indians had few choices because those who objected were not heard. When the chiefs learned of the coming legislation, they complained, but the commissioner of Indian affairs ordered the agents to prevent tribal representatives from traveling east to oppose the policy. So, even though many on the reservations wanted no part of allotment, few in Washington heard their voices because often Indians could not pay the costs for a trip to the capital. Within a few years, survey crews had completed their work and the agents began to allot land to each family or individual. The process varied widely but usually followed one of two patterns. In some places, individuals chose the land and moved onto it. In others they ignored the agent's orders and so he assigned land to them; for example, at Cheyenne River in Dakota, one man remembered, "They allotted land to us and wherever our land was, [that] was our homestead." Occasionally tribal groups chose their lands all in the same place and then continued living communally.

Once allotment went into effect, many reform groups thought that what they called "the Indian problem" had been solved, and so they turned their attention to other issues. However, Native Americans, the government, and white settlers all saw frequent changes in the policy and its implementation. The program aimed at making the Indians farmers, but often reservations had poor soil or lay in areas that suffered droughts regularly. After trying and failing to harvest more than scanty crops, many Indians looked for other ways to use their land, and in 1891 Congress authorized them to lease it to nearby whites. This assured the landowners at least a modest income from their allotments without their having to work as farmers at all and struck directly at the heart of the reformers' assertions that the family farm would lead Indians to accept American values. Congress continued to modify the program and in the 1906 Burke Act permitted officials to withhold citizenship from some Indians to protect them from being swindled out of their land. Whatever actions the government took, swindlers and land thieves stayed ahead of it, so that the tribal land base that stood at about 138 million acres when allotment began shrank to only a third of that during the next four decades. After allotment went into effect in the 1890s, Interior Department clerks failed to keep careful records of income from Indian trust lands and not until after 2010 has this issue begun to be settled.

Changing Reservations

On the reservations, a new generation of younger, often boarding-school-educated people joined village chiefs in exercising authority. Like the older, more traditional leaders, they sought to protect their people and customs. Frequently this meant using the new reservation situations in ways that differed from what their elders might have done or the bureaucrats might have expected. Even where Indian police and judges lacked much support, their actions tended to bring varied bands together, if only to decry what fellow people did. At Cheyenne River in Dakota, police and band officials from all parts of the reservation met periodically, tying disparate groups together. Within a couple of decades, members of the Blackfeet, Mineconjou, San Arc, and Two Kettle bands of Lakota began to drop some of their strong band identification as they came to live and work together. By 1903, leaders of the separate bands agreed to organize a twelve-person tribal business council, with representatives from each area on the reservation. The council had the authority to approve tribal financial dealings and to fend off land grabs by area politicians, and gradually the elected councilmen came to replace traditional band leaders in dealing with federal officials.

Other examples abound of people ignoring, avoiding, or twisting to their advantage policies set for them by outsiders. Residents of the Round Valley Reservation in California faced Methodist missionaries determined to assimilate them quickly. At first, the Pomo people there looked at Round Valley as a seasonal refuge where they received government food and clothing. They and other bands living there also saw the reservation as their homeland, much the same as the people at Cheyenne River had done. Statements from several band leaders all expressed similar ideas. James Sherwood, the Pomo leader, said, "We want land, plow, garden, and work." "We want our own farms," another stated, while a third echoed these sentiments, adding, "We want to do something for ourselves." Despite such statements, the Indians had no desire to abandon their band or tribal identity. They saw their agent Henry Sheldon as a tyrant and opposed him repeatedly, refusing to work for the wages he offered. This proved so successful that at one point he complained they would laugh at him when he offered wages lower than they demanded. They stole grain as well as other goods from the agency storage. When the agent tried to prevent them from holding traditional ceremonies at two sweat lodges they had built, Pomos broke or damaged the reservation equipment and stopped working until Sheldon got it repaired. In these ways they directed activities despite what the agent and missionaries wanted.

Not all western tribes became farmers. Among the Nez Perce people in Idaho, many preferred to raise cattle, and by 1890 tribal members owned at least seven thousand head. However, they lacked the capital to fence their lands, and by then at least as many cattle from the herds of nearby ranchers also grazed on Indian grassland. Tribal members whose farms failed, or who had no money for cattle-raising, often leased their land to others. This brought ever-larger numbers of non–Nez Perce animals onto the reservation and caused increasing tensions between the Indians and their neighbors. Farther east, in Utah, the Northern Utes faced pressures from whites to surrender or lease their land. A few tribal members who became ranchers gained influence because they worked with agency officials and even white stockmen some of the time. William Wash, one of the Indian ranchers, often served as a Ute spokesman when land-use issues arose. For example, in 1913 Ute stock owners opposed any further leasing of tribal land to whites, and he presented their arguments. "The Indian has always held it [the land]," he said; "they do not want to lease it at all." Wash and his neighbors represented the changing face of their part of Indian country at the turn of the century.

Wherever they lived, Native Americans faced wrenching economic and social change. Men from the hunting cultures of the plains groups had few outlets for their interests and often fewer chances to gain satisfaction or prestige in traditional ways. If they rejected agriculture, most lacked enough money to buy cattle. If they considered working as Indian police or scouts, they faced ridicule or ostracism for serving the government rather than their own people. Many accepted part-time or day-labor jobs herding for nearby ranchers, hauling hay, or repairing fences. Women turned their attention to gardening and, under the direct scrutiny of the field matron service, to homemaking. A few managed to escape the boredom and poverty of the reservations by traveling with one of the Wild West shows then operating. William Cody (Buffalo Bill) and Gordon Lillie (Pawnee Bill) hired men and women to show several aspects of Indian life. Dressed in buckskins and wearing feathered headdresses, the men roped cattle, raced horses, and attacked stagecoaches to the delight of eastern and foreign audiences. The women practiced Native crafts, set up tepees, and demonstrated clothing, jewelry, and hairstyles. During most of the 1880s the Buffalo Bill show included eighty to one hundred Indians each season. In 1885 even Sitting Bull traveled with Cody's show for a time, receiving a trained horse from the entertainer.

Other Native Americans got jobs entertaining crowds attracted by the advertising for medicine-show outfits that crossed the East selling patent medicines and a little excitement. Begun in 1881, the Kickapoo Medicine Company, the largest of these groups, operated thirty outfits. Each of these included a purported doctor with a name like Yellowstone Joe or Nevada Ned and dressed in western garb, along with a scout and anywhere from twenty to thirty Indians, including men, women, and children. The tribal people wore Indian costumes, danced, and drummed for interested audiences who saw them as exotic. Few medicine shows tried their magic in the West, fearing that the pioneers might kill everyone in the group, but they crisscrossed much of the East. After the entertainment had attracted a large crowd, the doctor gave his sales pitch for the cure-all medicine Kickapoo Sagwa. A phony drink made of colored water with a few spices and a little alcohol to give it some zip, the elixir appears to have sold well and probably did little harm to its users. The medicine or Wild West shows helped Indians get off the reservations and out from under the eyes and rules of their local agents. Reformers and government officials both objected to Native Americans traveling with these groups, and although the *Standing Bear v. Crook* decision of 1879 allowed Indians freedom of movement, reformers tried to end such activities. During the 1890s Commissioner of Indian Affairs Thomas Jefferson Morgan called on agents to "discourage" reservation residents from accepting these jobs, but his directive did not end the practice. Indians continued to work as entertainers in both Wild West and medicine shows at least until the outbreak of World War I.

Even while several thousand Native Americans managed to escape the dreary life of the reservation every year, the vast majority could not. At many agencies, tribal shamans continued to practice the ceremonies that officials had declared illegal. Prophets urged their adherents to remember traditional rites and beliefs. In the Northwest, Smohalla visited many tribes and urged his listeners to reject white ideas and practices. When responding to demands that Indians give up hunting and turn to farming, he retorted, "You ask me to plow the ground. Shall I take a knife and tear my mother's bosom?" Ideas similar to that circulated among many tribal groups as they continued to resist agency rules and pressures for acculturation. The Ghost Dance of 1898–90 received the most attention, but Indian people all across the West sought help for their new circumstances.

Of all the cultural and religious responses to the forces of change in Indian country, the Peyote Cult or religion became the most widespread and has lasted to the present. Tribal people in the Southwest had used fruit or "buttons" from peyote, a cactus that grows there and in northern Mexico, in ceremonies for generations, perhaps even centuries. It produces mild hallucinogenic dreams or visions and, for some people, vomiting and headaches as well. In some ways its effects recall the so-called black drink that Muscogean groups in the Southeast used for countless generations to cleanse themselves as a part of worship. Most scholars think that the Comanches brought peyote back from their raids into northern Mexico and introduced it to other groups on the southern plains. Apparently early reservation users tried the buttons as a way to escape their wretched conditions, but by the late nineteenth century a set of religious ideas and practices had developed around the drug. Quanah Parker, the outspoken Comanche leader, urged its acceptance in Oklahoma. Gradually the ceremonies came to include singing, prayers, drumming, meditation, and the use of peyote as a sacrament in the combined Indian and Christian practices that evolved. Unlike the Sun Dance or potlatch ceremonies, which took place in public and drew plenty of attention, the peyote rites could be conducted in homes, sweat lodges, or other settings away from the prying eyes of agents or reservation police. So the practice spread, offering religious solace as well as a sense of rebellion against the pressures to assimilate.

The new "Peyote Road" attracted unwanted attention from reformers and federal officials alike. Even though the teachings associated with it stressed hard work, monogamy, and the avoidance of alcohol, reformers complained that Indians were wasting time at the ceremonies when they should be working. They also feared the "demoralizing effects of all-night seances" and the possibility that using this new substance might "make the Indian contented with his present attainments [and] seriously interfere with his progress" toward full assimilation. Both federal and state authorities tried to end peyote use but without success. In 1898, Oklahoma Territory banned the substance, and the U.S. Department of Agriculture used federal agents at the Mexican border to intercept and destroy shipments of the buttons into the country. Facing continued attacks, adherents of the new beliefs organized in 1918 as the Native American Church in Oklahoma. After that the group spread slowly as it faced opposition from some Indian traditionalists because its ceremonies include some elements of Christianity. Yet despite the objections of reformers, government officers, some shamans, and other tribal leaders, the Native American Church reached across reservation borders and continues to provide Indians with focus and support today.

By the early twentieth century other trends began to break down tribal isolation as well. After more than a generation of forced attendance at white schools, hundreds of boarding-school graduates had moved into the cities, traveled to distant places, and gone to college or beyond. Some of these Indian physicians, lawyers, journalists, and writers left the reservations and shifted their focus. Rather than working to retain specific tribal cultures they wanted to bring tribal people together. Their efforts produced a multi-Indian movement to improve the lives of all Native Americans and to bring their ideas to the general public. In 1911 an impressive group of educated, literate, and articulate young people met to organize the Society of American Indians. Founded and led by such people as Carlos Montezuma, Thomas Sloan, Henry Roe Cloud, Charles Eastman, and Gertrude Bonnin, who wanted to break down barriers between and among tribes and to show them which issues they faced in common, in 1916 the society began to publish the *American Indian Magazine*. Deep splits within the leadership soon weakened the group, however. They argued bitterly about how much to cooperate with federal officials. Montezuma focused his anger on the Bureau of Indian Affairs, and when the others objected to his outspoken attacks, he left the organization and began publishing his own journal. U.S. entry into World War I and continuing tensions within the leadership doomed the Society of American Indians, and by 1923 it had collapsed.

During its short life it demonstrated the difficulties Native Americans had in moving beyond individual tribal matters to broad national issues, but at the same time it laid the groundwork for later multitribal organizations.

Carlos Montezuma (Wassaja) c. 1866–1923

Born into a Yavapai village in central Arizona, Wassaja was captured at age five in 1871 by raiding Pima Indians who then sold him to an itinerant Italian photographer, Carlos Gentile, for thirty dollars. Gentile soon adopted the boy and renamed him Carlos Montezuma, and together they traveled in the Southwest briefly. In 1872–73 they joined Ned Buntline and Buffalo Bill, with little Carlos acting in some of their theatrical productions. Living in the Midwest during much of the 1870s, Carlos attended school in several cities, and in 1878 Gentile put him in the care of the Rev. George Ingalls in Illinois. Carlos graduated from high school the next year and in 1880, at age fourteen, he enrolled at the University of Illinois. Four years later he graduated, then studied medicine in Chicago, and in 1889 he completed his courses at the Chicago Medical College and became a licensed physician. He spent several years as a reservation doctor in the West and in 1893 he moved east to the Carlisle Indian School to work with Richard Pratt. Three years later he returned to Chicago and opened a private practice. By 1900 he had become a spokesman for Indian rights and was at work to help secure an Arizona reservation for the Yavapai people (the Fort McDowell Indian Reservation was created in 1903). His experiences among western Indians turned him into an outspoken critic of government programs, and in 1911 he joined several other young, educated Indians to found the Society of American Indians. They published the *American Indian Magazine* that supported education and acculturation and opposed peyote use. Montezuma demanded that the Indian Office be abolished, and when his colleagues disagreed in 1916 he began his own publication, the newsletter *Wassaja*. He worked for better reservation living conditions and repeatedly attacked government programs for mistreating tribal people. In failing health in December 1922, he moved back west to the Fort McDowell reservation where he died on January 31, 1923.

Source: Peter Iverson, *Carlos Montezuma and the Changing World of American Indians* (Albuquerque: University of New Mexico Press, 1982).

New Challenges

In many ways reservation Indians avoided having to comply with directives from Washington and the meddling of teachers, missionaries, and agency employees, but some things could not be ignored. In 1917 the United States entered World War I, and that action had major long-range effects on Native American life. For several decades before that conflict, army officers serving in the West had suggested creating all-Indian units in the military, similar to the all-black regiments already in operation. Despite the existence of companies of Indian scouts for years and even a few all-Indian companies during the 1890s, most American planners rejected this approach. While considering how to use Native Americans in the military, they heard sharp criticism of the idea from the pan-tribal Society of American Indians (SAI), still in its infancy. That pro-assimilationist group opposed segregated units, arguing that "much of the popular clamor for a spectacular Indian regiment or battalion arises from the showman's brand of Indian as seen in the circus." Nevertheless, some all-Indian National Guard units from Oklahoma preferred their uniqueness and wanted to remain segregated. The SAI's argument aside, Indians from almost all tribes participated in the war effort.

When the United States entered the war, the Selective Service Act of May 1917 applied to all citizens, and since allotment had given individuals who took the land citizenship for at least a full generation by that time, most Indian men became eligible for the draft. Many of them hurried to join the army, and enlistments exceeded the numbers drafted during the war. To the dismay of missionaries and educators, armed service seemed to call for the very skills and ideas they had worked to suppress. Military officials claimed that Indian soldiers had superior abilities with weapons and as trackers, and many became snipers. As the war neared its end, the commissioner of Indian affairs at the time, Cato Sells, bragged that three-quarters of the Native Americans then in service had enlisted. In Europe some local commanders used men from the reservations as messengers and radio operators, having them speak in their own languages to confuse and frustrate the Germans. This came a full generation before the so-called Navajo Code Talkers of World War II fame. The figures vary, but it seems likely that as many as sixteen thousand men left the reservations for military service.

Not all groups cooperated wholeheartedly. The Six Nations Iroquois living in New York, for example, issued their own declaration of war against the central powers, claiming that they had never surrendered their tribal independence, and so they joined the war effort as separate nations. Despite calls such as that by Gertrude Bonnin, editor of *American Indian Magazine*, to "stand by the flag, red men, it is your flag," in scattered places young Indians objected to the draft. In western Utah and eastern Nevada, some Goshutes refused to register for the draft and threatened violence. After an investigation of local issues, it became clear that much of the resistance came because the men thought they had not become citizens and so were exempt from the draft. In early 1918 a sheriff's posse supported by a platoon of soldiers took the last of the protesters off to jail, ending the impasse. In 1917, some Oklahoma Indians had participated with whites and blacks in the short-lived Green Corn Rebellion against the draft, and while much of their protest stemmed from economic changes in agriculture, they had denounced both the war and conscription. At one meeting, some two hundred people listened while Ellen Perryman attacked the war. "To hell with the Government and the Allies," she said. "The Indians are not going to the slaughter fields of France." Certainly not all Native Americans loved the country that had mistreated them for so long.

The war changed many things for Native Americans on reservations. Because of Indians' participation in the conflict, in 1924 Congress passed legislation giving U.S. citizenship to any Native individuals not already having it. Of at least equal importance, many of the men who did not go off to the military, along with some of the women from the reservations, got war-related jobs away from home. No sooner had the United States entered the war than the government called on farmers and ranchers to increase food production. Commissioner Sells saw the Indian participation in war programs as just another way to hasten Native people along the path to acculturation and as a new chance to pressure them to become part of the national economy. He sent officials to lecture about the latest farming techniques, give advice on soil conservation, and offer small cash prizes for increased crop production. Patriotism swept across some reservations as tribal people there worked to increase their crops. In Montana, Blackfeet leader Medicine Owl assured the Blackfeet agent that "we will plant more corn to feed your soldiers and we will raise more goats and sheep [so] that your soldiers may be clothed." The acres in production jumped sharply, as some groups put land being rested back into production and others tried to raise two crops in a single year. By the time the government and farmers got their efforts under way, the war ended. In 1919 surplus crops brought lower prices. Using marginal land and leasing more acres to white farmers and ranchers in an effort to increase war production hurt the economic base of many reservation groups.

The postwar era saw increased quarreling among reformers over how to treat Native Americans. The thousands of Indian bureaucrats opposed most changes as threats to their jobs. Missionary groups, educators, and social conservatives denounced any move to slow or stop assimilation programs aimed at crushing tribal cultures. They received plenty of support from the popular *Saturday Evening Post*, which attacked proposals to change Indian policies. Church publications such as *Missionary Review* labeled Native Americans "pagan worshipers" and called for increased missionary efforts. Traditional ceremonies and dances drew the most criticism, being seen as backward cults that included "horrible, sadistic, and obscene" practices. After inspecting some of the New Mexico pueblos in 1926, new commissioner of Indian affairs Charles Burke denounced the residents as "half animals" and ordered the arrest of some leaders, saying their actions violated regulations. Growing anticommunist feelings during the 1920s led to personal attacks: those who defended tribal freedom of religion were called "antiAmerican, and subversive . . . agents of Moscow."

At the same time other reformers began to oppose the forcible destruction of the reservations and all things Indian. Groups such as the General Federation of Women's Clubs focused much of their attention on improving reservation conditions. The author Hamlin Garland wrote positively about tribal cultures and urged that the government stop outsiders from "regulating the amusements and daily lives of the natives." In 1923 John Collier, a social worker, helped organize the American Indian Defense Association, which differed from earlier reform groups in that it supported religious freedom and cultural pluralism for Native Americans. Collier and other like-minded reformers drew public attention to scandals over oil leases to business as well as to squatters who threatened tribal lands in New Mexico. Increasing public attention persuaded federal authorities to examine reservation conditions, and in 1926 the secretary of the interior hired the Institute of Government Research in Baltimore to review Indian policies and their results. Lewis Meriam headed the team of investigators that fanned out across the country. Two years later, in 1928, they published their findings as *The Problem of Indian Administration*, usually known as the Meriam Report. A scathing attack on almost all aspects of federal programs, it called for changes and improvements in such things as education, housing, diet, and public health, bringing national attention to long-ignored problems facing reservation dwellers. Within a year, and before serious reforms could begin, the economic collapse of 1929 and the Great Depression that followed brought the economy and the government to a standstill. Any implementation of the Meriam team's findings had to wait for the New Deal a couple of years later.

Suggested Readings

Adams, David Wallace. *Education for Extinction: American Indians and the Boarding School Experience, 1875–1928*. Lawrence: University Press of Kansas, 1995.

Britten, Thomas A. *American Indians in World War I: At War and at Home*. Albuquerque: University of New Mexico Press, 1997.

Cahill, Cathleen D. *Federal Mothers and Fathers: A Social History of the United States Indian Service, 1860–1933*. Chapel Hill: University of North Carolina Press, 2011.

Hagan, William T. *Indian Police and Judges: Experiments in Acculturation and Control*. New Haven: Yale University Press, 1966.

———. *Quanah Parker, Comanche Chief*. Norman: University of Oklahoma Press, 1993.

Hertzberg, Hazel W. *The Search for Indian Identity: Modern Pan-Indian Movements*. Syracuse: Syracuse University Press, 1971.

Hoxie, Frederick E. *The Final Promise: The Campaign to Assimilate the Indians, 1880–1920*. Cambridge, England: Cambridge University Press, 1995.

Iverson, Peter. *"We Are Still Here": American Indians in the Twentieth Century*. Wheeling, Ill.: Harlan Davidson, 1998.

Leiker, James N., and Ramon Powers. *The Northern Cheyenne Exodus in History and Memory*. Norman: University of Oklahoma Press, 2011.

McDonnell, Janet A. *The Dispossession of the American Indian, 1887–1934*. Bloomington: Indiana University Press, 1991.

Moses, L. G. *Wild West Shows and the Images of the American Indians, 1883–1933*. Albuquerque: University of New Mexico Press, 1996.

Zanjani, Sally. *Sarah Winnemucca*. Lincoln: University of Nebraska Press, 2001.

CHAPTER 7

From Reservations to Activism, 1930–1973

The New Deal Era and Beyond

W hen Franklin D. Roosevelt swept into office as president in 1933, his administration tried to institute changes that would lift the nation out of the Depression, and Indian affairs received their share of attention or more. While much of the economy neared collapse, conditions on many reservations fell below the minimum standards found anywhere else in the country. The 1928 *Meriam Report* had presented the state of health, education, and economic life in Indian country in chilling detail. Many of the isolated reservations had become rural poverty pockets. Per capita income stood at between $100 and $200 per year, contrasted to the national average of $1,350. The authors of the report called on the government to drop its acculturation program and stop demanding that all tribal people become Americanized. They urged that most of the boarding schools be closed and that the children be taught in day schools near their homes. Their report called for allocating more money to feed the schoolchildren, because their diet rarely included fruit or vegetables and cost the government only eleven cents per child each day.

The investigators found that the general health and living conditions on many reservations proved even more dismal than at the schools. Poor housing and a poor diet lowered people's resistance to diseases of all kinds. Measles, pneumonia, and tuberculosis swept through tribal communities. For example, the tuberculosis rate in Arizona stood at seventeen times the national average, while pneumonia killed the Yakamas in Washington at a rate twenty times that of the rest of the population. Trachoma, a serious eye disease, caused widespread vision problems, and the available treatments often resulted in blindness. Mortality rates among Indians soared well beyond those of other groups and the population in general. Even worse, the infant mortality rate of 190.7 per one thousand live births far exceeded those of blacks (114.1 per thousand) or whites (70.8). The researchers charged that the differences stemmed from the miserly congressional appropriations for Indian health care. The total health-care budget stood at $756,000, and this provided only about fifty cents per person to cover treatment costs for an entire year. These figures brought no national outcry, but they gave such a negative description of reservation life that it became possible for reformers to demand and get large increases in federal funding once the New Deal began its work.

John Collier, a vocal proponent of Indian rights during the 1920s, became the new administration's commissioner of Indian affairs. He accepted the idea of cultural pluralism and worked to end all efforts at breaking down what was left of tribal cultural ideas and practices. When Collier rejected calls not to abolish the Office of Indian Affairs (OIA), Alice Lee Jemison, a young Seneca woman from New York, complained that "we are weary unto death of the propaganda for a continuance of the bureau to 'protect' the Indian." Yet under Collier's leadership the Indian Office hired more Native Americans than ever before and gave them increased authority. Collier encouraged the use of tribal languages as well as social and religious ceremonies, a clear change from the earlier persecution of traditionalists who had tried to retain elements of their cultures. His orders overturned a century of efforts by religious and other reformers who had sought to destroy such "heathen" practices. Indian students at federal boarding schools no longer had to attend Christian worship services either. These actions opened a debate over what Indian policy should attempt, and many tribal people objected to the commissioner's ideas and actions. Christian Indians agreed with shocked missionaries who attacked Collier's actions as "Christ-mocking, communist-aiding, subversive." Although he sought to help the tribes and to give them more direct control over their affairs in ways that had not been tried, Collier failed to discard the old view that bureaucrats knew what was best for Indians. So, while he appeared to be taking a new direction, at times his approach proved as top-down and authoritarian as the methods of reformers of earlier generations.

Yet the commissioner wanted to help tribal groups recover after the long-time efforts to destroy their culture, and he wanted to end or reduce the discrimination they faced. He hoped to encourage Indians "to develop their own life in their own patterns . . . as noble elements in our common life." One step he took to achieve this goal was to allow religious freedom on the reservations. This meant that people could revive long-outlawed traditional rites such as the Sun Dance, potlatch, and other ceremonies. Rather than forcing Indian men to cut their hair, the new approach encouraged them to wear it long if they chose. In tribal communities, traditional religion and health care had often merged, as shamans conducted both healing and religious ceremonies. For years agents, physicians, and missionaries had tried to suppress these practices and criticized the Indian Shaker Church in the Pacific Northwest and the Native American Church on the southern plains as pagan and dangerous. Now they saw the new policies as turning the clock back, as undoing the past century-long efforts to acculturate Indians. One observer denounced those who favored legalizing tribal ceremonies as "idiotic, exceedingly stupid, and ignorant." Yet, during the 1930s, as they came to realize that most Indian religions encouraged family stability and abstinence from alcohol, some health-care workers and bureaucrats changed their minds. As a result, these pan-tribal religious groups came to be seen as helping to improve reservation life, and gradually whites recognized some Native healers as having legitimate places in their communities.

Tribal languages, arts, and crafts all received encouragement, a complete reversal of efforts to destroy or replace them. The Indian Office hired linguists to record tribal languages. Then, moving beyond the mere preservation and study of those languages, staff turned to producing bilingual materials that could be used in Indian schools. These stunning changes led to widespread criticism of Collier and associate reformers as communists, atheists, or worse. Nevertheless, the spirit of change then sweeping through the upper levels of the Office of Indian Affairs continued. As Native medical practices and religious ceremonies were accepted and encouraged, so were many forms of tribal art and crafts. Building on established programs at the Museum of New Mexico in Santa Fe, Collier encouraged tribal cultural expressions, which led to an upsurge of interest in such activities. Potters, weavers, basket makers, silversmiths, and carvers began producing what became a flood of cultural and artistic works. A few people revived totem-pole carving in the Northwest, while Navajo weavers and Pueblo potters used both traditional patterns and techniques as well as new ones. In 1933 the Indian Office supported small demonstrations and exhibitions of weaving, pottery making, and other crafts at the Chicago World's Fair. Two years later, Congress established the Indian Arts and Crafts Board to help Indians promote and market their products.

Having stopped federal programs aimed at destroying tribal cultures, Collier and his allies worked to protect the changes they had brought about by getting Congress to pass new legislation. In 1933 the New Deal's Civilian Conservation Corps (CCC) included an Indian Division that offered young men steady employment with food, clothing, temporary housing, and a modest salary for six months at a time. Without this program some reservation dwellers would have had none of those things. Living at seventy-two CCC camps scattered across the West, these workers labored on a wide variety of projects that included building water reservoirs, digging and enlarging wells, reforesting overgrazed land, marking trails, clearing forest underbrush, fencing land, and assisting with anti-erosion projects. Yet, while the conservation efforts of this program protected and even improved some tribal lands, other federal actions hurt reservation social and economic practices and sparked bitter criticism.

When massive wind erosion hit the country during the 1930s Dust Bowl years, federal employees viewed some Indian ranching and grazing practices as wasteful and harmful to the environment. This led to erecting new fences to keep animals away from already overgrazed lands—a worthy goal but one that disrupted some tribal stock-raising practices. The Navajo Stock Reduction Plan probably caused more anger about Collier's direction of the Indian Office among Indians than any other single action he took. Bureau officials on the scene saw the range as having been nearly destroyed by the Navajos' large sheep and goat herds, which numbered about eight hundred thousand animals. They tried to persuade the Indians to sell or slaughter some of their livestock so the grazing lands could recover. However, the Indians blamed the continued drought, not their animals, for damage to the range. More important, they saw their livestock as a measure of their wealth and community standing, so they resisted federal efforts to kill their animals. They objected bitterly to how the program actually worked. Those with large herds could simply cull the weakest and least-desirable animals. Poorer Navajos, however, often had only ten or fifteen sheep and they had to surrender animals from those small herds. A decade later, nearly half of the animals had been sold or slaughtered. Despite his efforts to help Indians, Collier became their favorite target. Later one Navajo elder recalled that all had gone well until the commissioner came along "and stomped his big foot on our sheep, goats, and horses—and crushed them before our eyes." On some parts of the reservation, bitterness over the stock-reduction plan and its implementation remains to the present day.

Alice Lee Jemison, 1901–1964

Daughter of a Cherokee father and a Seneca mother from a prominent family, she spent her childhood among the Senecas in western New York and became a journalist and lobbyist for the Seneca Nation. Unable to get any higher education, she gave up hope of becoming a lawyer and in 1919 married La Verne Jemison. Ten years later they separated and she became the sole supporter of her two children and aging mother. That year, 1929, she became secretary to Ray Jimerson, then president of the Seneca Nation. This started her career as an activist and public figure in Seneca and national affairs. From the start she followed Carlos Montezuma's ideas and attacked U.S. Indian policies repeatedly. Both of them pressed to have the Office of Indian Affairs abolished. They both used the phrase "the only good Indian bureau is a dead Indian bureau," because they thought that the bureau interfered with tribal sovereignty and harmed Indian people. During the 1920s growing Iroquois nationalism affected her ideas about tribal sovereignty, and her views never moved far from that goal. She gained valuable experience as a publicist and writer during the defense of two Seneca women charged in a 1930 murder. In 1934 she moved to Washington, D.C. and for much of the next ten years she denounced the Indian Office, its commissioner John Collier, and New Deal Indian policies repeatedly. Her attacks brought retaliation from Interior Department officials, who called her a fascist, an American Nazi, and even a Nazi spy. In 1940 she opposed the pre–World War II draft, claiming that the Iroquois were sovereign and that Indian men should wait until their tribes declared war before joining the military. Her bitter hatred of the Office of Indian Affairs and persistent attacks on the government reduced her national influence, but she represented a major stream of Indian opinion about the direction of federal policies at the time.

> Sources: Lawrence M. Hauptmann, *The Iroquois and the New Deal* (Syracuse: Syracuse University Press, 1981); Hauptmann, "Alice Lee Jemison: A Modern 'Mother of the Nation,'" in *Sifters: Native American Women's Lives*, ed. Theda Perdue (New York: Oxford University Press, 2001), 175–86.

The central piece of the Indian New Deal, the 1934 Wheeler-Howard bill (Indian Reorganization Act), incorporated many of Collier's hopes to refashion national policies for dealing with Native Americans. As the bill moved through Congress, its contents changed considerably, yet when enacted it shifted the course of federal policy substantially. At least in theory, cultural pluralism and encouragement of tribal rites and ideas replaced forced assimilation as central goals. Unfortunately federal officials developed new policies without bothering to ask what the tribes wanted. One of the most important provisions of the IRA was that it officially ended the nineteenth-century allotment program. Then it provided funds for tribes to repurchase some of the lands lost because of that policy, and within the first three years of its passage Native American groups added more than two million acres to their existing landholdings. The new law responded to continued demands that the government hire Indians for many jobs on the reservations. In fact it moved beyond that and instituted the practice of preferential hiring within the Office of Indian Affairs and related offices.

The New Deal efforts to reconstitute tribal governments proved important in bringing long-term changes to the reservations. They provided Indians a chance to write tribal constitutions and form reservation-based governments, but they ignored traditional village and band leadership customs and even modern business councils that had developed early in the twentieth century. To establish new governments, tribes had to vote within one year in favor of taking that step. Hoping to explain what was happening and to allay suspicions, Collier traveled west to ten locales in Indian country. To his surprise, many reservation groups expressed only lukewarm support for this new style of tribal government, and some opposed it openly. The Iroquois in New York attacked the effort, and many of the Plains Indians rejected it as well. During the next several years voters in 174 tribes approved going ahead, but another 78, including the Navajos, the largest group, voted against new governments. In these reservation elections many individual Indians chose not to vote, but eager federal officials counted their abstentions as votes in favor of the new constitutions. This tactic may have changed the results in some close races. In several places the effort to create new tribal governments further divided already badly split reservation groups. Partially assimilated and Christian groups opposed the effort as communistic and as steps backward and away from Americanization. Successful allotment farmers feared that they might lose their land to the proposed new governments. At the same time, others complained about moves to reduce or destroy the roles and status of traditional clan and tribal chiefs and shamans in local affairs. Most of this opposition caught the bureaucrats by surprise and worsened existing divisions within tribal communities. Despite the confusion, debate, and rancor, most present-day tribal governments got their start under the IRA or the 1936 Oklahoma Indian Welfare Act, the exception being Alaska Native groups.

World War II

Although some of the New Deal programs helped, Indians like other Americans did not escape the effects of the Great Depression until World War II revived the national economy. Native Americans had left their homes for jobs in nearby cities prior to the war. That conflict accelerated the movement, as thousands of reservation dwellers sought employment and another twenty-five thousand left to serve in the military. In 1940 Congress passed a selective service act, which brought back the old arguments about whether to place Indian young men in their own units or to integrate them. John Collier suggested that as many as forty-two thousand men from the reservations might be eligible for the draft. Not surprisingly, given his ideas about tribalism, he recommended that all-Indian units be established. Tribal members split on the issue, but Navajo Tribal chairman J. C. Morgan supported it, because he thought that segregated units were a way to get young men with weak reading skills into the army. He feared that if they served in regular companies, many of the young Indian men might encounter discrimination, because they had little off-reservation experience. Writing about the issue, Morgan noted that the "Navajo will cheerfully accept any assignment . . . but it would seem wise to consider the advantages of maintaining the Navajo as an indigenous regiment." Selective Service officials ignored the suggestion, and Native Americans served alongside other Americans throughout the war.

Most tribal members supported the war effort wholeheartedly, but some groups and individuals objected to the draft. Utah Paiutes and Mississippi Choctaws claimed that they lacked citizenship. In the summer of 1941 a Choctaw elder wrote that "Choctaw Indians never vote or pay poll tax. The white friends here say we are not allowed to vote. . . . If we are not citizens, will it be right for [us to fight]?" Religious scruples kept some from cooperating. Five Hopi traditionalists refused to register on religious grounds, claiming that tribal teachings predicted a major war. Those beliefs warned that the tribesmen were "to show their bows and arrows to no one" at that time. The judge rejected their defense and sentenced them to a year and a day in federal prison. At Taos Pueblo in New Mexico the men considered their long hair to have religious significance, but they too had to serve. In one incident, John Collier intervened to get a twenty-six-year-old rain priest from the Zuni tribe the same treatment other clergymen received. Among the Tohono O'odham people in Arizona, an aged leader urged the men not to register, so the authorities arrested him and another villager for encouraging resistance to the draft.

The German-American Bund and some communists tried to encourage noncompliance with the draft too, but their activities seem to have had little result. Among the Six Nations Iroquois Confederacy in New York, long-standing issues brought some objections. These groups questioned the authority of the U.S. government to order their men into a war. The Iroquois had long claimed to be independent sovereign nations within the United States and Canada, and the Mohawks, Senecas, and Tuscaroras all referred to earlier treaties to claim that they lacked citizenship. Saint Regis Mohawk tribal leaders stated that "under our treaties with the United States of America, we are a distinct race, nation and people owning and occupying and governing the lands of our ancestors and under the protection of the federal government in reciprocation for our friendship." John Collier urged them to register as aliens and then take their claims to court, which they did. In 1941 the U.S. Second Circuit Court of Appeals ruled against their claims in *Ex parte Green*. At the same time, federal officials suggested that a small delegation from these tribes come to Washington, where they could announce their own tribal declarations of war against the Axis powers, and this seems to have lessened some of the opposition.

Only a small minority of Native Americans had serious objections to military service, and most supported the war as enthusiastically as the rest of the population. Within six months after the declaration of war, about seventy-five hundred Indians had entered the military. By the conflict's end, twenty-five thousand Native men and women had served in the armed forces. Of these, over twenty-one thousand served in the army, many of them as volunteers. They helped invade the beaches of Normandy on D-Day, raise the flag on Iwo Jima in the Pacific, and pursue the Germans across North Africa. Some units used Native Americans as radio operators, because they could send messages in their tribal languages. In the Pacific, the Navajo Code Talkers used a special coded version of their language that even other Navajos could not understand. When the Japanese invaded the western Aleutian Islands, tribal people in Alaska served in what they called Eskimo territorial guard companies on the mainland. Clearly, Indians fought wherever American military forces operated during the war. Native American women served as nurses, as WACs (army auxiliary corps members), or WAVEs (navy auxiliary corps members), doing support work for combat units.

Wartime service gave many young Native people much more experience with other Americans than they had had before. They traveled far from home, often overseas. They gained respect for their actions and a sense of accomplishment and personal worth from their wartime duties. Four decades later, in 1997, surviving Navajo Code Talkers marched in President Bill Clinton's second inaugural parade, and in 2001 they received citations from President George W. Bush six months after he had taken office. Rituals that long predated the present century got renewed attention, as reservation communities welcomed veterans home. Among the Lakotas and the Kiowas on the plains, returning servicemen received traditional honors of war, and their presence helped to revive the nearly defunct warrior societies on many reservations. Certainly the veterans enjoyed this attention, but they also faced the traumas that resulted from modern war. Alcoholism, an inability to settle back into former patterns, and dissatisfaction with treatment on or near the reservations plagued some for years.

Those who had remained at home during the conflict had new experiences too. Thousands left reservation communities to work in wartime industry or agriculture. Some of them held regular, full-time jobs for the first time. Almost all of them benefited from steady wages but they also faced discrimination, poor housing, and loneliness while away from home. They could not always leave their work to attend traditional ceremonies or celebrations on the reservation. Used to being surrounded by friends and family, or certainly near them most of their lives, some who went to cities for the first time found life there isolating and stressful. Those who stayed on the reservations faced the same kinds of shortages and rationing as other Americans, but their long-term poverty before the war made such experiences even more difficult than for some others.

Expecting to find changes when they returned home after the war, Indian men faced disappointment. Unemployment, poor housing, mediocre medical care, and discrimination still existed. Not only had few changes taken place, the strong feelings of American nationalism that had developed became a major threat to tribal survival in the next two decades. As early as 1943, opponents of John Collier's programs began a renewed attack on him, on the Indian Reorganization Act, and on tribalism itself. Congressional hearings that year led to calls to abolish the Indian Office and to begin the process of what some people described as getting the government "out of the Indian business." Supporters of this approach claimed that Indians had proved themselves fully capable of dealing with the rest of American society during the war, so they deserved to be treated equally. This meant reducing spending for tribal programs and ending government actions that fostered collectivism and paternalism toward the tribes. Religious groups such as the National Council of Churches called for an end to efforts that encouraged Indians to "return to the blanket" by practicing their "pagan" rites and dances. Popular magazines such as *Reader's Digest* published articles demanding that Native Americans be given the same freedom enjoyed by other citizens.

Indian Claims Commission

Such ideas sounded good. Few could publically oppose giving Native Americans equal treatment. Others argued that the government erred by continuing its supervision of tribal funds and reservation facilities. This approach laid the groundwork for a basic challenge to thinking about government responsibilities toward the tribes that had existed for generations. One observer described the mid-1940s attitudes as showing a renewed anti-Indian bias that wanted the tribes turned loose from federal programs "even if it means starvation for large numbers" of people. To give the tribes their freedom and cut federal expenses, in 1946 Congress established the Indian Claims Commission (ICC), a body that was to examine past dealings between the federal government and the tribes over land cessions, treaty payments, and other long-standing issues. When the new commission had settled past claims and injustices, the government expected to end its financial responsibilities toward Native groups.

Although established to complete its work in just five years, the ICC operated for more than thirty. During that time 176 tribal groups filed 370 separate claims, far more than congressional supporters of the program had anticipated. Each case went through several stages, with Indians, scholars, and lawyers all participating in the process. Reservation-based oral accounts had less influence than the paper evidence presented by researchers and the government, and it often took years for any particular group to work its way through the process from entering its claim to receiving any compensation. Tribes that had received less than the going market price for land taken during the nineteenth century had to provide evidence showing the land's value at the time the government took possession of it. The commissioners eventually would rule on how much more the Indians should have gotten and how much interest should be credited to their account. Some groups received millions, but not all won their cases. In the case of the Lakota Sioux, the tribe became eligible for more than $17 million as payment for having lost the Black Hills in South Dakota. The Lakotas rejected the settlement, however, demanding that their lands be returned, but the government refused and the issue remains unsettled today. Others also objected to getting cash rather than land, but few followed the Lakotas' example and turned down the federal dollars. When the claims process ended in 1978, the government had awarded around $818 million, settling just 285 of the 850 claims brought before it.

Termination

If it had worked as its congressional backers expected it to, the ICC would have ended the issue of Indian claims against the government. Instead, because its operations lasted so long and cost far more than anyone expected, they drew tribal attention to past federal misdeeds. While righting some past wrongs, the commission had a more sinister goal as well. It represented the first step in the broad-based effort to end all federal responsibilities toward the tribes and led directly to the termination policy that followed. By 1947, anti-Indian members of Congress had begun working toward abolition of the Indian Office and its programs. That year the Senate Civil Service Committee called for an end to federal services for some tribes, and demanded that the bureau prepare a list of reservations where people could operate without further federal assistance. The next year the Hoover Commission, examining governmental efficiency, recommended that all special programs for Indians be halted. By the early 1950s, western senators such as Arthur Watkins of Utah, Frank Church of Idaho, and Henry Jackson of Washington all supported the idea. With this broad base of support, what became known as "the termination era" soon arrived.

The movement's supporters rejected cultural pluralism. Like the nineteenth-century Indian affairs reformers, they demanded that Native Americans shed their differences and become part of the general society. Commissioner Dillon Myer, a pro-termination man, went so far as to close some reservation day schools, enlarge the boarding schools, and urge teachers and other staff members there to do whatever they could to assimilate their students. At least for a time, such orders appeared to roll the clock back fifty or even seventy-five years to the early reservation era. What contemporary observers overlooked was the fact that those who supported cutting the tribes loose from the federal government expected that business interests would be able to renew their exploitation of reservation natural resources, as they had done prior to the Collier era. Strangely enough, the supporters' actions resulted in reducing federal appropriations for their home districts and states. Actual termination of tribal status began with the 1953 passage of House Concurrent Resolution 108, which stated that Indians would be "subject to the same laws and entitled to the same privileges" as other citizens. Then it announced that Congress wanted to end existing wardship status for particular groups, and it listed tribes and bands in nine states that would lose federal services.

A few weeks later, President Dwight D. Eisenhower signed Public Law 280, putting the new policy into motion. Not surprisingly, no senior federal official had bothered to consult with any tribal leaders before termination went into effect. As a result, when Native Americans did learn about it, they had little specific information at hand. The first opposition came from the National Congress of American Indians. A relatively new group founded in 1944, it tried to mobilize tribes against the policy and linked tribal leaders across the country in attacking it. One Blackfeet spokesman described trying to plan for the tribe's future while facing termination as being like trying to cook "a meal in your tipi when someone is standing outside trying to burn the tipi down." Not all agreed. A minority of acculturated Indians cheered the policy, hoping that it would lead to the closing of the reservations and the incorporating of their populations into the general society. Years later, historian John Wunder described the process as the "most successful legal attack on Indian rights and sovereignty" since the nation's founding fathers had signed the Constitution.

Particular tribes such as the Menominees of Wisconsin and the Klamaths of Oregon suffered greatly after termination. Both groups had large timber reserves on their reservations, and federal officials thought that gave each group an economic base solid enough to cope with the changes. This proved overly optimistic. In Wisconsin the Menominee reservation became the state's poorest county. The tribal hospital could not meet state health standards and had to close. Because the tribe lacked a strong tax base, it could not provide for schools and other needed social services. Within a couple of years, the corporation that had been formed to manage tribal assets resorted to selling off prime vacation plots to wealthy people from the Chicago area. The tribal sawmill had to lay off many workers because the timber business could not support the payroll. Termination proved a disaster for the Menominees and they launched an all-out campaign that in 1973 succeeded in returning them to tribal status. In Oregon the Klamaths divided into two groups: one wanted to continue tribal forest management, and the other wanted to sell tribal timberlands and divide tribal assets on a per capita basis. Eventually both the Menominees and the Klamaths managed to be reconstituted as tribes, but only after much strife, suffering, and loss of resources. Dozens of other tribes and bands also experienced termination. Nevertheless, only about thirteen thousand out of nearly four hundred thousand Indians belonged to those groups, and their landholdings constituted just over 3 percent of tribal lands at the time. Still, the uncertainties over termination, the erasing of long-accepted treaty rights, and the intra-tribal bitterness that resulted all made *termination* a dirty word. At its height the policy ended federal relationships with one hundred tribes, bands, and rancherias, small local groups, that included 13,263 people.

Relocation

If the Indian Claims Commission was to pay off past federal debts to Native Americans and termination was to end other governmental responsibilities, then government planners needed something else to bring Indians into the general society. In 1948 they began a trial program offering to help Navajo people relocate to Denver, Los Angeles, and Salt Lake City. By the 1950s this led Commissioner Myer to establish a Branch of Placement and Relocation within his agency, now renamed the Bureau of Indian Affairs (BIA). Through this office he hoped to lure tribal members into the cities and away from the reservations, where they lacked any chance for well-paying jobs. The program represented a formal effort to accomplish what had been happening for decades: individual Indians had been moving to cities since before the 1920s. At first, some reservation dwellers viewed the relocation plans as just another federal plot to undermine tribal life and a part of the hated termination policy. Certainly, if successful, this effort would weaken their societies, tribal ties, language, and religion, so their fears had a solid basis. Still, given the isolation and lack of economic opportunity on many reservations, the new policy made some sense.

As it evolved over the next decade, the program established relocation centers in cities near large concentrations of Native Americans and in other selected urban centers. Places as widely separated as Minneapolis, Chicago, Tulsa, Los Angeles, Dallas, Cleveland, and Albuquerque had such offices. The BIA printed attractive posters showing young families moving to these and other cities and by 1960 had assisted about thirty-three thousand Indians in leaving their reservation homes. At first, about all the bureaucrats did was to give one-way bus tickets to Indians, and at times they purposely sent people to cities far from their particular reservations, hoping to discourage them from returning home. Some of the urban newcomers lacked job skills and experience, and finding work was not easy. So many gave up on city life that in 1956 Congress provided funding for urban Indian job training and placement services. This cut unemployment but failed to help with the many social problems facing Native Americans in large cities.

As a formal program, relocation lasted just about a decade and had only a modest impact. Individual and family movement far outstripped federal efforts, as two-thirds of those leaving reservations at the time did so without government assistance. The migration into the cities that had begun during World War I accelerated sharply so that by 1970 the Census Bureau reported that 44 percent of Native Americans lived off the reservation. That figure continued to climb, and by 2010 about two-thirds of American Indians in the United States resided in cities or towns, rather than on reservations. The experiences of those moving into urban areas varied widely. One Chicago dweller remembered that he worried about his children because of heavy traffic, but said, "I think that they got a better education here [than] they would [have received] back home." For him, the reservation had little attraction. "What is there back home?" he asked. "When I go back I see no jobs, nothing to do, everyone drinks." A middle-aged woman had the opposite reaction. "I wish we had never left home," she said. "This will never be home to me. It's dirty and noisy and . . . crowded."

Despite government expectations that the Native city dwellers would become fully assimilated, the program failed. Certainly leaving their reservations weakened tribal identity for some, yet often the city experiences had effects similar to those of the boarding-school era. Those who came from close-knit communities sought each other out when they came to town and organized Indian cultural or neighborhood centers. Usually not many individuals came from a single reservation or tribe at the same time, so the centers introduced people from many groups to each other. Soon they recognized that they shared customs and ideas more often than they differed, and this caused a gradual shift away from tribal self-identification to a more general awareness of themselves as Indians who shared interests and needs with each other that differed from those of other city groups. By the middle of the 1960s, these growing pan-Indian feelings gave rise to new Native American organizations that either began or became more active during the social unrest of that decade.

Migration changed the lives of those who moved to the cities, and it had mixed effects on those who chose to stay behind. On some reservations the young, educated, and independent people left, and those who remained were mostly the old, the very young, the sickly, and the unskilled. Where that was true, social and economic problems worsened. Some of those communities became poverty pockets with few skilled people and a shortage of money for needed social programs such as public health, housing assistance, and education. However, that was only part of the story. Often urban workers returned to the reservations for family occasions, tribal ceremonies, powwows, or just to visit. When they did so, they brought much-needed cash along. Others who had acquired more education or new job skills in the cities came home to help their families improve life there. Still, for some groups the situation remained grim for the next several decades.

Militancy and Change

During the 1960s, demands for many kinds of reform swept through American society, and this movement soon came to include Indians as well. Having benefited from improved education and their urban experiences, a new generation of Native Americans stood ready to speak out for changes in their lives and in their treatment by the government. Until that time, most tribal leaders or spokespersons for pan-tribal groups such as the National Congress of American Indians had protested occasionally but not as stridently as they came to do in this decade. The "new urban Indians" had gained experience in organizing and working together at the cultural centers that had developed in many cities. The regional powwow circuit that operated on the plains expanded well beyond that area, as both reservation dwellers and urban Indians looked for entertainment that offered them a sense of cultural identity and pride. At the same time, the Native American Church reached out to members living far beyond its original confines in Oklahoma. Young and articulate Native people had the skills and organizational experience to work toward new goals.

In 1961, at the American Indian Chicago Conference held at the University of Chicago, new ideas emerged for how to deal with the government and the rest of society. When established chiefs and other tribal leaders seemed too cautious, younger and more outspoken attendees denounced them as "Uncle Tomahawks" and "apples" (red on the outside but white on the inside). Dissatisfied with the conference discussions, the young militants left town, headed to Santa Fe, and convened their own meeting. There they founded the National Indian Youth Council, proclaimed a "Declaration of Indian Purpose," and then demanded what they called "self-determination." The founded a newspaper, *Americans before Columbus*, and used it to spread their ideas. Clyde Warrior, an Oklahoma

Ponca from a traditional family, became one of the new protesters' outspoken leaders. "We are not free," he objected. Those living on reservations, he said, have their "choices and decisions made by federal administrators, bureaucrats," and subservient tribal governments. Others living elsewhere had their "lives controlled by local power elites." Words like his struck a responsive chord among many tribal people, who increasingly turned to nontraditional public confrontation to attract public support for their demands.

As early as the mid-1950s, tribal fishermen in the Northwest had begun challenging Washington state laws limiting their salmon fishing on the Columbia and other rivers there. The 1854–55 treaties between the United States and the northwestern tribes had assured the Indians they could continue to fish at their "usual and accustomed grounds and stations." White commercial and sport fishermen had opposed this for decades, and the state government passed regulations that essentially cut off tribal people from their fishing rights. Several groups sued the state, trying to end the regulations, but lost. Feeling that the ruling ignored their treaty rights, the Makah tribal council asked the National Indian Youth Council to help them demonstrate. This led to a series of "fish-ins," which brought local Indians into direct conflict with police, sheriffs, and state game officials as the protesters demanded their rights to take salmon from the local rivers, and arrests followed quickly. The dispute attracted increasing media attention when one local official denounced the Indians bitterly. "We had the power and force to exterminate these people from the face of the earth" years ago, he said. "Perhaps we should have!"

Such statements and the continuing violence soon grabbed national headlines, bringing the participation of entertainer and civil-rights advocate Dick Gregory and movie stars Marlon Brando and Jane Fonda, whose presence attracted even more nationwide media attention. By 1970, continued Indian demands finally persuaded the Department of the Interior that it needed to support Indian treaty rights, and so the federal government and the tribes moved into federal court against the state of Washington. After a bitter legal fight that pitted the state and its fishing industry against the federal government and the tribes, Judge George Boldt ruled in favor of the Indians. The mid-nineteenth-century treaties, he said, had protected existing tribal fishing rights. Boldt's 1974 *United States v. Washington* ruling awarded one-half of the annual salmon catch to Indian fishers. That decision raised a firestorm of protest from whites who rejected the tribes' rights to any of the fish. White thugs bombed Indian fishing vessels, and frequent violence erupted before tempers cooled. Responding to white demands, the state of Washington appealed the ruling, but in 1979 the Supreme Court upheld Boldt's decision.

The growing militancy among many younger Indians led to clear divisions among tribal peoples but more over tactics than goals. Often the older, established leaders who participated in the National Congress of American Indians balked at public demonstrations. They saw themselves as differing from other minority groups seeking full integration into the national society. Instead they wished to retain a separate identity. The Indian wanted more than equality, one spokesman explained. "He is fighting to retain his superior rights as guaranteed to him by treaties and agreements as the original inhabitants." This attitude widened the gap between established reservation officials and the growing numbers of younger militants, who saw the turbulence of the civil rights movement era as a chance to help all Native Americans, but particularly those who now lived in the cities. Often urban Indians had weaker ties to tribal communities than those who still lived in Indian country.

As their actions and rhetoric became increasingly more strident, militants demonstrated against their own tribal leaders at national meetings of the National Congress of American Indians as well as against the federal, state, and local governments. They wanted to gain what they called "self-determination," a goal they shared with many reservation-dwelling people who were more conservative. By "self-determination" they meant control over the programs that directly affected their lives. To gain more attention, some Indians turned to direct action. An early example occurred in 1964 at Alcatraz Island in San Francisco Bay. Just the year before, the federal government had closed its prison there and declared the island to be "surplus property." Then officials learned that a small group of Sioux Indians had moved onto the island and claimed the right to settle it under the terms of the 1868 Treaty of Fort Laramie. That agreement had promised the Lakotas the right to use vacant federal property. U.S. marshals removed the small group quickly, but the Sioux then took their case into federal court. In 1968 they lost, and a year later they began a second occupation of Alcatraz. In November 1969, a small group calling itself Indians of All Nations landed on the island, hoping to establish an Indian cultural center there. Again federal officers removed them. About ten days later, seventy-eight more people, calling themselves Indians of All Nations, moved onto Alcatraz. In just a few weeks more than three hundred people representing about fifty tribes occupied the island. Although led by militants, the group tried to reach out to more-conservative Indians by defending tribal traditions and promising that the cultural center they expected to build would help retain the beliefs and languages of reservation groups.

The seizure became an immediate media success. At first, network TV news gave daily reports of activities on the island, and Indian leaders used this newfound access to national media effectively. Proclaiming that they were "attacking the whole system [of federal tribal relations]," they claimed Alcatraz by "right of discovery," set up a local government, opened a school, started a police force, began publishing a newspaper, and established a "Bureau of Caucasian Affairs," for dealing with the United States. When their actions drew attention from pilots of harbor cruise boats that visited the island, occupiers began charging tourists five dollars apiece for landing. At one point they shot an arrow at a boat of sightseers, and they also fired homemade rockets at Coast Guard vessels checking on them. These acts ensured continued national attention, but the militants failed to gain their primary objective—title to the island and permission to build a cultural center there. Nevertheless, the occupation got the full attention of the White House. One administration aide denounced the invasion as "confrontation politics" by "an irresponsible, but P[ublic] R[elations] conscious group." Another labeled it "superb showmanship." Several administration staffers proposed launching a commando operation with U.S. Navy Seals, a combined land and sea invasion with the Coast Guard and the Navy, and even a dawn invasion using tranquilizer guns against the occupiers. Leonard Garment, the official responsible for managing federal government response to the affair, stopped these ideas cold. He cautioned that "Alcatraz could become the biggest political sideshow of 1971" if a single Indian or federal marshal died. So, the government avoided doing anything aggressive. Instead, it cut off water and electricity to the island and waited for public interest to fade. On Alcatraz, differences over goals and tactics split the occupiers, and the college students who had led the occupation returned to their classes the next fall. When the daughter of Richard Oakes, one of the leaders, died after falling down a stairway in the former prison, the militants began to drift away. By June 1971, when federal marshals returned to the island, the remaining occupiers agreed to leave.

For much of the late 1960s and early 1970s, the militancy that had led to the Alcatraz incident spread across the country, causing repeated demonstrations and occupations. In New York State, for generations Mohawk tribal members had enjoyed the right to cross the border into Canada and return without question under the terms of the 1794 Jay's Treaty. When Canadian agents at tollbooths on the Cornwall Bridge now tried to make Mohawk travelers pay, the Indians objected, and in 1968 and 1969 tribal members blockaded the bridge several times. After the second incident, the Canadian government accepted their right to use the bridge without interference. Nevertheless, this issue remains as an irritant in Indian-white relations there. In 2009 and again in 2013 disputes over border crossings, bridge tolls, and the actions of customs officials in both the United States and Canada led to demonstrations by Mohawks and their supporters.

In 1968 Minneapolis Indian leaders such as Clyde and Vernon Bellecourt, George Mitchell, and Dennis Banks formed the American Indian Movement (AIM). Established to gain equal treatment for Native Americans in that city, the group expanded quickly. After its participation in the Alcatraz takeover, it became the most widely recognized militant Native American organization. Its actions encouraged protests across the country during the years ahead. Indians seized Fort Snelling in Minneapolis and Fort Lewis in Washington, occupied a lighthouse on Lake Superior, and marched in Lassen Volcanic National Park in California. On July 4, 1971, Lakotas protested against the loss of the Black Hills to the United States over a century earlier by climbing atop the heads at Mount Rushmore in South Dakota. Other Indians demonstrated at a Boy Scout program in Topeka, Kansas, objecting to the Boy Scouts' use of Indian dances for public entertainment. At Plymouth, Massachusetts, on Thanksgiving Day in 1972, Indians painted Plymouth Rock red and boarded the replica of the *Mayflower* there. Other groups tried to occupy BIA offices from California east to Pennsylvania while they denounced the agency for "bossing Indians around." Most of these protests sought to focus public interest on the social and economic needs of Native Americans and to call attention to the "many, many broken treaties and promises" that marked past federal dealings with the tribes.

That complaint led to the 1972 Trail of Broken Treaties, which brought militants east to Washington, D.C. In the autumn of that year, Vernon Bellecourt, one of the AIM leaders, agreed to coordinate the effort, which had support from nine pan-tribal groups. In the first phase, automobile caravans started out from Seattle, San Francisco, and Los Angeles. As the convoy traveled toward the capital, people from reservations and cities along the route joined in, so that by the time the group reached Washington, hundreds of protesters representing dozens of tribes presented their demands to the Nixon administration. They reached the District of Columbia just one week before the presidential election, making national leaders nervous. When only a few low-level BIA officials appeared open to their protests, the hundreds of militants sitting in the BIA building's auditorium seized the site. Some rampaged through offices, breaking windows and furniture, burning correspondence, and seizing tribal records. After barricading the doors, they proclaimed the building the Native American embassy. Earlier they had smuggled cans of gasoline and rifles inside, and so they could not be dislodged easily.

The occupiers' actions presented the administration with few choices less than a week before the election. By doing nothing, officials would appear weak and indecisive, but "any use of police power to evict [the Indians] would have been a holocaust," according to one Nixon advisor. Restraint had worked at Alcatraz, but that event did not unfold at the end of a reelection campaign. White House advisors decided to present a strong face to the public by denouncing the illegal trashing of the BIA building and records. Any potential use of violent action they deferred until after the election. Instead, they reviewed the protesters' list of complaints, which included unjust and broken treaties, issues of religious freedom (e.g., the use of peyote and eagle feathers in Native rites), calls for the restoration of tribal lands, and demands that more funds be spent for Indian health care and education. The protesters outraged President Nixon, who saw their actions as a repudiation of his efforts to help the tribes. One staff member said that "the President took the occupation very hard." Whatever he thought privately, his aides soon negotiated a settlement. The militants received $66,000 to pay for their return to their homes, and officials promised to study the demands that had been made.

Reactions to the Trail of Broken Treaties illustrate the divisions within and between Indian groups. Alaska Inuit leader Joseph Upicksoun called the entire event a "fiasco," while Hopi Clarence Hamilton labeled it the "Trail of Destruction."

Speaking for the National Tribal Chairmen's Association, Webster Two Hawk attacked the people who occupied the BIA headquarters as "irresponsible, self-styled revolutionaries," and he urged the government to prosecute all of the participants. Navajo tribal chairman Peter MacDonald testified that the demonstrators' actions resulted from the "rage and frustration" Indian people felt, and he pointed out that Native Americans had many real complaints over their treatment by the government and the rest of American society. At the same time, many of the militants returned home to cheers and enthusiastic welcomes in their communities because they had dared to attack the BIA and to show the entire nation their frustration and anger.

Although the caravan to Washington had achieved its central goals of delivering complaints and focusing public attention on Indian grievances, the protest seemed to die out as the caravan members drove home. They soon learned that the federal task force appointed to consider their grievances had rejected all twenty of them. As protests continued, two AIM leaders, Dennis Banks and Russell Means, went to the Pine Ridge Reservation in South Dakota to help traditional Lakotas defeat Richard Wilson, the tribal chairman there. His opponents accused Wilson of having a personal "goon squad" to intimidate his rivals and keep himself in office. This had resulted in a virtual civil war on the reservation, with Wilson's opponents charging that his thugs had beaten dozens and murdered at least sixty people there. A Lakota named Wesley Bad Bull Heart was killed by a non-Indian just off the reservation. When local officials charged the accused killer with manslaughter rather than murder, Indians protested what they saw as clear evidence of unequal law enforcement. Showing their frustration and anger, they attacked and set fire to the courthouse in Custer, South Dakota. Local unrest continued, as violence between AIM protesters and local police broke out in Custer City and Rapid City as well.

In the middle of this situation, Richard Wilson's "enforcers" attacked AIM leader Russell Means, and the next day, February 27, 1973, AIM supporters began an armed takeover of the town of Wounded Knee. They chose this community because of the symbolic importance of the 1890 massacre of Big Foot and his followers there by the U.S. cavalry and public awareness of that event resulting from Dee Brown's best-selling book *Bury My Heart at Wounded Knee*, which had been published in 1970. About two hundred activists, including AIM members and anti-Wilson traditionalists from Pine Ridge, occupied the village. They brought explosives, rifles, and shotguns to defend themselves, and within hours the BIA police and Wilson's police surrounded them. FBI agents, federal marshals, and U.S. troops joined the siege. The standoff brought an immediate flood of TV, radio, and print journalists to the scene. As one observer later said, "Wounded Knee received more attention in its first week than the entire previous decade of Indian activism." For the first several weeks, national newscasts offered a positive or at least neutral account of the situation. Civil rights leaders, black activists, and supporters from non-Sioux tribes trekked to South Dakota to endorse the occupation.

In March, traditional leaders at the scene announced the formation of the Oglala Sioux Nation, declaring its independence from the United States. While being interviewed for network news, Means stated the occupiers' determination to shoot anyone who crossed their border. He and other occupiers demanded that the existing tribal government at Pine Ridge be abolished, and that they be free to return to their traditional forms of tribal organization, as they claimed the Sioux treaty of 1868 promised. Tensions subsequently mounted. On the night of April 26, 1973, the two sides fired between six and eight thousand rounds at each other. It's a "miracle that no one has been killed," one federal observer noted. "Some morning we will wake up to see 8 to 10 people dead" here. While a few officials demanded that the government isolate the village, cut off all supplies, and move in with force, moderates directed federal actions. "We could end the siege in a day if the marshals attacked," one conceded, but "we don't need an Indian massacre on our hands."

By early May, federal and Indian negotiators reached an agreement. The government promised to discuss the 1868 treaty, to investigate Wilson's administration of the reservation, and to prosecute any people accused of wrongdoing. In return, the Wounded Knee leaders promised to lay down their arms and to accept possible federal arrests. Few reporters remained to describe the event. When the standoff ended, the FBI arrested nearly 250 individuals. The casualties during the takeover numbered only three: two occupiers had died and one FBI agent had been wounded and paralyzed.

Tensions and violence at Pine Ridge continued for several more years, but AIM lost most of the public support it enjoyed when the occupation began. Interest waned, to some degree the public turned against the demonstrators, and the militants seemed to lose their cohesion. Federal officials visited Pine Ridge as promised, but when the talks concluded, they told their listeners that the treaty system had lapsed in 1871 and that the government had to accept the existing tribal governments. Indian militancy remained, but it proved less focused than earlier. In 1975 gunmen murdered two FBI agents at Pine Ridge, and the government quickly charged AIM activist Leonard Peltier in the case. On the basis of what many considered shaky evidence, he received two life terms for the murders. By that time most Americans had lost all interest in the Native protests, riots in the cities had ended, the Vietnam War was over, and the whole country seemed eager for calm. At the same time the violent militancy had changed the public image of tribal societies forever. Whatever else one could say, that helped American Indians to face the future with a new confidence.

Suggested Readings

Child, Brenda. *Boarding School Seasons: American Indian Families, 1900–1940.* Lincoln: University of Nebraska Press, 1998.

Cornell, Stephen. *The Return of the Native: American Indian Political Resurgence.* New York: Oxford University Press, 1988.

Cowger, Thomas W. *The National Congress of American Indians: The Founding Years.* Lincoln: University of Nebraska Press, 1999.

Deloria, Vine, Jr., and Clifford Lytle. *The Nations Within: The Past and Future of American Indian Sovereignty.* New York: Pantheon, 1984.

Iverson, Peter. *"We Are Still Here": American Indians in the Twentieth Century.* Wheeling, Ill.: Harlan Davidson, 1998.

Philp, Kenneth. *Termination Revisited: American Indians on the Trail to Self-Determination.* Lincoln: University of Nebraska Press, 1999.

Rosenthal, Nicolas G. *Reimagining Indian Country: Native American Migration and Identity in Twentieth Century Los Angeles.* Chapel Hill: University of North Carolina Press, 2012.

Smith, Paul Chaat, and Robert Allen Warrior. *Like a Hurricane: The Indian Movement from Alcatraz to Wounded Knee.* New York: The New Press, 1996.

Smith, Sherry L. *Hippies, Indians, and the Fight for Red Power.* New York: Oxford University Press, 2012.

Townsend, Kenneth. *World War II and the American Indian.* Albuquerque: University of New Mexico Press, 2000.

Wilkinson, Charles. *Blood Struggle: The Rise of Modern Indian Nations.* New York: W. W. Norton, 2005.

CHAPTER 8

Tradition, Change, and Challenge since 1970

Jealousy and Backlash

By the early 1970s most Americans had lost patience with the turbulence of the preceding decade. They longed for an end to the riots, demonstrations, and strident demands that bombarded them through television newscasts and their daily papers. When the Wounded Knee occupation ended, Native American militancy receded. Yet new federal laws and court decisions continued to broaden tribal governments' authority. The 1975 Indian Self-Determination and Educational Assistance Act gave tribes some of the independence that chiefs and militants had sought for years. Now, at least in theory, they dealt with federal officials on a government-to-government basis. This law reinforced the feelings of some whites that over the years fumbling bureaucrats and fuzzy-minded liberals had given the tribes too many benefits and far too much authority. They responded with a broad anti-Indian backlash that included violence in many parts of the country and continued sporadically for several decades.

Occasionally local officials in the West expressed anger and frustration when nearby reservation dwellers seemed to have reached near equality with other citizens. For example, in August 1979 a commissioner from Sanders County, Montana, fired off a letter to the Senate Select Committee on Indian Affairs. As others had demanded, he called on the senators to abolish the reservations because the government had "been taking care of RED MEN long enough." This assertion grew from the commissioner's belief that the tribes received special treatment and enjoyed more privileges than their non-Indian neighbors. When the self-determination act empowered tribes to regulate economic activity on their reservations, business leaders echoed those complaints. In January 1986 the Mobil Oil Corporation deleted a Colorado company from its list of approved subcontractors for work on the Navajo Reservation when it learned that the company's president had rejected tribal labor regulations that required hiring Navajo workers if they possessed the necessary skills. After calling the Indians "members of the vanquished and inferior race," this company president told tribal officials that he did not "recognize the legal existence of the so-called Navajo Preference in Employment Act of 1985 or any other part of the so-called Navajo Tribal Code."

Disputes over fishing and hunting rights listed in nineteenth-century treaties, the enforcement of state game laws, and the demands of local anglers and hunters all focused attention on what many whites perceived as "special treatment" for Indians. In 1974 Wisconsin state game wardens arrested several Anishinaabe (Ojibwa) men for spearfishing out of season. The Lac Courte Oreilles band sued, claiming that 1850s treaties guaranteed their the right to fish regardless of state regulations. After nearly a decade, a 1983 federal court decision upheld the Indians' right to spearfish when they chose. Sport fishers and northern Wisconsin resort owners reacted angrily, because they feared that Anishinaabe spearing of walleyed pike would harm both local fishing and the economy tied to it. Hundreds of protesters lined streams and lake banks to jeer, throw stones, and issue threats to the Indians while they fished. Pickup trucks sported bumper stickers reading "Save a Walleye, Spear a Squaw" as the spearing continued. Anti-Indian groups, including one in Wisconsin called Protect Americans' Rights and Resources, sued to overturn the 1983 decision, and the state offered to pay the Lac du Flambeau band $35.6 million if it would give up all but ceremonial rights to spearfishing. When the band refused, the suit continued, and in 1991 the federal judge fashioned an agreement under which the Indians and the state agreed on how many fish Native Americans could harvest each spring. The Lac du Flambeau band filed a countersuit against a group known as Stop Treaty Abuse (STA). In 1992 a court ruling in favor of the tribe prohibited the filing of more injunctions by sport fishing groups. Although it did not end the dispute entirely, this decision indicated clearly that the federal government would uphold some tribal treaty rights.

Similar protests erupted elsewhere, and during the late 1970s an anti-sovereignty movement developed. A national umbrella organization, the Citizens' Equal Rights Alliance (CERA), coordinated the activities of at least fifty member groups operating in thirty-three states and reportedly including at least a half-million members. In 1978 it published a manifesto entitled "200 Million Custers," which it distributed widely. The most outspoken and active of these groups included All Citizens Equal and Flathead Residents Earning Equality in Montana, the Committee for Equality in North Dakota, and Totally Equal Americans in Minnesota. In addition to leading local protests and circulating anti-Indian materials, members of these organizations flooded BIA offices with as many as six hundred protest letters a week. Frequently they worked to clog state and federal court dockets with nuisance suits, including twenty actions by Montana ranchers against the confederated Salish and Kootenai (Flathead) tribes over disputed water rights.

Bitter anti-Indian feelings developed in Washington State as well. Usually these stemmed from disputes over fishing and hunting issues or other land-use questions. One angrily worded manifesto attacked tribal efforts to limit or control hunting and fishing by non-Indians. "Uncle Sam is giving America back to the Indians," its authors raged. To these protesters it seemed as if federal bureaucrats were running a "nationwide, sinister juggernaut, exacting from Americans sacrifices of property, money, rights, and identity" and turning these over to the tribes. In Montana, some non-Indians living on the Flathead Reservation became outraged when Indians began enforcing new regulations.

After being arrested by tribal officers for hunting without a permit on his own land, one bitter resident defended himself, saying that "no Indian government is going to tell me what I can do on my own land or anywhere else. I don't recognize that government's authority at all." In 1981, Crow Indians in southeastern Montana blocked a highway bridge across the Bighorn River to keep non-Indians from coming onto their reservation to fish. CERA officers rallied public support, filed lawsuits, and even proposed legislation to reduce the authority of tribal governments.

When challenged by people who said that their actions had a racist base, many anti-Indian protesters rejected the charge. "Now don't you make us out to be racists and extremists," Del Palmer, one of the most outspoken, said. Almost immediately thereafter, however, he complained that "the time's coming that we're going to have . . . Indian this and Indian that in government. What would happen if our next governor was an Indian? We'd all be down the drain." Whether they believed it or just thought that the voters demanded such rhetoric, some elected Montana officials used that line of reasoning. One state legislator disagreed that white racism played any role in the disputes. At the same time, he chided Flathead attorney Pat Smith, saying, "Pat, your problem is, you don't think like a white man." William Covey, who had helped found the CERA in 1988, claimed that racists could be found on both sides. "If an Indian admits that he is a racist, that's O.K.," he said. But "if a non-Indian says he's a racist, that's terrible." Responding to such ideas, most Indian leaders remained calm, and one observer noted the controversy existed because "lots of whites are just plain jealous."

There can be little doubt that growing local sovereignty of Indians kept people in many parts of the country angry because of what appeared to be favoritism toward Native Americans and because of the increasing impact tribal courts and regulations had on people living on or near reservations. For example, the Chemehuevi Paiutes, who live just west of the Colorado River along Lake Havasu in eastern California, faced a storm of protest from whites residing on their land when the tribe raised land rental fees. The modest rents lagged far below those charged by neighboring property owners, but the new rates angered many of the leaseholders who had enjoyed the previously low charges. In the early 1990s the Seneca tribe in New York State encountered similar difficulties. A century earlier, in 1892, tribal leaders had leased the land on which the town of Salamanca now stood. The original agreement called for an annual payment of $17,000, which may have been a reasonable sum when it was signed one hundred years ago. However, by the 1990s the situation had changed drastically. Some Indian activists suggested that the town-dwellers might be evicted, and reporters from New York City poured in to record the dispute. A few angry whites considered destroying their homes or other property, but when the dispute ended, the city fathers agreed to a new lease in the amount of $60 million per annum. Disputes like these two meant that the public could not avoid the changing status and power of tribal governments.

Legislation and Court Actions

More isolated than most Indian groups, Alaska Native people received little attention until 1959, when that Alaska gained statehood. Within just a few years the Alaska Federated Natives organized several regional associations to protect their land and resource claims. Their demands led to the 1971 passage of the Alaska Native Claims Settlement, which upheld their rights to forty-four million acres of land and paid the groups some $962 million for other claims they held. That action came about as a result of new legislation and court decisions that focused on the concept of self-determination and related issues. Presidents Kennedy, Johnson, and Nixon all took an interest in Indian affairs. Johnson gave an address entitled "The Forgotten American," and he called for an end to termination. He then set up the National Council on Indian Opportunity and charged it with recommending new directions for federal-tribal cooperation. Continuing studies of reservation conditions produced reports on Indian health and educational opportunities that suggested important policy changes. The Indian Education Act of 1972 and the 1975 Indian Self-Determination and Educational Assistance Act provided new funding and greater attention to Indian needs and ideas than had been paid earlier.

Asking for and obtaining some local sovereignty brought unexpected and occasionally harmful results for tribal groups. The Navajos found, to their surprise, that the Indian Civil Rights Act of 1968 might be used against them. Apparently that is just what some of its congressional supporters expected. In 1968 a public quarrel between the white tribal attorney and one member of the tribal council occurred. When the council banned the attorney from the reservation, he sued to be allowed to return and won under the terms of the new legislation. Ten years later, in *Oliphant v. Suquamish Indians*, the court ruled that tribal governments could not try nonmembers for criminal actions on the reservation. That same year, however, the *Santa Clara v. Martinez* decision gave tribes the right to determine their own membership criteria. The case stemmed from traditional practices on which the Pueblo government had decided that only children of Santa Clara Pueblo men could be tribal members. When the Pueblos decided to exclude the Martinez children from the tribal rolls because their father was a Navajo, the family had sued. Although traditionalists and women's rights supporters expressed shock and dismay, the decision strengthened tribal courts in dealing with internal reservation matters. It also gave reservation governments immunity from suits filed against them under the 1968 Indian Civil Rights Act.

Indian religious practices continued to come under federal and state scrutiny despite the American Indian Religious Freedom Act. Peyote use drew mixed responses throughout the twentieth century. As early as 1940, the Navajo tribal council legislated against its use and possession on the reservation. Years later the Native American Church sued the tribe, but in 1959 a court in Arizona ruled that tribal leaders had the authority to block even the religious use of peyote. A few years later, the result differed after authorities arrested and then convicted John Woody and other Navajos for peyote use in California. In its 1964 *People v. Woody* decision, the Supreme Court of California overturned the convictions, ruling that California could not interfere with those who took the drug in a religious ceremony. Nevertheless, a 1990 decision showed how easily Indian religious freedom could be challenged. Two members of the Native American Church who worked as drug and alcohol counselors for the state of Oregon lost their jobs for taking part in a peyote ceremony at church. In *Employment Division of Oregon v. Smith* the U.S. Supreme Court ruled that the state could prohibit the religious role of peyote because it had the right to regulate drug use. This decision remained in force until 1993, when the Religious Restoration Act became law. Some disputes focused on the use of feathers from eagles and other protected birds, and in 1986 the U.S. Supreme Court ruled that tribal religious ceremonial needs for feathers did not entitle Indians to possess them outside the usual set of federal regulations. The issue of tribal rights to bird parts and feathers from protected species for religious ceremonies remains an unsettled and contentious one.

Resources and Economic Issues

After World War II, employment and economic self-sufficiency remained elusive for many Native Americans living on reservations. Most tribes held lands with comparatively little value and few resources, but some enjoyed better circumstances. During the 1950s tribal lands contained at least 3 percent of the oil and natural gas then located in the United States. In addition, Indians owned at least 10 percent of the known coal deposits in the country, amounting to between one hundred and two hundred billion tons. Some reservations had uranium deposits, valuable forests, or water resources potentially valuable to corporations and a possible source of income and jobs to tribal groups. Unfortunately, when corporations negotiated drilling or mining leases, some reservation leaders lacked the expertise to obtain fair payments. For example, the Peabody Coal Company persuaded the Navajo and Hopi tribes of the Southwest to sign contracts that paid them only 17.5 cents per ton of coal the company mined on their land. That miserly fee came at a time when coal prices were rising sharply, so that the tribes got less than a 2 percent royalty for their fossil fuel.

Responsibility for negotiating reasonable contracts lay with the BIA, and clearly that agency's officials were not up to the task. Often the office staff understood little more than their Indian charges did, and existing federal legislation allowed the contracts to operate for years before any changes could be made. In 1976 the Department of the Interior raised its leasing rates to 17 percent, roughly eight times higher than negotiated previously. Because they realized how bad the leases were, tribal leaders began to protest. On some reservations reformers and younger leaders attacked those who had signed the existing contracts, gaining leadership roles for themselves. Hoping to redo the leases and gain more funds for tribal needs, in 1974 some reservation officials formed a federation of tribes with natural resource holdings. A year later they broadened the group and founded the Council of Energy Resource Tribes (CERT). During its history, this organization had as many as twenty-five member tribes of more. It worked to gather information on resource production and worked to make the data available to interested groups. In early 1977, CERT chairman Peter MacDonald tried to turn the organization into a resource cartel modeled after OPEC, run by the Arab oil-producing nations, but the move failed. Still, MacDonald's effort brought new attention to reservation-based economic issues, and for a time some tribes increased oil production as well.

Although many Indians seemed to welcome resource development because of the new jobs they meant for their reservations, some objected. At Black Mesa in Arizona and on tribal lands in eastern Montana, serious questions arose about the environmental costs of large-scale mining. By the 1990s even some ranchers in eastern Wyoming joined their tribal neighbors in trying to head off Peabody Coal's large-scale strip mining on grazing lands that had been in their families for generations. For those who had worked as uranium miners during the 1950s and 1960s, questions over resource development became intensely personal. By the late 1970s, lung cancer swept through the ranks of former Navajo miners who had worked at Kerr-McGee mines in Arizona and New Mexico years earlier. "No one ever told us of the danger," one tribal council member remarked. The mines paid well and brought the only jobs that Indians there ever had, yet "now the people are dying."

In the Black Hills and nearby Montana and Wyoming, open-pit uranium mining left ruined landscapes and dangerous radioactive waste at the sites. By 1979 the Department of the Interior described contamination there as unsafe for animals. Meanwhile, Indian activists complained that the Black Hills were "not just another mine site," but rather "a spiritual center" for tribal people. In Arizona, Stewart Udall, former secretary of the interior, worked to obtain compensation for the families of miners who had died from cancer after working in the uranium mines. He visited Navajo communities, gathered information about the illnesses and deaths, and filed four suits on behalf of miners and people in Utah who lived downwind from atomic test sites. By 1990 courts had ruled against him in three of the suits. Still, his efforts paid off because that year Congress set up a compensation plan that would give $100,000 to miners who contracted cancer or to the families of those who died from it, and half that much to the so-called down-winders as well. Some people eligible for compensation never got any because they lacked evidence like weekly pay stubs and old medical records needed to file applications, so the issue has continued into the twenty-first century. As a cost-cutting measure, officials in the George W. Bush administration halted payments to all but the actual miners or their families, eliminated the down-winders from coverage, and they called for further study of the medical links between mining and atomic tests and increased risks of cancer.

Timber and other rights also continued to disturb relations between the tribes and their neighbors. In Wisconsin the Mole Lake Anishinaabe (Ojibwa) retained their treaty right not only to spearfish, as discussed earlier, but also to cut timber freely. By 1990, they had authorization to begin cutting in the Northern Highland–American Legion State Forest in the north-central part of the state. They planned to sell the timber to nearby sawmills but also hoped to build tribally operated mills. At the time, the five other Anishinaabe bands in northern Wisconsin had not yet decided whether to exercise their timber-cutting rights. Across the country other reservation groups' property claims antagonized or frightened their neighbors. For example, during the late 1980s in Tacoma, Washington, the Puyallup tribe held rights to more than three hundred acres of downtown property worth several hundred million dollars. In 1988 the fourteen hundred mostly poor tribal members voted to drop their claims in return for a promised $162 million in cash and land, with an additional promise of jobs. On the East Coast, in 1972 the Penobscot and Passamaquoddy Indians sued asking for 60 percent of the state of Maine, which had been taken from them illegally in the decades after American independence. This brought quick action from Congress, and in 1980 President Jimmy Carter signed the Maine Indian Settlement Act, paying the tribes $81.5 million as compensation and to give them funds to create a tribal land base.

Issues related to water supplies and to lands lost to flooding behind government dams continue to raise serious questions. Nearly all disputes dealing with tribal water rights are based on tribal claims that resulted from the Supreme Court's 1908 *Winters v. United States* decision. There the court found that whenever the federal government had established a reservation, that action also set aside enough water to allow the Indians to carry out their economic activities. It also guaranteed that the tribes would not lose their water rights if they did not immediately use them. The Tohono O'odham people of southern Arizona received an annual allotment of Colorado River water from the Central Arizona Project in 1977 in exchange for dropping their suit against non-Indian water users. During the 1980s more than fifty suits over tribal water rights clogged the courts, but in each new decision the reservation groups won. In 1989 the Shoshone and Arapaho people of Wyoming received a large grant of water. Fifteen years later, in 2004, the Gila River Community Water Settlement awarded the Gila River Indian Community in Arizona nearly $2 million for irrigation projects and more than six hundred thousand acre feet of water for its farms. The water-rights issues remain unclear, and claims from Indians and their neighbors in the West are so contentious that at present dozens of cases continue to work their way through the courts or other forms of arbitration.

Education

As tribal groups gained increasing control over their own affairs, they turned more of their attention to educational matters. When Native Americans moved to the cities, many encountered the negative stereotypes of Indians that appeared regularly in public-school curricula. A growing sense of Indianness and self-awareness of Red Power led to complaints about these classroom materials. Partly in response to this dissatisfaction, in 1964 Rupert Costo and Jeannette Henry Costo founded the American Indian Historical Society. Seeking to bring knowledge about their past to Indians, in 1970 they published *Textbooks and the American Indian*, which demonstrated the one-sided and inaccurate treatment public-school textbooks gave when discussing Native Americans as part of the nation's history. Not long after their book appeared, a broader examination of over one hundred U.S. history textbooks supported their charges. That study reported that "the notion of the blood-curdling, perilous, massacring savage" continued to be common in existing texts. To remedy that, within just a few years the Newberry Library of Chicago sponsored academic meetings in Washington, Chicago, and Los Angeles that brought university and college instructors together to develop strategies for incorporating historically accurate Native American materials into existing courses. Those efforts persuaded national textbook publishers to make numerous deletions and corrections and to insert accurate material into their products.

Creating an Indian Historical Society and putting pressure on textbook publishers certainly brought results. Yet many tribes and individuals continued to need help or change closer to home. Although federal programs sent increasing funds to local school districts, Indians rarely saw evidence that the money reached their children's schools. They began to question local administrators, and when that seemed to have no effect, they elected tribal members to school boards. In the West, large tribal populations made this easier than in much of the country, and by the mid-1970s at least seventy-eight school districts on or near reservations had Native American majorities on their boards. Others conducted sit-ins such as that carried out by Navajo parents in Ship Rock, New Mexico. Although these actions brought some response, the Navajo tribal government decided to establish its own school and in 1966 opened the Rough Rock Demonstration School. Founded with the idea that it should provide students with a solid base of tribal language and culture, Rough Rock offered bilingual classes and sought to develop tribally based instructional materials. Tribal leaders and school officials controlled all aspects of the curricula and went so far as to exclude non-Indian faculty at the school from any role in setting administrative policies.

Other tribes followed suit, as Indian-operated schools opened from the Midwest to the Pacific. In New Mexico several used bilingual instruction and tribally based classroom material. Tribes in Montana operated the Rocky Boy School, providing their students with Anishinaabe and Cree history, language, and lit-erature. Working with preschool children, the Viejas Indian School in Alpine, California, offered help similar to what Head Start gave other American pre-schoolers. It also operated after-school programs for older children. In upper midwestern cities, relatively heavy concentrations of Native Americans result-ed in efforts to begin similar institutions there. Anishinaabe and Dakota stu-dents had schools in both Minneapolis and St. Paul, and local Native Americans opened one in Milwaukee, Wisconsin, as well. Staff and administrators of these institutions tried to develop and incorporate teaching materials based on tribal culture, history, and language. Their success in doing so varied. Among some groups the students had little motivation because their parents did not use the tribal language at home. Other groups had few people who possessed both lan-guage and teaching skills. Some tribal elders complained that having to compete with the elements of TV-spread American popular culture made retaining their languages and cultures difficult at best.

In trying to overcome such problems during the late 1960s, some tribes decid-ed to found their own colleges. They hoped that such institutions would provide skilled workers and trained leaders to help run reservation affairs. The Navajos led this movement and in 1968 founded Navajo Community College in Many Farms, Arizona. In 1971 Congress passed the Navajo Community College Act. The tribal Board of Regents strove to ensure that Navajo history, culture, and language had a central place in the course offerings. In 1997 the school was re-named Diné (Navajo) College. The founding and early success of this institution encouraged other tribes and groups to open colleges, often—but not always—located on their reservations. The Tribally Controlled Community College As-sistance Act of 1978 provided federal encouragement and funding that enabled many groups to establish schools on their reservations. As of 2013, thirty-eight tribal colleges and tech schools operated in twelve states. These included each of the states along the Canadian border west from Michigan to Washington, Kan-sas and Nebraska in the Midwest, and California, Arizona, and New Mexico in the Southwest. Almost all of these institutions are community colleges offering the first two years of college academic classes as well as technical and vocational courses. Usually underfunded, they often lack good facilities or adequate equip-ment but all have strong support from the tribal communities, send many of their graduates to four-year colleges, and are sources of intense local pride.

Ada Deer

Born in 1935 at the Menominee hospital in Keshena, Wisconsin, much of Ada Deer's life has focused on affairs of the Menominee people and their reservation. Her mother, a nurse from a wealthy Philadelphia family, married John Deer while working on the reservation. When Ada was six, the family moved to Milwaukee seeking better jobs but soon returned. In 1953 she graduated from high school and enrolled at the University of Wisconsin, where she majored in social work and served on the Youth Advisory Council of the Governor's Human Rights Commission. After receiving her bachelor's degree in 1957, she attended Columbia University and in 1961 got a master's degree there. For much of the next fifteen years she sought to improve living conditions on the Menominee Reservation when the federal termination policy nearly destroyed the tribe. Working closely with Joseph Preloznik and others, she helped to found DRUMS, Determination of Rights and Unity of Menominee Stockholders, to oppose Menominee Enterprises, Inc., begun after the Menominee Termination Act of 1954 to manage tribal assets. In 1973 the effort succeeded, as President Nixon signed the Menominee Restoration Act. In 1976 Deer joined the faculty of the School of Social Work at the University of Wisconsin. After she lost several races for public office, in 1993 President Clinton appointed her as the first woman assistant secretary of the interior (director of the BIA). Four years later she served as the acting chair of the National Indian Gaming Commission. In 2000 she became the head of the American Indian Studies Program at the University of Wisconsin.

Sources: Nicholas Perloff, *Menominee Drums: Tribal Termination and Restoration* (Norman: University of Oklahoma Press, 1982); Nancy Oestreich Laurie, "Ada Deer Champion of Tribal Sovereignty," in *Sifters: Native American Women's Lives*, ed. Theda Perdue (New York: Oxford University Press, 2001), 223–41.

Many young Indians left reservations or urban enclaves to attend colleges and universities. Their presence there led to demands for American Indian Studies programs. In 1968, Native students at the University of Minnesota asked for classes in their own languages, including courses on Indians' roles in the state's history. Surprisingly, although this effort came at the time the American Indian Movement began in Minneapolis, the push to establish such courses remained peaceful. News of their success at Minnesota brought calls for similar offerings at schools across the country, and by the mid-1980s well over a hundred colleges and universities had incorporated them. The programs vary widely, from institutions that offer only a few undergraduate courses or a minor to others that award a PhD. These academic innovations have brought a new sense of urgency to many efforts designed to help the tribes retain their cultures. Critical language programs not only offer courses in tribal languages but also gather oral versions of ceremonies, poetry, history, and religious beliefs. Some work to produce dictionaries, grammars, children's stories, and other material that will help keep alive tribal languages that have only a few elderly speakers still using them.

Tribal Acknowledgment

As federal willingness to grant self-determination and limited local sovereignty to tribes continued, groups that wanted to be recognized as Indians came forward to press their claims. From the passage of the 1934 Indian Reorganization Act through the late 1970s, nearly thirty tribes achieved that goal. Some persuaded an interested congressional representative to introduce legislation to help them, and a few benefited from executive actions granting them tribal status. Once that happened, their members became eligible for BIA programs and access to the Indian Health Service. A few groups received other benefits too. In 1980, for example, the Houlton Band of Maliseets in Maine, numbering about 350 people, gained tribal recognition. This enabled them to share in the Maine Indian Land Claim settlement and brought the band about $1 million. With those funds they purchased some land and reestablished a formal presence in the state. Their success brought them legal status as Indians and the opportunity to take part in existing federal programs.

As ethnic awareness permeated American society by the last quarter of the twentieth century, Native Americans wanted to have their ethnic identity made public, and at the same time they looked forward to receiving the benefits that tribal status would give them. Even before the Maliseets won their struggle in Maine, observers had called for some established framework that could be used to settle claims related to Indian identity. As a result, in 1978 Congress established the Federal Acknowledgment Program. Its name has changed slightly since then, but the process it began continues to the present. In some ways the procedure resembles that of the Indian Claims Commission that operated right after World War II. Tribes must apply and go through a series of hearings, where they present the evidence gathered in support of their application. Many of the petitioning groups consist of people who claim to be the descendants of tribes or bands assumed to have disappeared generations or even centuries ago. Perhaps their ancestors purposely hid in the forests or mountains as they tried to survive. Some became so thoroughly acculturated that their neighbors had no idea they were Indians. Others represent substantial intermarriage with non-Indians, including blacks and Cajuns, over generations. For many reasons, at some time in the past they ceased to be recognized as "real" Indians.

Federal Acknowledgment Program officials, expecting to sort through the claims of perhaps a few dozen groups, set up a list of requirements they thought would make it easy to decide which people qualified for federal recognition.

They were wrong. What began as an open process became one that demanded increasing amounts of data, often nearly impossible for the applicants to obtain. During the first ten years of the program, 111 separate applications reached BIA officials' desks. This number continued to grow, and at present more than two hundred groups still await action. Not only did the larger than expected number of applications clog the process, long-recognized tribes became increasingly worried about the recognition of new one. They reasoned that federal funds for Indian-related programs would remain stable, and if the number of new tribes grew, then the existing ones would lose some of their funding. Members of recognized tribes had come to fill most positions at the BIA, and some of these bureaucrats reflected the biases of their home communities.

Despite such difficulties, as of 2013 the program continues to operate. To prove their Indian heritage, applicants must submit documents that show that they have always been considered Indians, have lived in a particular place continually, are descended from a historically known group, have had some tribal government or authority over the members, and possess some criteria for group membership. These requirements call for just the sort of materials the applicants have the most difficulty producing. Because their ancestors tried to fade into the countryside to avoid conflict with their white neighbors, now they have great difficulty in securing the required documents. Once considerable intermarriage with either local blacks or whites occurred, small tribes often lost their spoken language, and the descendants of such unions came to be seen merely as neighbors rather than as tribal members. Certainly the need to produce evidence that some type of tribal government existed and functioned for generations remains a major stumbling block for many of the petitioners. In 2013 the number of federally recognized tribes stands at 566, a number that has not increased in several years, and barely half of the twenty-some groups that went through the process had achieved recognition. More than thirty years after the Federal Acknowledgement Program began, critics continue to denounce the entire process.

Responding to the repeated complaints about it, in August 2013 the BIA proposed new guidelines to streamline the program. Yet like almost every effort to modify the process, critics have attacked the new rules even before they can be put into effect. In Kent, a small western Connecticut town, citizens have opposed the land claims of the tiny Schaghticoke tribe for years. A decade ago they fought Indian efforts to gain recognition, fearing that the tribe might gain title to property in the town. Now they have persuaded their local selectman and their congressional representative to resist the new plans. They worry that the tribe will open businesses to compete with the local merchants, and might even build a casino in the middle of the small community. Other Native groups share the whites' doubts about having more tribes recognized, often because they feel their own land claims or casino operations will be threatened. Along the Columbia River in Washington State tribes living upstream worry that if groups near the

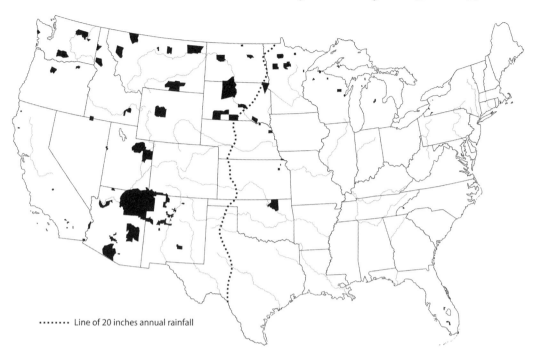

········ Line of 20 inches annual rainfall

Larger Indian reservations, 1980–1990

mouth of the river gain official recognition, that would cut into the number of salmon available to tribes farther from the coast. Clearly this issue is far from settled.

Gambling and Casinos

By the twenty-first century, tribal leaders faced a variety of contentious issues that often put them at odds with their non-Indian neighbors. As it had in the past, gaming or casino gambling drew much public attention and debate. Tribal cultures have included small-scale gambling for centuries, so when some groups opened their bingo halls to the public, few Indians gave it much thought. Reservation gambling facilities as they exist today started in 1979, when the Seminole Tribe of Florida began awarding $10,000 prizes at their newly opened reservation bingo hall near Fort Lauderdale. At the time, state law limited bingo payments to only $100, and so Florida officials moved quickly to close what they considered to be illegal tribal games. When the Seminoles sued, a federal court ruled that the state had no jurisdiction over the size of bingo payouts. The tribe opened several more bingo halls and soon had nearly ten thousand players pouring millions of dollars into its treasury. Within the next decade, other reservation groups began opening various gambling facilities as leaders saw the potential for income and employment for their people.

During the 1980s California authorities tried to close existing Indian gaming facilities and to prevent the development of any new ones, but they failed. In 1987 one band sued the state, and the resulting *California v. Cabazon Band of Mission Indians* decision declared that California had no authority over reservation activities. The next year Congress passed the Indian Gaming Regulatory Act, which established a National Indian Gaming Commission to oversee tribal gaming issues and operations. The legislation provided funds through the BIA as loans to help tribes build facilities ranging from modest bingo halls to multimillion-dollar resorts. In less than a decade over one hundred tribes had opened some kind of gambling facilities in twenty-four states, and by 2011 at least 240 tribes had 460 gambling operations. Their gross annual revenues exceeded $27 billion. Granted, nearly 40 percent of the earnings came from only a few tribes, but Indian leaders recognized the immense popularity of gambling and began referring to it as "the new buffalo" for their people.

The federal legislation set up three classes of gambling that tribes might offer, but nearly all of the resulting disputes focus on what they call Class III gambling. This includes modern, sophisticated games such as slot machines, blackjack tables, and other Las Vegas–style games. States that allow any gambling had few choices but to accept Indian practices if such operations remained on tribal land. In California the governor objected and refused to negotiate compacts between the state and the tribes, but the federal court decision there forced state authorities to sign gaming agreements. In 1998, at least 65 percent of California voters supported Proposition 5, which allowed Indian gaming in that state. Casino operators in Nevada objected to the spread of Indian competition in their customer-rich neighboring state but had little recourse. On the East Coast, Donald Trump sued in federal court to shut down tribal competition to his Atlantic City operations, but he lost.

The most spectacular success came to the Mashantucket Pequots in Connecticut. In 1983 they received federal acknowledgment as a tribe and since then have enlarged their membership from fewer than one hundred people to about three hundred in 2013. By the 1990s they had added some fifteen hundred acres to their tiny reservation, and in 1992 they opened Foxwoods Casino there. Within easy driving distance for nearly fifty million people, their gaming operation became an instant multimillion-dollar success. At first, Connecticut governor Lowell Weicker rejected their efforts to install slot-machine gambling at the casino. When tribal leaders offered to donate $1 million each year from their profits to help support assistance programs for economically depressed small towns in the state, he withdrew his objections. Within just a couple of years Foxwoods generated hundreds of millions of dollars, which the tribe used to build a resort complex, a museum, and a historical research facility. It has subsidized national multitribal meetings and given money to help build the National Museum of the American Indian in Washington, D.C., and it stands as the showcase for successful Indian gaming operations.

A few isolated groups have realized only small profits and several have actually closed their gaming facilities because they lost money, but various issues continue to make commercial gambling on reservations contentious. In 1990 at the St. Regis Mohawk Reservation in northern New York, Mohawks fought bitterly over building casinos. Elected leaders opposed reservation-based gambling, while Warrior Society members backed it. Before the dispute ended, two people were murdered and a newly built casino building burned. Twice since then reservation voters there have rejected building a new casino, and tribal members remain sharply divided over the matter. In New Mexico, members of the Mescalero Apache Tribe sued to have the laws allowing reservation-based gambling declared unconstitutional. In Arizona in 2001, the operators of dog- and horse-racing tracks brought suit, hoping to prevent the governor from negotiating gambling contracts between the state and Arizona tribes. The court ruled in their favor and sent the matter back to the legislature to be reworked. Although many tribal leaders see the right to offer casino gambling on their reservations as demonstrating a new degree of tribal sovereignty, issues surrounding gaming still generate heated debate. For example, in the 2002 general election, Arizona voters faced three separate gaming initiatives on their ballots. Despite those efforts to block gaming, none of these halted the building of large profitable casinos that now operate in both the Phoenix and Tucson metropolitan areas.

Repatriation of Tribal Remains

By the 1970s, Indian activists had stepped up demands for holdings in American museums, archaeology laboratories, and university research collections to be returned to the tribes. They objected to the display, storage, and study of funerary items, sacred objects, and skeletal remains that had been found on tribal burial grounds during the preceding two centuries. Archaeologists defended themselves, saying that they were trying to preserve tribal cultures. The activists responded by charging that, to the scholars, the only real Indians were long-dead ones. Most of the argument focused on artifacts and remains gathered from Indian burial sites during the nineteenth century by amateur pot hunters and military officers. Thousands of such items had reached the Smithsonian Institution or other museums and research centers, and only gradually was that trend reversed. Beginning with the 1906 Antiquities Act and moving through the Historic Sites Act of 1935 and the 1966 National Historic Preservation Act, the laws began to limit what might be collected, as well as where collecting might take place and under what circumstances. Once Congress passed the 1978 American Indian Religious Freedom Act, such discussions became central to the disposition of the more than half a million tribal skeletal remains and sacred objects of all sorts held by museums. In 1987, Robert McCormick Adams, former secretary of the Smithsonian Institution, announced that curators, anthropologists, and archaeologists had "an obligation to return skeletal remains in our collections to tribal descendants."

Since then, two new laws have taken the requirements much further and changed the situation entirely. In 1989, legislation creating the Smithsonian Institution's National Museum of the American Indian called for the return of skeletal and funerary remains to the appropriate tribes when connections to those groups could be found. The next year Congress passed the Native American Graves Protection and Repatriation Act. It directed that U.S. agencies and other organizations that receive federal funds identify and return artifacts and skeletal remains to the tribes whenever possible. That directive effectively included nearly all of the museums, historical societies, and universities in the country and so had a greater effect than all the earlier legislation put together. It called on museums and other repositories to examine the Indian materials in their possession and then to notify tribes if the collections included items that might have come from their ancestors. For the first time in generations, perhaps ever, curators went through dusty storage bins and seldom-visited archives, taking inventories of what they had. The results of that effort astonished many in the museum world, because neither they nor their predecessors had ever conducted such a thorough evaluation of their holdings. Often they had only a vague idea of what their collections included.

Professional archaeologists and curators feared that the new laws might lead to what they considered unreasonable tribal demands for everything on museum shelves. In some places they fought the spirit of the law whenever possible. For example, the museum staff at the University of California at Berkeley denounced the new rules. Frank Norick, a researcher there, became outraged and complained that "science should not be sacrificed on the altar of religious beliefs!" Despite similar denunciations elsewhere, increased public awareness and continuing federal pressure brought much of the debate to a close. Within just a few years, the National Museum of Natural History had returned more than 18,500 cultural items and skeletal remains to tribes across the country, including groups of Hawaiian Islanders. Often, tribal elders held public ceremonies to rebury skeletons identified as belonging to their ancestors. Of equal importance, sacred objects such as pipes, wampum belts, religious masks, and medicine bundles have been sent back to tribal authorities as well. At present, tribal leaders and scholars have reached agreement on many issues that divided them bitterly only a decade or so ago. In some cases Indians have declined materials being returned because they lack the facilities, trained personnel, and funds to care for the items effectively. In 2013 two Paris auction houses offered Hopi Kachina (Katsina) masks for sale. Tribal leaders appealed the sales, saying that these were living, sacred beings, not just ceremonial objects, but the sales proceeded. Hearing their plea, one of the buyers gave the items he had bought to the tribe. Debates over which materials need to be returned to tribal groups and what group should get a particular item continue.

Religious Sites and Rights

Related directly to the return of medicine bundles and other religious materials, the disputes over the protection of particular Native groups' sacred sites continue to fuel debates and spark demonstrations into the twenty-first century. This issue first received public attention during the early 1950s when the Indian Claims Commission proposed to settle the government's quarrel with the Lakotas over the Black Hills. The ICC offered millions of dollars for the lands illegally taken from the tribe, but the Lakotas rejected the settlement, demanding that the land be returned. Since then, Native Americans have become increasingly outspoken about their religious sites and the need to return them or preserve them for tribal use. During the 1980s, when the Peabody Coal Company began large-scale strip-mining of coal in the Four Corners area of Arizona, New Mexico, Colorado, and Utah, both the Hopi and Navajo tribes objected. Traditionalists opposed the mining because it destroyed the land itself. To them, "the Mesa, the air, the water, are Holy Elements" to be prayed to for the "well-being of each generation." Others complained that pollution from the operations hid the sacred San Francisco Peaks so that they could not view the mountains. In the 1983 *Wilson v. Block* decision the tribes lost a suit in which they tried to halt construction of a ski resort in the same mountain area. During the winter of 2012–13 the tribes protested the use of effluent water for snow-making on the same mountains by a ski resort near Flagstaff, so the disputes continue.

   In other places the results of similar disputes varied. The Chumash Indians of Southern California won a delay in the construction of a proposed natural-gas terminal at Point Conception on the coast. At the end of the 1970s a consortium of power companies began planning for the facility. The Chumash Indians enlisted help from nearby activists, and the resulting site occupation and demonstrations caused enough negative publicity to postpone the project. By 1980, falling utility prices made the plant economically unfeasible, so construction halted. The tribes lost their battles to protect particular sites in several other locales. During that decade the U.S. Forest Service decided to open a road in Northern California, in order to improve access to timber and recreational areas nearby. However, its own expert testified that the road might destroy sites essential to holding ceremonies that "constitute the heart of the Northwest [Indian] religious beliefs and practices." When California tribes sued, lower courts supported their religious claims. However, in 1988, the U.S. Supreme Court ruled against them, finding that the American Indian Religious Freedom Act offered no protection in this case. Construction of the road never took place, but the case set a legal precedent against Indian rights that may be used in the future.

Sometimes religious disputes divided reservation communities and instigated harsh feuds. In Arizona the Hopi villages split in 1989 when the tribal council approved a gravel pit for workers at the tribally owned construction company to use as a source for highway material. The pit did not occupy a sacred site, but it lay near the area from which the Snake Society priests gathered live snakes for their annual ceremonies. The priests complained that the site was the "nesting place" of the snakes and that the council had reached its decision "without consulting us." They feared that "if we let go of any part of our religion, our Hopi way of life will be discontinued." With that level of anxiety, the tribal leaders found a compromise to the dispute. Farther south in Arizona, astronomers from universities in the United States, Italy, and Germany chose Mount Graham as the best place in the country for a new multi-mirror observatory. The first investigation of the site produced no objections. In fact, several Apache elders said that it had no religious significance for their people. Others in the tribe thought differently, however, and a bitter fight over building the observatory broke out. A group known as the Apache Survival Coalition sued to halt the project. Later environmentalists joined the suit, claiming that the construction threatened the survival of the endangered Mount Graham red squirrel. These objections failed to stop the project, and in 1988 Congress approved it. Six years later a federal court ruled against the Apaches, allowing construction to continue. By 2008 the universities had added all of the telescopes and mirrors planned for the site.

Team Mascots

Throughout much of the twentieth century, high school, university, and professional athletic teams across the country used Indian names and symbols. Although some tribal groups may have objected earlier, in 1972 AIM leader Dennis Banks and others attacked the use of Indian mascots as racist and demeaning. Threatening suits against the owners of the Atlanta Braves and Cleveland Indians baseball teams for using Indian caricatures as mascots and for marketing these mascots on team souvenirs, the activists focused national attention on the issue. College teams across the country had such nicknames and mascots as Indians, Redmen, Illini, Seminoles, and Warriors. Professional teams in baseball, basketball, football, and hockey competed as Braves, Black Hawks, Chiefs, Indians, Redskins, and Warriors. Some thoughtful tribal leaders pointed out that except for the Fighting Irish of Notre Dame, few teams, if any, used non-Indian national, ethnic, or racial groups as their symbols. They denounced the use of tribal terms or supposed Indian attributes, calling these acts of cultural thievery.

To them teams that used such mascots were guilty of stealing parts of tribal culture. Many Indians found the caricatures more objectionable than the mere use of the names. The Atlanta Braves celebrated each home run they hit by having "Chief Noc-a-homa" come out of his tepee and dance. At the University of Illinois, "Chief Illiniwek" amused crowds at football games, and fans of the Florida State University Seminoles and of the Atlanta Braves did "the tomahawk chop" to celebrate their teams' achievements.

When protesters objected to universities and professional teams promoting such images and actions, many fans and alumni reacted angrily. They considered such complaints attacks on tradition and good fun. After all, some said, teams used their mascots to recognize Indian bravery and courage, and many people laughed off the complaints. Native American students at Dartmouth, Illinois, and Stanford Universities took the issue more seriously, and they campaigned to have the mascots dropped. At both Dartmouth and Stanford they succeeded, and the teams now play under new nicknames. The authorities at Illinois, however, refused to act. In fact, in 1989, when the protests reached their peak there, the university chancellor defended Chief Illiniwek as a "dignified, respected, [and] even [a] revered symbol" of the school's teams. The dispute there attracted so much attention that before it ended, the state legislature adopted a resolution supporting the university administration.

Despite strong fan support for using tribal names and traditional symbols to represent their teams, criticism grew. The National Congress of American Indians had denounced using tribal symbols for decades. In 1999 the NAACP passed a resolution opposing such names and symbols, and in 2001 the U.S. Commission on Civil Rights issued a statement attacking use of Native American mascots. Universities such as Wisconsin and Iowa refused to schedule games against teams with Indian names. In 2005 the National Collegiate Athletic Association labeled Florida State University's use of "Seminoles" for the team name as "hostile and offensive." Florida governor Jeb Bush defended the school and called the NCAA's action "ridiculous" and insulting to the team and the tribe. In this case the Seminole Tribe of Florida authorized the school to use its name, and a few other tribes have done that. In 2005, the NCAA ordered teams with Indian mascots or symbols to find new ones or be excluded from national post-season tournaments, unless authorized by the specific tribes. During the next several years almost all complied with this directive. The last major holdout, the University of North Dakota, stopped using "Fighting Sioux" as their name in 2012 after a statewide vote on that issue.

Meanwhile, professional sports clubs proved even more resistant to dropping their team names and symbols than the schools. Major league baseball and pro football continue to remain at the center of this controversy, partly because of their long and well-advertised seasons. Critics of the Cleveland Indians baseball team attack its logo—Chief Wahoo—as demeaning and racist, and in 1997 Native groups protested when that team reached the World Series. Many people continue to object to the Atlanta Braves, "Chief Noc-a-homa," and the toma-hawk chop, seeing them as demeaning to Indians. In football, the Washington Redskins continue to receive the most protests. Given the negative uses of that "Redskin" in American history, most people find it difficult to accept the team owners' defense that its use honors Indians. Still, despite the demonstrations and protests over their names, these teams continue to defend them, have apparent-ly not suffered any financial damage, and cling stubbornly to their symbols. In March 2002 *Sports Illustrated* published the results of a survey it had conducted, showing that almost no white fans and even most Indians had few objections to teams using tribal names or mascots. So the debate continues.

Mishandling Trust Funds

Many of the contentious issues that separate Indian groups from the rest of American society focus in some way or another on the question of tribal sover-eignty. Laws, federal court decisions, and disputes between tribal governments and local or state authorities all play roles in the ongoing drama. The most con-tentious current dispute between tribes and the federal government grew out of the mishandling of Indian trust funds after the 1887 passage of the Dawes Act. That legislation initiated a system for government supervision of Indian land leases and tribal funds, which has operated ineffectively ever since. For several generations, reservation leaders asked agents and other officials about their money but got few answers. By the 1980s the growing ethnic awareness that resulted from the Red Power movement and from self-determination policies encouraged some Native Americans to demand an accounting. When federal officials refused, Elouise Cobell, a Montana Blackfeet, raised money for a fed-eral court suit. The case went to trial in 1996, and the special investigator found that Department of the Interior employees had destroyed hundreds of cartons of records needed by the tribes and the court. In 1999, Judge Royce Lambreth found Secretary of the Interior Bruce Babbitt and Secretary of the Treasury Rob-ert Rubin in contempt for refusing to cooperate with the investigation and fined each of them $625,000. He described the bureaucrats' handling of tribal funds as showing "a shocking pattern of deception," and he ruled that the government was required to prepare quarterly statements accounting for its handling of tribal funds. When an appeals court upheld Lambreth's decision, the George W. Bush administration dropped further legal action.

Appeals and other legal maneuvering kept the dispute moving, and in 2006 an appeals court removed Judge Lambreth from the case because of his one-sided, pro-Indian remarks and perceived lack of objectivity. By 2009 the government and Native American Rights Fund lawyers reached an agreement that called for the United States to appropriate $3.4 billion in damages. Of that the settlement, $2 billion was set aside for tribes to buy back land Indians had sold or lost since the 1890s. The other $1.4 billion was to go directly to individuals who suffered because of the Interior Department's mishandling of their trust funds. As bureaucrats struggle with incomplete and often incorrect records, some have questioned the wisdom of assigning the Interior Department—which lost track of the accounts in the first place—as the office most qualified to handle the new funds. For the tribes, trying to buy back land held by individual Indians or families is a major challenge. Often a dozen or more people have partial claims to a single plot, and getting them all to agree to sell is difficult. Still, in the summer of 2013 the government is beginning a decade-long effort to purchase ten million acres of land—an area twice the size of the state of Maine—for 150 tribes. Ongoing investigations will provide the data for making the decisions about who will get the final awards.

Sovereignty or Assimilation

A variety of issues continue to separate American Indians from the rest of society. Both radical and traditional leaders have sought to expand their tribal sovereignty, but for vastly different reasons. Unemployment, poverty, poor education, and health concerns all demonstrate that tribal members do not share equally in the national wellbeing. In some parts of the country, overt racism and discrimination still exist, but for the most part, in the major urban centers where most Native Americans now live, these are no longer a major issue. During the last several decades of the twentieth century, many Americans became more interested in their own ethnic and family backgrounds, and this seems to have fostered more widespread tolerance. For Indians, this means that American society is more ready than ever to welcome them as one more ethnic group in the national social mix. A clear example of this happened on December 27, 2012, at Mankato, Minnesota. There, 150 years to the day after the United States hanged thirty-eight Dakotas for their part in the 1862 Dakota War, a public ceremony dedicated a memorial to the men who died there on the gallows. The ethnic awakening that has swept through American society has also affected American Indians, no matter where they live. Many appear to want increasing ties with their tribal groups, and this is particularly true for those living away from the reservations. Since 2000, Indian rodeos, the powwow circuit, language classes, drum groups, and on-reservation religious and cultural ceremonies all have experienced increased attendance.

At the same time, some actions by tribal people have moved them directly into the American mainstream and even beyond. By 1989 Indian delegates had helped write parts of the UN Declaration on the Rights of Indigenous People. On November 22, 2002, the space shuttle *Endeavor* carried John Herrington of the Chickasaw Nation, the first Indian astronaut, to the international space station. Indian actors and moviemakers have produced films such as *Smoke Signals* and

Skins. Others have participated in a Hollywood film depicting the Navajo Code Talkers of World War II and a 2002 television version of the Tony Hillerman novel *Skin Walkers.* In 2013 Johnny Depp costarred in camp version of *The Lone Ranger,* although some Indians thought that his version of Tonto was too stereotypical. Earlier, in 2005, the National Museum of the American Indian opened its doors to the public on the Mall in Washington, D.C. Meanwhile, tribal governments are trying to clarify their relations with state governments and Washington too. In a case involving a non-Indian South Carolina family that adopted a Cherokee baby, the Supreme Court ruled in their favor, but the father appealed to Cherokee authorities and has retained custody of the child in Oklahoma. For a time the tribe was in a dispute with U.S., South Carolina, and Oklahoma courts over the infant's future. However, in 2013 the courts ruled against it and returned the child to its adoptive parents. Clearly, this variety of Indian participation in national activities shows that the future positions tribal people will take remain unclear at best. What is certain is that Indians have not disappeared, and in the twenty-first century they will continue to have far more to say about their lives and places in American society than they had in the past.

Suggested Readings

Ambler, Marjane. *Breaking the Iron Bonds: Indian Control of Energy Development.* Lawrence: University Press of Kansas, 1990.

Basson, Lauren L. *White Enough to Be American? Race Mixing, Indigenous People, and Boundaries of State and Nation.* Chapel Hill: University of North Carolina Press, 2008.

Brown, Michael. *Who Owns Native Culture?* Cambridge: Harvard University Press, 2003.

Cobb, Daniel M. *Native Activism in Cold War America: The Struggle for Sovereignty.* Lawrence: University Press of Kansas, 2008.

Cramer, Renee Ann. *Cash, Color and Colonialism: The Politics of Acknowledgment.* Norman: University of Oklahoma Press, 2005.

Echo-Hawk, Roger. *Battlefields and Burial Grounds: The Indian Struggle to Protect Ancestral Graves in the United States.* Minneapolis: Lerner, 1994.

Eichstaedt, Peter H. *If You Poison Us: Uranium and Native Americans.* Santa Fe: Red Crane Books, 1994.

Nabokov, Peter. *When Lightning Strikes: The Lives of American Indian Sacred Places.* New York: Viking Press, 2006.

Nesper, Larry. *The Walleye War: The Struggle for Ojibwe Spearfishing and Treaty Rights.* Lincoln: University of Nebraska Press, 2002.

Spindel, Carol. *Dancing at Halftime: Sports and the Controversy over American Indian Mascots.* New York: New York University Press, 2000.

Wunder, John R. *"Retained by the People": A History of American Indians and the Bill of Rights.* New York: Oxford University Press, 1994.

Index

References to illustrations appear in italics